What Democrats Talk About When They Talk About God

What Democrats Talk About When They Talk About God

Religious Communication in Democratic Party Politics

Edited by David Weiss

LEXINGTON BOOKS

A division of

ROWMAN & LITTLEFIELD PUBLISHERS, INC.
Lanham • Boulder • New York • Toronto • Plymouth, UK

Published by Lexington Books
A division of Rowman & Littlefield Publishers, Inc.
A wholly owned subsidary of The Rowman & Littlefield Publishing Group, Inc.
4501 Forbes Boulevard, Suite 200, Lanham, Maryland 20706
www.lexingtonbooks.com

Estover Road
Plymouth PL6 7PY
United Kingdom

British Library Cataloguing in Publication Information Available

Library of Congress Cataloging-in-Publication Data

What democrats talk about when they talk about God : religious communication in democratic party politics / edited by David Weiss.
    p. cm.
  Includes bibliographical references and index.
  ISBN 978-0-7391-3826-7 (cloth : alk. paper)—ISBN 978-0-7391-3827-4 (pbk. : alk. paper)—ISBN 978-0-7391-3828-1 (electronic : alk. paper)
  1. Religion and politics—United States. 2. Christianity and politics—United States. 3. Democratic Party (U.S.) I. Weiss, David, 1961–
  BR526.W48 2009
  201'.72—dc22
                                                    2010027794

Printed in the United States of America

♾ ™ The paper used in this publication meets the minimum requirements of American National Standard for Information Sciences—Permanence of Paper for Printed Library Materials, ANSI/NISO Z39.48-1992.

Contents

Introduction

What Do *Democrats Talk About When They Talk About God?*

David Weiss

The juxtaposition of religion and politics in the United States simultaneously fascinates and frustrates us. The two are not to mix, we are told; certainly, we are expected to acknowledge, if not uphold, the metaphorical "wall of separation" between church and state. If we are not to discuss either our religion or our politics in polite company, worse still is to publicly air our views on their intersection. Yet over the past few decades that very intersection—religion-*in*-politics—has been anything but a private matter.

Since the 1960s the religious affiliations and the private (yet publicly declared) beliefs of our politicians and office holders have been matters of public declaration and debate and, as a result, of political strategizing. Marking this change—which occurred little more than a decade after candidate John F. Kennedy promised voters that he would not let his Catholic upbringing or his Church's leadership influence how he might govern as U.S. president—were the open pieties of Jimmy Carter and his self-description as "born again"; the rise of the Moral Majority, a nondenominational Christian "parachurch" organization expressly devoted to the shaping of political policy; and the brilliant decision by Ronald Reagan's 1980 presidential campaign team to not only target the Moral Majority but to give its members and other like-minded "people of faith" a degree of visibility, voice, and, thus, validity in the political process unseen in over half a century.

The successful mainstreaming of politico-religious rhetoric during the Carter and Reagan years paved the way for the founding of other parachurch groups, such as the Christian Coalition and Focus on the Family, George H. W. Bush's invocation of Augustine's "just war" doctrine to describe U.S. military action in the Persian Gulf, the confessional nature of the Clinton presidency, the overt religiosity of George W. Bush's public rhetoric (epitomized by his

1

declaration that his favorite philosopher is Christ) and his call for the founding of a White House Office of Faith-Based Initiatives, and the Karl Rove strategy to target the conservative Christian "base" of the Republican party in the 2000 and 2004 Bush campaigns. Even during the 2008 election season, as scholars, pundits, and theologians were declaring the end of the era of the religious right and its influence on American politics,[1] religious communication remained a *sine qua non* of the campaign trail. All of the 2008 candidates, both Republican and Democratic, took pains to show that they were deserving of the trust and endorsement of the still-powerful churches and parachurches (groups who continued to make their influence felt even during the early years of the Obama administration) in the health care debate and elsewhere.

A great deal of scholarly, journalistic, and political writing has been devoted to the centrality of religion and religious communication in contemporary politics, particularly as evidenced by Republican candidates and officeholders. What has mostly gone missing, however, is any serious recognition that Democrats have had plenty to say as well. This book offers a unique look at what Democrats talk about when they talk about God, their personal beliefs, and their views on the many points of intersection between church and state (and religion and politics).

That little has been written to date on religious rhetoric in Democratic Party politics is understandable. After all, since the Carter presidency, few Democratic candidates or officeholders have sought to directly associate organized religion, parachurches, spiritual beliefs (or "religious values" with themselves), their campaigns, their messages, or their supporters. By contrast, the Republican Party has basked in its self-proclaimed monopolies on religion, values, and "people of faith" as its core constituency. (As Iowa Republican Party cochairman Leon Mosley exhorted his delegation at their 2004 national convention, "Remember, We're the GOP: God's Own Party.") Republican politicians and officeholders regularly proclaim themselves to be guardians of traditional mores and protectors of the place of religion in the public sphere. During the first decade of the 21st century, the president who installed an Office of Faith-Based Initiatives in his White House, the U.S. Attorney General who publicly sang hymns, and the primary candidate who declared that it would be easier (and, by implication, more desirable) to rewrite the Constitution than to "change the word of the living God" were all Republicans, not Democrats.[2] And as the *New York Times* reported in February 2008, exit polls asked Republican primary voters—not Democratic primary voters—if they described themselves as born-again or evangelical Christians (Steinfels, 2008). Should we be surprised, then, that Democrats have been so peripheral in so much of the current public discussion surrounding, celebrating, or critiquing the resurgence of religious rhetoric in U.S. public and political life?

Yet while it may be true that for most of the last 50 years, Democratic presidents and candidates have been reluctant to make religious communication a central part of their rhetoric, things are clearly changing. Since the turn of the current century, religion has become—for better or worse—a directly addressed, at times even central, component of Democratic presidential campaigning. As several contributors to this volume demonstrate, in both 2000 and 2004, the presidential and vice presidential candidates spoke regularly about religion and religious beliefs while on the campaign trail. Parallel to and influencing such changes in the Party has been the rise of the "religious left," liberal and progressive churches and parachurch organizations that have been (re)claiming core Christian principles as their own and showing how those principles can and should apply to campaigning and governance. As a result of these changes, during the 2008 primaries and general election campaign, the candidates not only spoke about religion of their own volition—they were given frequent opportunities by media outlets and other organizations to do so. In June 2007, Sojourners, a leading Religious left group, sponsored a preprimary event whose express purpose was to get Democratic front-runners Hillary Clinton, John Edwards, and Barack Obama to speak about their religious upbringings, practices, and beliefs. Almost a year later, the nondenominational organization Faith in Public Life sponsored its own, nearly identical event—broadcast on CNN—called the "Compassion Forum," at which Clinton and Obama each spoke for roughly an hour about their faith and personal values. *Time* Magazine featured a July 2007 cover story entitled "How the Democrats Got Religion" (Gibbs & Duffy, 2007)—and then, five months later, ranked it the #2 religion story of the year. The Pew Forum on Religious Life in November 2007 provided a platform for John Kerry to discuss his faith and reflect on how his own religious (mis)communication in 2004 might have contributed to his failure to win the presidency. And in July 2008, during the final months of the general election campaign, *Newsweek* offered a cover story on Obama entitled "What He Believes."

As news organizations are wont to do, each of these stories, forums, and events were covered as if their contents were exclusively *new* and, for the most part, one-dimensional. Yet as this book demonstrates, religion and religious communication in Democratic Party politics have roots that are centuries old and contemporary expressions that are as diverse as the members of the party itself.

PREVIEW OF THE BOOK

Given the seemingly permanent prominence of church-and-state issues in American public and political life—and, more recently, the intensification of public, journalistic, and scholarly fascination with these issues—*What*

Democrats Talk About is uniquely situated to be used by what might be best described as a specialized crossover audience: engaged citizens interested in one of the most compelling sociopolitical issues of our time *and* scholars and students of communication, political science, religious studies, sociology, and history.

The chapters that follow explore the historical and philosophical roots and the wide variety of contemporary manifestations of religious communication in Democratic Party politics, policy, and campaigning. Part I, entitled "Historical and Philosophical Perspectives," lays the groundwork for the book—and, thus, for the broader study of contemporary Democratic Party religious communication—in two important ways. In Chapter 1, Paul Haridakis takes us back to the very roots of the party by exploring the public and private expressions of faith of its founder Thomas Jefferson. As Haridakis demonstrates through a close reading of Jefferson's public documents and private correspondence, the Founding Father who coined the term "wall of separation between church and state" was deeply committed to his own personal journey of faith and understanding and a staunch opponent of religious intolerance, positions that have influenced Democratic Party political expression and policy formation for more than two centuries. Chapter 2, by Penni Pier, also explicates the historical context for current-day politico-religious communication albeit in a rather different way. In her chapter, Pier provides an overview of the interactions, intersections, and conflicts between religion and U.S. politics since the country's founding and explores the psychological roles played by religion in the lives of individuals and nations. Having done so, she then traces the divergent paths taken by the Democratic and Republican Parties, particularly during the 20th century, in regard to religious association and expression.

The presidency and the presidential campaign trail have always been among the most visible venues for politico-religious communication in this country. Part II, entitled "Past Presidents and Presidential Hopefuls," explores the way a number of recent presidential contenders and one past president have talked to prospective supporters about God and personal belief. In Chapter 3, I look at the ways John Kerry talked before and during the 2004 election about his own religious views and his positions on the proper place of religion in governance, policy, and public life. As I demonstrate, Kerry manifested three distinct, incompatible, and even mutually exclusive religious personae while traveling the campaign trail, leaving voters bewildered about the candidate's own character and the ways in which his stands on church-and-state issues differed from those of his opponent, George W. Bush. Chapter 4, written by Paul Raptis, Tom Preston, Allison Ainsworth, and me, also focuses on religious communication during the 2004 presidential campaign, but not that which was offered by that year's Democratic candidate. Rather, our chapter offers a metaphorical analysis of a speech given by former president Bill Clinton in a New York City church on the eve of the Republicans' national convention. As Raptis and his colleagues show, Clinton skillfully deployed a wide variety of metaphors and biblical allusions in order to discursively unite Democrats with religion, praise the values of the Democratic Party and its nominee John Kerry, and call into question the GOP's exclusive claim to the religious high ground.

In Chapter 5, Brent Roberts and Dan Gross explore the public religious communication of John Edwards, Kerry's running mate in 2004, as well as a contender for the Democratic presidential nomination in his own right earlier that year and then again in 2008. Edwards, never one to be reticent in expressing his faith publicly, became progressively more emphatic about his religious views over the course of his two attempts to become his party's nominee. Moreover, as Roberts and Gross demonstrate, Edwards's positions on social issues—the elimination of poverty, civil rights, access to education—were rooted not only in the particulars of his own religious upbringing but also in the traditions of the early 20th-century "social gospel" movement, thus offering additional support for one of this volume's overarching themes: the historical continuity of religious communication as a component of Democratic Party politics and policy. The final chapter of this section, by Christina Knopf, explores the many fascinating and revealing contradictions in the rhetoric of Al Gore. Having performed a cluster criticism on a set of 22 speeches delivered after Gore's exit from public office, Knopf shows how the former vice president, a public figure more commonly associated with reason than spiritual feeling, makes careful distinctions between faith and religion, offering an understanding of liberal democracy that requires the former but not necessarily the latter. At the same time, Knopf demonstrates how Gore's love of both facts and faith has posed philosophical and political challenges for him and his would-be supporters.

A central theme that emerges in Part II—leading Democrats' progressive interpretations of faith and religious values and the applications of those interpretations to politics and policy—is further developed in Part III, entitled "The Religious Rhetoric of Barack Obama," which focuses on the religious rhetoric of Barack Obama both before and since his ascent to the White House. As all of the contributors to this part show, not since Jimmy Carter has the country seen a Democratic elected official for whom it seems so comfortable and so natural (if not always entirely convincing) to talk publicly about religious belief and its place in governance and the public square.

In Chapter 7, Jim Petre and Lenore Langsdorf analyze then Senator Obama's keynote address at the 2004 Democratic National Convention. They demonstrate that even in that early moment in the national spotlight, Obama revealed his spiritual side, using his rhetorical gifts in ways that invited audiences to envision alternatives to the politics of the George W. Bush administration. Using as a theoretical lens Cornel West's (1989, 1993) notion of "prophetic pragmatism," Petre and Langsdorf argue that Obama's speech successfully offered an inclusive political rhetoric combining a progressive interpretation of faith-based politics with elements of an American theodicy that can be seen in the writings of Ralph Waldo Emerson and John Dewey as well as West himself.

In Chapter 8, Biff Rocha and Jeffrey Morrow also explore a keynote address delivered by Barack Obama: the address given at the 2006 "Call to Renewal" event sponsored by Sojourners, the organization founded by progressive clergyman and author Jim Wallis (2005, 2008). While acknowledging Obama's rhetorical talents, Rocha and Morrow argue that the "Call to Renewal" speech was problematic in a number of ways, both religious and rhetorical, including its confusing use of Christian testimony, its reliance on hostile-audience techniques, and its troubling interpretations and applications of the *Aqedah,* the Old Testament account of Abraham's sacrificial binding of Isaac. Rocha and Morrow use their analysis of the Obama speech as a platform from which to explore broader questions about the respective roles of religion and secularity in contemporary political and public life.

Chapter 9 explores another connection between Barack Obama and Sojourners founder Jim Wallis, now a consultant to the Obama administration and an advisor to the president's Office of Faith-Based and Neighborhood Partnerships. In this chapter, Sam Boerboom analyzes the 2009 University of Notre Dame commencement address delivered by the newly inaugurated president, a speech that garnered a great deal of public attention due to the juxtaposition of its central theme, political approaches to the issue of abortion, and its place of delivery—the campus of a prestigious Catholic university. Using the theoretical lens of articulation (Grossberg, 1992) to explicate Obama's attempts to forge a common ground among people holding opposing views on a controversial topic, Boerboom demonstrates the influence of Wallis's strategy of "conservative radicalism" on Obama's abortion position while also drawing parallels to a 1963 address by John F. Kennedy calling upon Americans and Soviets to jointly pursue peace.

Part IV, entitled "Religion in Gubernatorial and Congressional Campaigns," of the book steps away from presidential politics in order to explore how religious communication was used—and critiqued—in the campaigns of two other leading national-level Democratic politicians. In Chapter 10, Sara Ann Mehltretter explores the unique approach to religious communication taken by Tim Kaine in his successful 2005 Virginia gubernatorial campaign. Kaine, a liberal Democrat and practicing Catholic, made a rather daring move on the campaign trail, recounting his past experiences as a Catholic service worker in terms of a personal conversion narrative and missions testimony, a rhetorical form heretofore associated almost exclusively with evangelical Protestants. As Mehltretter demonstrates, this gave Kaine a way to speak openly and frequently about matters of personal faith and, in doing so, to connect to a wide range of voters, including many who might otherwise have been reluctant to support him.

Finally, in Chapter 11, Julie Woodbury investigates the 2006 campaign of Keith Ellison, Minnesota's first black member of the U.S. House of Representatives and the nation's first Muslim member of that body. Like John Kennedy in 1960 and John Kerry in 2004, Ellison, too, would have preferred to keep his religion a nonissue on the campaign trail; but this was not to be. As Woodbury demonstrates, while Ellison's political opponents and numerous pundits attempted to frame the candidate's religion as a barrier to proper public service, Ellison offered a view of himself and his politics that was consistent with both the tenets of his faith and the principles enshrined by the founders of our nation.

As a whole, *What Democrats Talk About When They Talk About God* provides a counter-argument to the prevailing view that religion, religious faith, and religious communication are exclusive to Republican Party policy, politics, and governance. In various ways, each of the contributors to this volume shows that, for good or bad, religion is now—as it has been for centuries—a component of rhetoric, campaigning, and governing by Democrats as well. In painting a picture of the diverse, even contradictory, ways that religious language has been and continues to be used by members of the party often mislabeled as irreligious, *What Democrats Talk About* also shines a light on new directions—largely but not exclusively progressive—in politico-religious communication that might be taken up by candidates and politicians of any party.

NOTES

1. See, for example, Dawkins, 2006; Dionne, 2008; Ellingsen, 2007; Harris, 2006; Hitchens, 2007; and Wallis, 2008.
2. George W. Bush, John Ashcroft, and Mike Huckabee, respectively.

REFERENCES

Dawkins, R. (2006). *The God delusion.* New York: Houghton Mifflin.

Dionne, E. J., Jr. (2008). *Souled out: Reclaiming faith & politics after the Religious Right.* Princeton, NJ: Princeton University Press.

Ellingsen, M. (2007). *When did Jesus become Republican? Rescuing our country and our values from the Right: Strategies for a post-Bush America.* Lanham, MD: Rowman & Littlefield.

Gibbs, N., & Duffy, M. (2007, July 12). How the Democrats got religion. *Time.* Retrieved from http://www.time.com/time/politics/article/0,8599,1642649,00.html

Grossberg, L. (1992). *We gotta get out of this place: Popular conservatism and postmodern culture.* New York: Routledge.

Harris, S. (2006). *Letter to a Christian nation.* New York: Knopf.

Hitchens, C. (2007). *God is not great: How religion poisons everything.* New York: Hachette.

Steinfels, P. (2008, February 2). Evangelical Democrats, exit polls, and a matter of balance. *New York Times.* Retrieved from www.nytimes.com/2008/02/02/us/politics/02beliefs.html

Wallis, J. (2005). *God's politics: Why the right gets it wrong and the left doesn't get it.* San Francisco: HarperCollins.

Wallis, J. (2008). *The great awakening: Reviving faith and politics in a post-religious right America.* New York: HarperOne.

West, C. (1989). *The American evasion of philosophy.* Madison: University of Wisconsin Press.

West, C. (1993). *Beyond eurocentrism and multiculturalism: Prophetic thought in postmodern times.* Monroe, ME: Common Courage Press.

Part I

Historical and Philosophical Perspectives

Chapter 1

The Religious Explorations of Thomas Jefferson and His Public and Private Expressions of Faith

Paul Haridakis

The First Amendment provides, in part, that Congress shall make no law establishing religion or preventing its free exercise. Through these two clauses—the establishment and free exercise clauses—the First Amendment sets forth the principle that governance and religion should not be entangled. Nonetheless, the extent to which government action can deal with religious issues without being unconstitutionally entangled with them has been hotly contested.

Government interest in, and the exercise of control over, subjects dealing with religion predates our Constitution. Religious freedom, ostensibly one of the primary reasons for many Europeans coming to the New World, was almost immediately repudiated by those new arrivals. Numerous colonial laws disenfranchised those who deviated from the religious norms of the colonies of which they were a part. Some colonial laws punished religious nonconformity through mechanisms such as invalidating the right of those holding nonconforming religious views to participate in colonial political affairs. Others were more severe, such as execution for heresy (see Tedford & Herbeck, 2001, pp. 18–20).

Despite the subsequent adoption of the U.S. Constitution and its First Amendment guarantee of religious liberty, the tension pertaining to the separation of church and state has remained a part of U.S. political and social life. It continues to be played out in contexts such as controversies over prayer in schools, initiatives to add intelligent design to public school curriculums, permitting religious displays on public property, and the like.

Interestingly, one historical figure whose views are valuable and perhaps critical to understanding this ongoing tension is our third president, Thomas Jefferson. Jefferson's public and private expressions pertaining to religion, due to the breadth of his intellectual and philosophical interest in religion, highlight the deep roots of controversy regarding how political leaders and institutions in the United States deal with religion in the political realm, and are surprisingly relevant today. For example, one major debate taking place currently is the controversy surrounding the teaching of evolution versus intelligent design in the public schools (Hall, 2006). Jefferson himself confronted a similar controversy in the early 1800s when he had trouble obtaining a censored text dealing with the creation of the world (ultimately securing the book from the publisher). Recently, Jefferson's name came up again when it was disclosed that the first Muslim to be elected to Congress took his oath of office on a Qur'an once owned by Thomas Jefferson ("Rep. Ellison's Oath," 2007; see also Julie Woodbury's chapter in this volume).

Thomas Jefferson was a staunch advocate of the separation of church and state. His views on this constitutional conundrum have had a considerable influence on individual U.S. Supreme Court justices and Supreme Court cases implicating the establishment clause of the First Amendment. (For a review of representative cases, see Reiss, 2002.) Jefferson also was a firm believer in the idea that an individual's belief is a private, rather than public, matter. Allegedly, he once told a writer working on a biographical sketch of Jefferson not to discuss his religious views, as they were "known to my God and myself alone" (quoted in Sheridan, 1983, p. 4). Jefferson's reticence to publicly express his own faith attracted scorn. During the presidential election of 1800, for example, federalists and some of the clergy who supported them used Jefferson's failure to be more explicit in his embrace of Christianity as a way of degrading him "as an unbeliever who was unworthy to serve as chief magistrate of a Christian nation" (Sheridan, 1983, p. 10).

Although Jefferson was not verbose in his public communication regarding his religious beliefs, his private expressions of faith over the course of his lifetime, often articulated in letters to friends and family, were quite extensive and revealing. An exhaustive review of both his public and private communications regarding faith cannot be covered in one chapter. Similarly, the depth and intensity of the overarching discussion pertaining to the role of faith in politics or the separation of church and state cannot be addressed adequately in a single chapter. The purpose here is simply to provide some representative examples of Thomas Jefferson's public and private religious expressions, and some major themes in each, that evidence that early in our nation's history our third president was at the center of such debates. Accordingly, his views may provide a context for understanding them today. They also may assist us in putting in context discussion of religion by later presidents and candidates for that office and the broader discussion of the role of faith in politics. In addition, as the Democratic party's first president[1] (his two predecessors—Washington and Adams—were federalists), Jefferson's views are particularly germane to considering what Democrats talk about—or don't talk about—when they talk about religion.

JEFFERSON'S RELIGIOUS LEANINGS

Jefferson probably was raised Anglican as a child. It has been suggested that he had a disaster of conscience as a teen, shifting to a more vague religious view "based on reason" (Holland, 2004, p. 185). Exactly what Jefferson's religious views were and how they changed over the course of his lifetime has been the subject of debate and speculation for over 200 years. He has been variously described as an atheist (Neem, 2007, p. 139), a deist (Sheridan, 1983, p. 39), a "freethinker" (Jacoby, 2004, p. 5), and a nonbeliever, among others. It is difficult to argue persuasively that there is definitive proof for any particular classification of Jefferson's religious leanings. Jefferson, at least subsequent to becoming president, referred to himself as a Christian, although it does not appear that he ever ascribed to the divinity of Jesus (Fox, 2002; Holland, 2004; Sheridan, 1983). On balance, the wealth of evidence suggests that Jefferson was not a nonbeliever. He was also intensely interested in gaining an understanding of religious beliefs of different types. His intellectual curiosity in the views of the Stoics, Epicureans, Muslims, Buddhists, Jesuits, Unitarians, and adherents of other religious and moral philosophies has been widely discussed. Jefferson acquired numerous copies of the Bible and the New Testament over the course of his lifetime. (For a review of his extensive personal library, see Sanford, 1977.) Jefferson's contact with the Qur'an seems to have occurred during the 1760s, perhaps around the time he was completing his formal legal studies. It has been suggested, however, that he may have harbored some concern about strict adherence to this or any other single religious text, particularly after his experience in dealing with the envoy of the Sultan of Tripoli regarding Barbary pirates' acts of terrorism toward U.S. trade ships (Hayes, 2004).

Jefferson was a firm believer in freedom of conscience. His public documents, such as his *Notes on the State of Virginia* (1785/2003a), the *Declaration of Independence* (1776/2003b), and the bill he drafted and introduced in Virginia for establishing religious freedom, disclose that he was monotheistic. In many of his public addresses, including both his first and second inaugural addresses, he also referenced God in the singular (though he did not always use the word "God" specifically).

It has been suggested that Jefferson entertained the idea of tying the United States to the philosophy of Jesus (Fox, 2002; see also Neem, 2007). While that didn't occur, he did spend much private time thinking about Jesus' philosophy and separating Jesus' moral teachings from the baggage in which Jefferson felt it had been enveloped by religious leaders (e.g., priests, ministers) over the centuries. For example, in an 1801 letter to Moses Robinson (reprinted in Adams & Lester, 1983), he wrote "the Christian religion when divested of the rags in which they have inveloped it, and brought to the original purity and simplicity of it's benevolent institutor, is a religion of all others most friendly to liberty, science, and the freest expansions of the human mind" (p. 325).

As one distills Jefferson's public and private communication regarding religious beliefs, one thing seems certain: for Jefferson, "religious liberty" was "the foundation of *all* liberties" (Gaustad, 1998, p. 682). He opposed governmental efforts that did not maintain a separation of church and state. Although he felt strongly that the government should stay out of private religious affairs, he also opposed attempts by clergy to commingle religious beliefs and government affairs. However, Jefferson did not want any interference with the right of individuals to choose and exercise their private religious beliefs. This tripartite view—the separation of government from religion, the separation of religion from government, and the private nature of religious beliefs—was consistently reflected in his public and private expressions of faith.

SOME EXAMPLES OF PUBLIC EXPRESSIONS OF FAITH

Religious pronouncements are significant in many of Jefferson's public writings. In 1774 he wrote the *Summary View of the Rights of British America.* In it he noted that "The God who gave us life gave us liberty at the same time" (quoted in Gaustad, 1998, p. 682). In 1776 he wrote the *Declaration of Independence* (1776/2003b), in which he referred to "nature's god" and the "creator" from whom we are endowed with "inalienable rights" (p. 21). As president, he closed both his first and second inaugural addresses with references to God. He concluded his first inaugural address by stating, "may that Infinite Power which rules the destinies of the universe, lead our councils to what is best, and give them a favorable issue for your peace and prosperity" (Jefferson, 1801/2003c, p. 335). In the closing of his second inaugural address, he referred to "that Being . . . who has covered our infancy with his providence, and our riper years with his wisdom and power" (Jefferson, 1805/2003d, p. 363). Together, such statements reflect his belief in God and commitment to religious liberty as a natural God-given right.

However, some of Jefferson's public expressions dealt with the separation of church and state very directly. For example, the bill he introduced in his home state of Virginia that ultimately became that state's statute for religious freedom in 1786 provided an explicit guarantee of freedom of religion. As Gaustad (1998) described it, "Jefferson's bill called not for toleration, but for freedom, not for mere disestablishment, but for a full and complete separation of the civil from the ecclesiastical" (p. 684). Hearing of its passage while in France, Jefferson was delighted to see such disestablishment after centuries during which he felt "the human mind had 'been held in vassalage by kings, priests, and nobles'" (quoted in Gaustad, 1998, p. 684).

This theme of complete separation was perhaps most pronounced in his letter to the Danbury Baptists. In October 1801, shortly after he was elected president of the United States, the Danbury (Connecticut) Baptists wrote to President Jefferson supporting religious liberty but expressing concern that the Constitution was not specific as to protecting religious liberty as an inalienable right ("The Danbury Baptists' Letter," 2002). In response, President Jefferson called religion "a matter which lies solely between Man & his God." He suggested further that the First Amendment's establishment and free expression clauses built a "wall of separation between Church & State."

Jefferson's short direct response to the Danbury Baptists has garnered considerable discussion, articles, and debate. According to Neem (2007), the Christian Coalition has challenged the argument that Jefferson meant to separate religious expression from the public sphere. Others have suggested that Jefferson supported a wall separating church and state to further the goal of religious liberty, and if that goal could be advanced "by a limited, strategic union of church and state, Jefferson was willing to breach the 'wall'" (Dreisbach, 1990, p. 210). Also, because the First Amendment only applied to the federal government at the time Jefferson wrote his letter, it has been proposed that he may not have been referring to a separation between *state* governments and the church or matters of religion (Dreisbach, 2002).

The fact that Jefferson zealously advocated religious liberty in his public communication, but did not publicly endorse Christianity specifically or embrace the notion that the United States was or should be a Christian nation, led to harsh attacks, such as the smear campaign during the presidential election of 1800. For whatever reason, Jefferson did not reply satisfactorily to claims that he was an atheist or did not believe in Christianity. In his public communication, when he did embrace freedom of conscience, he tended to treat it as a private matter. Even after the electoral smear campaign, he was reserved when referencing his religious ideas publicly. For example, in his first inaugural address, he referred to "blessings" such as "the love of man," and "an overruling Providence" rather than God, and he praised religion rather than Christianity (see Jefferson, 1801/2003c, pp. 333–334). Similarly, he closed his letter to the Danbury Baptists by referring to "the common father and creator of man" ("The Danbury Baptists' Letter," 2002).

SOME EXAMPLES OF PRIVATE EXPRESSIONS OF FAITH

Although Jefferson was hesitant to disclose his own faith publicly, in his private correspondence Jefferson was quite explicit in articulating his views regarding Christianity, religion, and his own journey of conscience. Many of Jefferson's private expressions of faith that have emerged and been assessed over the years appear in private correspondence to family, friends, and others with whom he shared some religious and/or moral beliefs. In addition to his body of letters referencing religion, Jefferson also completed two significant biblical compilations: *The Philosophy of Jesus of Nazareth* (completed during his presidency; reconstruction printed in Adams & Lester, 1983, pp. 55–105) and *The Life and Morals of Jesus of Nazareth* (completed toward the end of his life; reprinted in Adams & Lester, 1983, pp. 127–297). He also wrote *A Syllabus of an Estimate of the merit of the doctrines of Jesus, compared with those of others* (reprinted in Adams & Lester, 1983, pp. 332–334), which he shared with some members of his family and close friends. These are the places where we get the best glimpse of his beliefs.

In these and other private correspondence, as opposed to his public statements, Jefferson disclosed the nature of his faith. One rather consistent theme was his argument for adherence to a simple and basic Christianity, stripped of its orthodoxy, based on the moral teachings of Jesus, and informed by the Enlightenment notions of reason. For example, in a letter to Moses Robinson shortly after he took office, he indicated that Christianity, in its pure and simplistic form (devoid of the "rags" added to it), was the religion most supportive of liberty (see Holland, 2004, p. 202). He also suggested to Robinson that before New Englanders would join the Republicans it would first be necessary that they throw off the "dominion of the clergy" (quoted in Neem, 2007, p. 146).

Jefferson's views in this regard were influenced, in part, by the writings of Joseph Priestley. Jefferson was particularly fond of two of Priestley's works: *The History of the Corruptions of Christianity* and *Socrates and Jesus Compared* (discussed and cited in Sheridan, 1983). In the former, Sheridan explains that Priestley, a Unitarian, presented Christianity as a simple and straightforward religion. There was one God. God used Jesus to make known to the world the nature of God and to teach people to lead a moral life for which they would be rewarded after death. For Priestley, other vestiges of

Christianity, such as original sin and the divinity of Jesus, were notions added by others. In *Socrates and Jesus Compared,* Priestley ultimately concluded that Jesus was superior for many reasons, not the least of which was (a) his commitment to one true God, in juxtaposition to Socrates' polytheism, and (b) the certainty of life after death in juxtaposition to Socrates' apparent lack of such certainty.

The two works had a tremendous impact on Jefferson's religious thinking. During his first term as president, Jefferson discussed his views of Christianity and the moral teachings of Jesus in correspondence with Priestley and another close friend, Dr. Benjamin Rush, a Philadelphia physician with whom he had served in the Continental Congress. To Priestley, Jefferson suggested that reason, justice, philanthropy, and "belief of a future state" were aspects of Jesus' teachings on which to focus in order to get Christianity back to its true roots (reprinted in Adams & Lester, 1983, pp. 327–329).

Writing to Rush, he provided his view of those roots. In a particularly detailed and insightful letter to him in April 1803, Jefferson included his *A Syllabus of an Estimate of the merit of the doctrines of Jesus, compared with those of others* (reprinted in Adams & Lester, 1983, pp. 331–334; cited in Sheridan, 1983, pp. 22–23). In his letter, he described himself as a Christian—committed "to the genuine precepts of Jesus himself" (p. 331). In his *Syllabus,* he lauded Jesus for his moral teachings and proposed "the doctrine of a future state" as an incentive for leading a moral life (p. 334).

Such correspondence suggests Jefferson was critical of self-serving followers who perverted Jesus' simple doctrines. He seemed particularly critical of self-serving orthodoxy added to Jesus' basic precepts by Christian churches and clergy over the centuries. Returning to the simple message of Jesus, which to Jefferson was superior to any alternatives, was rational.

This approach to his own faith, marked by what he considered to be a rational application of Christianity, remained a constant theme in his private communication with friends and family over the course of his lifetime. In addition to Rush, Jefferson shared his *Syllabus* with his daughters and a few other close relatives and friends (Sheridan, 1983). In his *Syllabus,* Jefferson lauded ancient philosophers' precepts regarding matters such as individual restraint and self-discipline, but felt that they were insufficient in addressing social harmony. He praised Jews for their monotheism, but found them deficient in their views of social harmony between nations and people. Thus, although he was well read in religious works and admired the philosophical expressions of ancient Greek, Roman, and Hebrew philosophers, particularly Epicureans and Stoics, he most admired Jesus as the greatest moral reformer (see Holland, 2004; Sheridan, 1983). His private letters and individual journey of faith consistently evidence that he saw Jesus' teachings as a paramount moral/ethical code.

During his presidency, Jefferson went so far as to cut out passages of the New Testament that he felt reflected Jesus' fundamental moral precepts and paste them into a compilation that he had bound and entitled *The Philosophy of Jesus of Nazareth* (see Sheridan, 1983, for an extensive discussion of this document; see also Holland, 2004). He never published it. Rather, he used it privately for his own moral guidance. This work, along with his *Syllabus,* provides important information about Jefferson's views during his first term as president. From these, one can speculate about his views of Christianity and the role he hoped Jesus' moral teachings could play as a moral guide for the nation, particularly with respect to social harmony and interaction.

Toward the end of his life, Jefferson compiled another work of extracts from the Gospels, *The Life and Morals of Jesus of Nazareth.* Whereas *The Philosophy of Jesus of Nazareth* provided moral lessons for Jefferson, *The Life and Morals of Jesus of Nazareth* may have been even more personal. He apparently did not share it with others; its existence only came to light after he died (Sheridan, 1983).

Prepared perhaps around 1820 (the exact date is not known), this biblical compilation of New Testament extracts may have been inspired, in part, by Jefferson's correspondence with John Adams, a correspondence that began in their later years (1812 to the early 1820s, after each had retired from politics). Adams and Jefferson corresponded at length regarding religious matters. In an 1813 letter to John Adams (reprinted in Adams & Lester, 1983), Jefferson indicated that he had relied on Priestley's opinions of Jesus as the foundation of his own faith (see also Holland, 2004). Jefferson shared both his *Syllabus* and "The Philosophy of Jesus of Nazareth" with Adams. In several letters, Adams, who also was critical of Christian orthodoxy, apparently encouraged Jefferson to continue his analysis of Christianity (see Sheridan, 1983, for a reference to several letters between Jefferson and Adams).

Because Jefferson did not reveal the existence or content of his *Life and Morals of Jesus of Nazareth* to others, including Adams, it is difficult to conclude that Jefferson's creation of the document was anything other than a very private exercise. This effort, however, when considered along with his compilation of scriptures in *The Philosophy of Jesus of Nazareth* and his *Syllabus,* evidences Jefferson's studious individual interpretation of scripture and suggests a man deeply committed to his own journey of faith and understanding. It is a journey that left him committed to (a) the belief in a benevolent God, (b) the recognition of Jesus as the greatest moralist in history and purveyor of God's values, and (c) the rewards of life after death for adherence to God's benevolent supreme moral framework as communicated by Jesus.

That moral framework was beautiful in its logic and simplicity. Toward the end of his life, in an 1822 letter to Benjamin Waterhouse (reprinted in

Adams & Lester, 1983, 405–406), Jefferson indicated that the love of God and one's neighbor "is the sum of religion" (quoted in Holland, 2004, p. 191). This view, to him, was logical as well. For example, in an 1823 letter to John Adams, Jefferson indicated that he found it was impossible, when one viewed the design of the universe and life on earth, not to believe in the existence of a supreme being (reprinted in Adams & Lester, 1983).

LASTING IMPACT

Perhaps Jefferson's strict adherence to maintaining the privacy of his religious beliefs undermined his goal of establishing a nation guided by the rational application of the morals of Jesus, stripped of its orthodoxy. With the exception of scholars who have explored Jefferson's private expressions of faith, few are even aware of his views. Perhaps this was inevitable and consistent with Jefferson's approach to maintaining the private nature of religion. As a political leader, had Jefferson made his private views known through his public communications, such an action would have been at odds with his strict commitment to the separation of governance and religion.

Despite his zeal in concealing his private religious leanings, Jefferson was not reluctant to express publicly his views on religious liberty. He maintained a lifelong commitment to the natural rights of man. For Jefferson, freedom of conscience was at the forefront of such rights. In his public communication he left no doubts about his views in this regard. They stand out in his public expressions as a revolutionary (*Declaration of Independence*), legislative leader (his Virginia bill for establishing religious freedom), and president (his letter to the Danbury Baptists). As a result, unlike his private expressions of faith, Jefferson's public communications regarding religious liberty have had a profound impact.

Nowhere is that impact seen more explicitly than in the development of U.S. Supreme Court jurisprudence pertaining to the establishment clause of the First Amendment. Jefferson's views on the separation of church and state have influenced the Court's interpretation of that First Amendment clause. As Smith (2003) put it,

> In case after case, the Court has struck down various practices of the state governments that it has concluded evince a prohibited "entanglement" between religion and government. While the boundaries of the prohibition have frequently shifted during the last fifty years, the framework the Court has used in analyzing such questions has been built on the separation metaphor. (p. 372)

Although the Supreme Court has not always been consistent in decisions regarding what is or is not an unconstitutional entanglement of government action and religion, Supreme Court cases dealing with the issue consistently reflect Jefferson's influence.

For example, in perhaps the first major religion clause case of the 19th century, the U.S. Supreme Court drew on Jefferson's ideas regarding the separation of religion from civil affairs. In *Reynolds v. United States* (1879), the U.S. Supreme Court upheld the conviction of a Mormon man for bigamy. In writing the Court's opinion, Chief Justice Waite drew on Jeffersonian thought gleaned from his Virginia bill for establishing religious freedom and his letter to the Danbury Baptist Association. In relying on Jefferson's separation metaphor, Chief Justice Waite concluded that Jefferson was referring to opinions, not actions. Thus, according to the Court's interpretation of Jefferson's position, "Congress was deprived of all legislative power over mere opinion, but was left free to reach actions which were in violation of social duties or subversive of good order" (p. 164). Therefore, the government could address actions such as polygamy without running afoul of the First Amendment.

In the mid-20th-century case of *Everson v. Board of Education* (1947), the Court dealt with the constitutionality of application of a New Jersey statute that reimbursed parents for transportation of their children to school. The statute was challenged to the extent that it reimbursed parents for transportation of their children to parochial schools. The Court ruled that reimbursing parents of students attending parochial or other religious schools did not violate the First Amendment. Citing *Reynolds,* the Court again rooted its decision on Jeffersonian notions: "In the words of Jefferson, the clause against establishment of religion by law was intended to erect 'a wall of separation between church and State'" (p. 16). Accordingly, the Court concluded that the state could not exclude parents *"because of their faith, or lack of it,* from receiving the benefits of public welfare legislation" (p.16). Justice Black, writing for the Court, asserted that the First Amendment "erected a wall between church and state. That wall must be kept high and impregnable. We could not approve the slightest breach" (p. 18).

In *Lemon v. Kurtzman* (1971), the Court condensed its establishment clause-related jurisprudence guided by the Court's reasoning in *Everson*— and by extension, its reliance on Jefferson's separation metaphor. The *Lemon* Court articulated a three-part test for determining when government action does not violate the establishment clause of the First Amendment. It ruled that government action is permissible only when (a) it has a secular purpose, (b) "its principal or primary effect . . . neither advances nor inhibits religion," and (c) it does "not foster 'an excessive government entanglement with religion'" (pp. 612–613).

By the same token, some jurists have suggested that reliance on Jefferson's separation metaphor for interpreting the First Amendment is misplaced and/ or misapplied. For example, although not rejecting the influence of Jefferson entirely, former Justice Sandra Day O'Connor questioned the traditional establishment clause analysis of *Everson* and its progeny which is based upon the separation metaphor. In her concurrence in *Lynch v. Donnelly* (1984) (a case in which the Court rejected the claim that a Christmas display on public property violated the First Amendment), Justice O'Connor suggested that the *Lemon* test should be clarified. Specifically, she proposed that the establishment clause is violated only when the government endorses or disapproves religion. This, arguably, is a less stringent standard than complete separation.

In a dissent he penned in *Wallace v. Jaffree* (1985), Chief Justice Rehnquist more directly distanced Jefferson from the First Amendment. He noted that Jefferson was in France (as ambassador) when "the Bill of Rights were passed by Congress and ratified by the States" (p. 92). He therefore raised doubt that Jefferson's views, expressed for example in his Virginia bill for establishing religious freedom, were incorporated into the First Amendment. He thus discounted Jefferson as a useful source for interpreting the meaning of the First Amendment.

These are just a few examples of cases that reflect the lasting impact of some of Jefferson's public expressions related to religious liberty. The point here is not to review the voluminous body of cases that have dealt with the entanglement of government action and religion or referenced Jefferson's wall of separation metaphor. It is to suggest, however, the continued presence of Jeffersonian thought in the interpretation of the First Amendment. Whether individual Supreme Court justices have supported or diminished the importance of Jefferson's public expressions on state-religion separation in that interpretation, the debate itself evidences Jefferson's lasting influence on how we in the United States think about and ensure religious liberty.

CONCLUSION

Public perception of Jefferson's religious views probably alienated some voters and encouraged the support of others. He garnered criticism. He barely won the presidential election in 1800. He and Aaron Burr tied in the popular vote. He became president only after the electoral college selected him by a one-vote margin over Burr. We can only speculate about the effect his religious views (or lack of understanding of them) had on his popular support among voters or the role it played in his election to the presidency. But there is little doubt that he has remained a central figure in the debate over the extent of the necessary separation of church and state in our constitutional democracy.

Jefferson's view of the separation of church and state may have been a minority view among 19th-century politicians (see, e.g., Hamburger, 2002). The fact that the Danbury Baptists wrote to the newly elected president to elicit his response to their concerns is evidence of the lack of clarity on what has become one of the most important interpretations of the establishment clause. Had Jefferson not advocated such a complete separation, the way with which we deal with religion in politics today might be far different.

The goal here was not to reach conclusions on this issue, but simply to consider the relevance of Jefferson's public and private expressions of faith. In Jefferson's public communication, it is difficult to discern any of his individual beliefs or faith, beyond those that can be gleaned from his public expression of monotheism. He did publicly espouse the existence of God. Further, he professed that God (by various names, e.g., "Almighty God," "Creator") provided our inalienable rights and freedom. However, he did not express the extent or changing nature of his personal religious beliefs—at least publicly.

Perhaps this separation between his public and private expressions of faith is one of Jefferson's clearest messages for future candidates of his party. It highlights that the founder of the Democratic Party and its first candidate to be elected president of the United States was committed to religious liberty. His was a message of tolerance for all faiths of the country's citizens. He wrote in his *Notes on the State of Virginia,* "it does me no injury for my neighbor to say there are twenty gods or no god. It neither picks my pocket nor breaks my leg" (quoted in Sheridan, 1983, p. 11).

The fact that Jefferson kept separate his public communication regarding religion and his own individual beliefs provides an example for Democratic candidates today who also may strive to embrace a variety of views rather than cater to a particular religious orientation. But it is difficult to draw effective lessons from Jefferson's experiences. They also suggest that a political candidate's failure to state his or her private beliefs may lead to erroneous speculation about those beliefs. On the other hand, stating those beliefs can lead to direct attacks on them. In short, the problem for both Jefferson and Democrats today (and Republicans, for that matter) is that religion in the United States has always been a highly emotional and divisive issue.

NOTES

1. The Party was officially known as the Democratic–Republican Party from 1798 to 1844, when the name was finally simplified. See, for example, "Party History" (n.d.) at http://www.democrats.org/a/party/history.html.

REFERENCES

Adams, D. W., & Lester, R. W. (Eds.). (1983). *Jefferson's extracts from the gospels: "The Philosophy of Jesus" and "The Life and Morals of Jesus."* Princeton, NJ: Princeton University Press.

The Danbury Baptists' letter and President Jefferson's response (2002, January). *Church & State*, p. 13.

Dreisbach, D. L. (1990). Thomas Jefferson and bills number 82–86 of the revision of the laws of Virginia, 1776–1786: New light on the Jeffersonian model of church-state relations. *North Carolina Law Review, 69*, 159–211.

Dreisbach, D. L. (2002). *Thomas Jefferson and the wall of separation between church and state.* New York: New York University Press.

Everson v. Board of Education, 330 U.S. 1 (1947).

Fox, R. W. (2002). Jefferson, Emerson, and Jesus. *Raritan, 22*, 62–75.

Gaustad, E. S. (1998). Thomas Jefferson, religious freedom and the Supreme Court. *Church History, 67*, 682–694.

Hall, R. W. (2006). Unnatural selection: The fundamentalist crusade against evolution and the new strategies to discredit Darwin. *University of Florida Journal of Law & Public Policy, 17*, 165–187.

Hamburger, P. (2002). *Separation of church and state.* Cambridge, MA: Harvard University Press.

Hayes, K. J. (2004). How Thomas Jefferson read the Qur'an. *Early American Literature, 39*, 247–261.

Holland, M. S. (2004). "To close the circle of our felicities": Caritas and Jefferson's first inaugural. *Review of Politics, 66*, 181–205.

Jacoby, S. (2004). *Freethinkers: A history of American secularism.* New York: Metropolitan Books.

Jefferson, T. (2003a). Notes on the state of Virginia. In *The Thomas Jefferson reader* (pp. 51–181). Old Saybrook, CT: Konecky & Konecky. (Original work published 1785)

Jefferson, T. (2003b). Declaration of independence. In *The Thomas Jefferson reader* (pp. 21–26). Old Saybrook, CT: Konecky & Konecky. (Original work published 1776)

Jefferson, T. (2003c). First inaugural address. In *The Thomas Jefferson reader* (pp. 332–335). Old Saybrook, CT: Konecky & Konecky. (Original work published 1801)

Jefferson, T. (2003d). Second inaugural address. In *The Thomas Jefferson reader* (pp. 359–363). Old Saybrook, CT: Konecky & Konecky. (Original work published 1805)

Lemon v. Kurtzman, 403 U.S. 602 (1971).

Lynch v. Donnelly, 465 U.S. 668 (1984).

Neem, J. N. (2007). Beyond the wall: Reinterpreting Jefferson's Danbury address. *Journal of the Early Republic, 27,* 139–154.

Reiss, D. (2002). Jefferson and Madison as icons in judicial history: A study of religion clause jurisprudence. *Maryland Law Review, 61,* 94–176.

Rep. Ellison's oath on Jefferson's Qur'an: An elegant epilogue. (2007, February). *Church & State,* p. 14.

Reynolds v. United States, 98 U.S. 145 (1879).

Sanford, C. B. (1977). *Thomas Jefferson and his library: A study of his literary interests and of the religious attitudes revealed by relevant titles in his library.* Hamden, CT: Archon Books.

Sheridan, E. R. (1983). Introduction. In D. W. Adams & R. W. Lester (Eds.), *Jefferson's extracts from the gospels: "The Philosophy of Jesus" and "The Life and Morals of Jesus"* (pp. 3–42). Princeton, NJ: Princeton University Press.

Smith, D. G. (2003). Thomas Jefferson's retrospective on the establishment clause. *Harvard Journal of Law & Public Policy, 26,* 369–383.

Tedford, T. L., & Herbeck, D. A. (2001). *Freedom of speech in the United States.* (4th ed.). State College, PA: Strata Publishing.

Wallace v. Jaffree, 472, U.S. 38 (1985).

Chapter 2

Deities, Divisions, and Democrats

The "Political Left" and Religion

Penni M. Pier

The presidential election of 2008 was a watershed event in American politics for a variety of reasons, such as unexpected upsets in the primaries, the presence of viable female candidates, and the election of the first African American president, to name a few. However, less obvious may be the rhetorical strategies Democrats used to bring evangelicals back into the fold. In order to understand how religion served as a significant rhetorical tool in the most recent presidential election, it is important to review the role religion has historically played in politics and how the change in the American political landscape beginning in the mid-20th-century came to bear on the 2008 presidential election.

RELIGIOUS INFLUENCE AS AN INTEGRAL COMPONENT OF THE POLITICAL LANDSCAPE

The United States has a rich history of triangulating religion, the formation of public policy, and the procurement of elected office. During the colonial period this triangulation was influenced by the Puritans, who created an inextricable link between politics and religion. The Puritans' desire for the freedom to engage in specific religious practices reflected their displeasure with the Church of England's lack of respect for an adherence to biblical text, which they believed to be the cornerstone of civilian life. For the Puritans religious practices were central to their worldview and served as a foundation for public policy (Suarez, 2006).

Due to Puritan influences (which remained after independence from British rule), the early American sociopolitical landscape did not reflect a desire to separate church from state; rather, the freedom to reconcile one's private and public persona was paramount (Wald & Calhoun-Brown, 2007). These early settlers believed that they were founding a government and a nation that would be ruled by laws that could, and should, be justified by scripture. Steeped in the political and rhetorical traditions of religious leaders such as Luther and Calvin, the settlers in the New World eschewed the authority of the Church of England in light of what they viewed to be a corrupt governing institution, in the process making an indelible mark on American politics by legitimizing religion as central to public policy and government infrastructure (Holmes, 2006; Sullivan, 2004). As the geographical scope of the New World expanded, local governments were often recognized only if churches had been established prior to a petition for recognition. Such emphasis on parish churches as a marker of legitimacy for the establishment of local magistrates and governing structures serves as an exemplar for the enmeshed nature of religion and government during this era.

The concept of a formal, or universal, religion exerting influence over matters of sociopolitical import has morphed over the past 200 years into what some would consider a more palatable "civil religion" where the values and virtues of a candidate are weighed in light of public opinion with regard to fitness for office (Gentile, 2006; Wald & Calhoun-Brown, 2007). In his classic essay Bellah (1967) asserts that American civil religion refers to "beliefs, symbols and rituals" that are woven into the fabric of the political landscape. It could be argued that adherence to, or at the very least the espousal of, identifiable religious views on the part of candidates is a fundamental characteristic of the modern candidate's fitness for office. The function of civil religion becomes important in American culture because it serves as a point of legitimization for acts performed on behalf of the country and its citizenry, much as the Puritans had intended. Governmental structures and institutions have a vested interest in presenting controversial actions in the most positive light, and if those policies and procedures are seen as sacred or done with God's blessing for the nation, the explanations and rationalizations given for such actions are more palatable to the citizenry, providing that the citizenry values "the sacred" (Ward & Calhoun-Brown, 2007). Therefore, to remain a righteous nation, contemporary politics (and its leaders) must visibly and reverently value the sacred, although not necessarily a sacred as defined by a specific denomination.

Americans, in general, hold a paradoxical view of religion. Rhetorically a separation of church and state is considered essential. Yet religion profoundly influences public policy and daily life and is so embedded in the American psyche that the symbiotic nature of the two goes unnoticed and unexamined (Sullivan, 2004). Conventional wisdom has turned a blind eye to the active role religion plays in contemporary American politics. However, image restoration research has long argued that the character of a political candidate, which could include moral fitness for office and religious affiliation, can be a compelling issue for voters and may serve as a point of either acclamation or attack during any given campaign cycle (Benoit, Blaney, & Pier, 1998; Benoit, McHale, Hansen, Pier, & McGuire, 2003).

American political history is peppered with examples of the importance and influence of religious tradition. The late 19th and early 20th centuries provide such examples of the religious undercurrents in policy associated with the abolitionist and the prohibition movements, both of which at the very least were based on Christian influence, if not doctrine (Reichley, 2001; Stewart, 2066). The mid-20th-century provides an exemplar of such religious fervor and subsequent image restoration, through the controversy surrounding John F. Kennedy's elevation to the presidency in light of his ties to Catholicism. While these snapshots of American political history may seem archaic and even irrelevant in the contemporary political landscape, to dismiss the importance of religion as an integral element of 21st-century political campaigns—or to see it as something new—is fanciful at best. As evidence of the continuing influence of religion in American politics, one need only examine the presidential campaigns at the close of the 20th century to know that religion remains a central consideration to anyone seeking political office (Reichley, 2001).

THE PSYCHOLOGICAL NEED FOR RELIGION

In order to understand the importance of religion to contemporary politics and political discourse, it is essential to grasp how central a sense of human purpose and social identity are to American culture. There is a tendency for political scholars to emphasize positivist approaches in the examination of human action and behavior. Goodheart (2009) argues that making only positivist inquiries, questions to which there is a predisposition to finding or fixing a definitive answer, strips away meaning and purpose essential to human nature. Cognitively, one's worldview, specifically how individuals view human nature, is tied to more metaphysical questions of the purpose of life (Caprara, Schwartz, Capanna, Vecchinoe, & Babaranelli, 2006). Religion is often used to provide answers to metaphysical inquiry because faith transcends positivist approaches to understanding human existence. The psychological need to feel as if human existence has purpose is so fundamental that social structures are integrated into existential schemas. Social identity theory posits that all individuals have a fundamental need to feel cognitively connected to other human beings; this is done primarily through group affiliations where in-group members share core values and beliefs (Patrikios, 2008). Individuals may affiliate with numerous social groups as an expression and formation of their personal identity; this would include both religious and political groups. These social spheres to which individuals belong by their very nature overlap and influence one another. Therefore, it can be argued that religious affiliations, or sensibilities, are inextricably linked with political identity.

Among scholars of religion the concept that American politics, and indeed culture, is headed toward secularism has largely been discredited. Cladis (2008) argues that religion is part and parcel of the American political landscape and psyche. Religion cannot be relegated to one private sphere and political identification to another; it is impossible to compartmentalize the two. Furthermore, it has been argued by several scholars that religion is necessary to sustain democracy. Gangle and Smick (2009), for example, suggest that "the right to be" is essential in a democracy. The concept of a meaningful existence is an existential one that finds legitimization through praxis. Thus, a political theology is created, where the system of government is seen as a mechanism to protect the human element. Such a political theology can have both scientific and religious outcomes without having to be reduced to absolutes. The human mind feels no dissonance with the scientific/religious tension because it allows for the reverence and protection of the individual and his or her purpose in life by the government (Gangle & Smick, 2009; Goodheart, 2009). Bottum (2010) posits that religion is essential to American democracy because the business of politics needs a semblance of morality to make it palatable to the citizenry. Although moral judgments often find their roots in religion, Bottum (2010) argues that there is enough universality among religious beliefs and value systems to sustain such a democracy. Goodheart (2009) extends the argument by asserting that historically the electorate believed that churches were a check on the (im)morality of the government. Furthermore, he argues that citizens need to believe that they have some influence over government—and religion is a mechanism by which that can be accomplished.

The inextricable link between religion and democracy provides a context for understanding how individualization, the personal beliefs, traits, and characteristics of each voter, is central to political choice and electoral decisions. While the concept of religion may live in the psyche, it cannot be recognized or categorized without action. For values to have meaning they must have an actionable anchor (Mitchell, 2007). It is reasonable to argue that religious belief and values can find an actionable anchor in the political process and, more specifically, in the act of voting. Furthermore, it can be argued that, if one's religious motivations are linked to political involvement, the more intrinsic the motivation, the more vested one may be in the political process (Eisenstein, 2006). Therefore, cognitively, religion can serve as an important element of electoral decision making; individualization becomes central in political choice (Caprara, Schwartz, Capanna, Vecchinoe, & Babaranelli, 2006). Because self-identified basic human values and traits are core aspects of the individualized voter, in order to feel affinity for a candidate the voter must be able to identify with the candidate's projected values and traits. In short, religion is a widely accepted, even expected, contributing factor to voting behavior (Patrikios, 2008). Religion and politics are mutually transactional, and contemporary scholars of electoral politics must address the role that religion plays in political campaigns.

THE INVENTION OF THE CONSERVATIVE REPUBLICAN AND THE SECULAR DEMOCRAT

Linguistic labels given to an organization or coalition are inherently socially co-constructed; an individual's perceptions of these labels are filtered through personal value systems that are themselves tempered by the amount of knowledge that one has about the organization in question. The Republican and Democratic parties are no exception. The values, labels, and assumptions attributed to each party are rhetorical inventions created over decades of political campaigning. Exploring the history behind the rise of parachurch groups such as the Moral Majority and the Christian Coalition, as well as various secularist and humanist groups, is vital to understanding the rhetorical situation that the Democratic Party currently finds itself in with regard to religion.

It is a common assumption among the electorate, promulgated by media coverage, that the Republican Party is synonymous with evangelical or religious conservatives, while the Democratic Party is home to the secular voter. Hart (2001) notes that secularism is not inherently hostile to religion or Christianity; rather it is an acknowledgment of the heterogeneous culture of the United States. However, these rhetorical descriptors persist despite the fact that many influential Democratic leaders label themselves as evangelicals (Lindsay, 2007). It is important, then, to note that the "religion divide" between the two parties is merely a rhetorical convention that is based loosely on historical events both within and outside of the Democratic Party, such as changes in voting patterns, the civil rights movement, and the founding of national religious coalitions. Furthermore, scholars argue that it is problematic to categorize those who lean "right" as religious conservatives. Likewise, the term *left,* often used to label an individual as antireligious or wholly secular, is also problematic.

> Religion in public is not . . . a novel development in U.S. history. But the shape of the current debate about religion in public *is* something new. . . . Although "the" religious right was to some extent fostered by Republican Party officials who sought to create a large conservative voting block, this alliance is often unstable, and the religious right is not a monolithic group. Nor is the left that opposes it and this in itself should give some sense of why it is problematic to describe the United States as polarized between "the right" and "the left." (Cladis, 2008, p. 877)

Regardless of the problematic nature of creating a rhetorical religious dichotomy between the two parties, such labels do exist. Political candidates who want to succeed must be cognizant of them.

THE RISE OF EVANGELICAL POLITICS IN THE DEMOCRATIC AND REPUBLICAN PARTIES

In the first half of the 20th century, little attention was given to the role religion played in political parties because conservative Protestants were "virtually indistinguishable" from mainline Protestants (Hart, 2001). It was not until the civil rights movement that religious liberalism found a voice in mainstream politics (Winston, 2007). Coalitions between religious groups began to form in the 1960s to push reforms such as the Civil Rights Act of 1964 and the Voting Rights Act of 1965. Throughout this era of legislative reform, religious justification was used to address issues of racism, poverty, labor laws, and, toward the latter half of the decade, the Vietnam War. It was during this time that mainstream media began making links between mainline religious groups and the advocating of specific public policy. Additionally, in order to accomplish and promote "liberal" causes, mainline activists allied themselves with secular liberals (Reichley, 2001). While historically religious liberalism has been associated with the Democratic Party, the Republican Party was not always exclusively associated with conservatism; an active and successful liberal wing of the party existed until the 1960s (Shelley, Zerr, & Proffer, 2007). Religious liberalism and its associations with the Democratic Party fell out of favor after the deaths of Martin Luther King, Jr., and John F. Kennedy. It has been argued that historical accounts of this era of religious liberalism tend to focus on policy rather than religious motivations behind the push for civil rights legislation (Butler, 2004). However, it can also be argued that omitting the religious underpinnings from historical accounts of this era has contributed to the stereotypes traditionally attributed to Democrats with regard to religion.

An evangelical presence became visible in 1972 (specifically in the Democratic Party) as evidenced by significant shifts in voting patterns. The reason for these shifts is twofold. First, evangelicals were instrumental in campaigning, protesting, and lobbying for civil rights legislation in the 1960s; they found that as a voting bloc they could have a significant impact on public policy and therefore began to take more active roles in the campaign process. The other impetus for the shift was a reaction to foreign policy and the Vietnam War. It was also at this time that secularists first appeared as a political force. At the 1972 Democratic National Convention there was a religious and cultural divide between secularist and religiously traditional delegates (Bolce & DeMaio, 2006). Such a fundamental division threatened the unity of the Party by giving rise to the antifundamentalist voter and the inevitable clash with the evangelical voting bloc that ensued. It could be argued that this schism in the Democratic Party allowed Republicans to build more effective evangelical coalitions within their own party as well as to appeal to disenfranchised Democratic evangelicals.

Although the Democratic Party experienced dissonance at its 1972 National Convention, Jimmy Carter's 1976 election saw the first organized movement by evangelicals to support a presidential candidate. During the next four years issues related to marriage and the family came to the forefront, catalyzing the emergence of the religious right in the 1980 election cycle (Suarez, 2006). Taking his cue from King, Rev. Jerry Falwell founded the Moral Majority in the late 1970s and early 1980s. At its heart were strong, conservative positions on prayer in school and abortion. Evangelical voters identified with Falwell's movement because there was an emphasis on serving one's local community and the idea that by accepting personal responsibility to serve as an advocate for one's fellow citizens, one could achieve a sense of agency in the political process (Winston, 2007). Evangelical support thus shifted from Democrat Jimmy Carter to Republican Ronald Reagan in 1980. Although Carter self-identified as an evangelical Christian, he was reluctant to support or advocate policies—including policies on such controversial issues as abortion and school prayer—that would stifle citizens' religious freedoms. In contrast, during the 1980 campaign, Reagan espoused the view that American freedom was bestowed by God and that policies should therefore reflect biblical directives. This position struck a resonant chord with evangelicals (particularly those who had supported Carter in 1976 and subsequently felt disappointed and even betrayed by him once he was in office) and was reflective of the goals of the Moral Majority (Bauer, 2008).

The Moral Majority was a national political force by the mid-1980s; by 1984, with the reelection of Reagan, evangelicals were considered synonymous with the Republican Party (Lindsay, 2007; Winston, 2007). Nevertheless, the group's popularity declined in the decade's later years because the social issues that were the foundation of the organization were not actively pursued by Reagan or George H. W. Bush, whose focus had turned to issues such as tax reform and foreign policy. Falwell disbanded the Moral Majority in 1989. However, the Christian Coalition, led by Pat Robertson and Ralph Reed, continued to exert political pressure and influence throughout the 1990s (Hart, 2001; Reichley, 2001). Although neither of those groups remains a force to be reckoned with, the continuing presence of similar active coalitions in and affiliated with the Republican Party—combined with the virtual absence or even acknowledgment of an evangelical base in the Democratic Party, along with the privileged voice given to secularists by the Democrats—has reinforced public perceptions of the respective moral and religious alignments of the two parties.

THE 2004 ELECTION AND THE REEMERGENCE
OF THE RELIGIOUS DEMOCRAT

The 2004 conventions highlighted the rhetorical polarity between the two parties. The Democrats built a platform around tolerance and equality, while the Republicans focused on freedom as a cornerstone of American life. The Republican mantra of freedom was tied specifically to a strong military and to the belief that the United States served as a moral exemplar for the rest of the world. As Stuckey (2005) notes, "Republicans promised a nation that would promote individual economic achievement, foster governmental involvement in social issues such as the prevention of gay civil unions and the promotion of 'Christian' values, and unilaterally advance U.S. interest in foreign policy" (p. 640). Although the issues advocated by the religious right and endorsed by the Republican Party had shifted from the 1990s focus on abortion and school prayer, the underlying assumptions that the United States was built upon a belief in the religious justifications behind domestic as well as foreign public policy were central to their political ideology.

By 2004, savvy Democrats understood the power of the religious voter and were actively seeking to close the perceived religious gap between the two parties by praising faith-based organizations and deliberately invoking God's name in stump speeches, as well as embracing pro-life Democrats. Such efforts were in vain as 2004 saw not only the defeat of the Democrats' presidential candidate, John Kerry, but also significant losses in the U.S. Senate, the House of Representatives, and state and local elections nationwide. Public perceptions of the lack of moral values of Democratic candidates played a significant role in their demise (Spielvogel, 2005). Reacting to what they perceived as one-sided coverage in the 2004 elections and the inaccurate characterization of the Democratic Party as exclusively secular, religious Democrats began to organize groups and sponsor conferences dedicated to explaining how their religious beliefs informed and shaped their political agenda (Seymour, 2008). While the 2004 election did not end with victory for a majority of the Democratic candidates, it clearly marked a turning point in the Democratic Party with regard to embracing religious rhetoric on the campaign trail and set the stage for the reemerging evangelical Democrats to become major players in the 2008 presidential campaign.

COURTING THE EVANGELICAL VOTE IN 2008

After the failures of 2004 the Democratic Party acknowledged that religious Democrats, including evangelicals, could be an influential voting bloc and made efforts to court them in earnest. In recognition of the importance of faith among the electorate, during the primaries the Democratic candidates regularly mentioned their faith in stump speeches (Healy & Luo, 2007), participated in religious forums, and organized what Bauer (2008) refers to as "faith tours" in key states. In June of 2008, Obama's campaign actively targeted young evangelicals. The senator gave stump speeches in community halls and church basements and stressed the importance of social justice, a concept that young evangelicals could identify with biblically (Laidlaw, 2008a). Throughout the 2008 election, the Democratic candidates' unapologetic attitude about their religious affiliation was a deliberate rhetorical strategy that resonated with voters (Seymour, 2008).

Religious Democrats were vocal and involved in the political process in the 2008 election, due in part to the fact that Democratic candidates made religion an important element of their campaigns ("Democrats Hibernated," 2009). Young evangelicals were central players in the 2008 election. Unlike the evangelical generation that preceded them, they tended to be focused on more universal issues such as hunger and poverty rather than specific policy issues such as abortion and tax credits, as illustrated by the comment offered in this journalistic report from the campaign trail:

> Young evangelicals are finding new ways to express their faith. They refuse to be held hostage to the hot-button issues that defined religion and politics for their parents, such as abortion and gay rights. "There's 3,000 abortions in

America every day," LaTondresse [himself a young evangelical] says. "But 30,000 kids die a day of hunger, preventable disease and lack of clean drinking water, [and] 47 million Americans don't have health care." In such a situation, he can no longer support the old policies of the Republican Party. "The stakes are too high to narrowly define my morality around just two issues." (Laidlaw, 2008b, p. ID07)

Rhetorically, a door was opened for Democratic candidates in the primary; they could appeal to younger evangelical voters on the basis of broad values that would resonate with them in a personal way.

Strategies to bring evangelicals into the Democratic fold continued into the general election. In an effort to capitalize on the evangelical vote and put to rest the stereotype of Democrats' hostility to religion, the Democratic Party planned several interfaith programs and events during the convention (Kreiger, 2008). However, courting the evangelical vote involved walking a fine line; it was important for both parties to avoid associations with the religious fringes in order to appeal to political moderates. For example, Republican candidate John McCain tried to distance himself from the controversial evangelical leader John Hagee, while Barack Obama repudiated the sentiments espoused by his former pastor, Jeremiah Wright (Brinton, 2008). Still, the 2008 election solidified the fact that evangelical voters were an influential voting bloc—and no longer the province of only one party.

RHETORICAL AND POLITICAL CONSIDERATIONS FOR THE DEMOCRATIC PARTY IN THE 21ST CENTURY

Contemporary politics can be contextualized in what Button (2006) terms a "post-secular" era, which simply means that there is a renewed recognition of religious affiliation among voters. Therefore, candidates seeking elected office in the 21st century cannot afford to ignore voters with a religious bent. Since G. W. Bush's 2000 election, religious rhetoric on the campaign trail has become a staple. Domke and Coe (2007) illustrate the importance of using language that resonates with the religiously inclined voter:

> G.W. Bush's talent for connecting with conservative Christians helped him win the presidency in 2000—he received nearly eighty percent of white evangelicals' vote in that election—and, once he took office, that language became a hallmark of his public communications. (p. 54)

Furthermore, as Domke and Coe (2007) argue, there is an expectation that the president will be the national spokesperson in times of crisis or tragedy and that "an ability to speak the language of religious leaders can be especially powerful" (p. 54). For example, G. W. Bush's successful 2004 campaign solidified the fact that post-9/11 voters had come to expect the invocation of God terms. Throughout the 2004 campaign, voters continually heard rhetoric that linked justifications for foreign policy with religious morality (Murphy, 2005). In sum, it is important to recognize that in contemporary American politics, with the increased visibility of evangelical voters and the success of the religious rhetoric used by both G. W. Bush and Obama during the campaign, the religious element of America cannot be ignored if a political candidate wishes to be viable.

Twenty-first-century candidates must also be cognizant of the religious diversity that exists in the United States, as well as the increased polarity between Judeo-Christian and non-Western religions. The mid-1960s saw an increase in the number of immigrants from non-Judeo-Christian backgrounds, such that Buddhists, Hindus, and Muslims have now reached a critical mass in the United States (Prothero, 2006). Such increases in religious diversity can challenge the historical perspective of America's collective identity as that of a civil society built on Judeo-Christian values and perspectives (Goff, 2004). Many Judeo-Christian voters may not be able to reconcile what they perceive to be a nation founded on their understanding of "God" with a changing religious landscape in the United States. As Wuthnow (2005, p. 80) writes, referring to a study conducted in 2003 with a national sample of over 2,900 respondents,

> Still, the view that American democracy and Christianity go hand in hand is very widely held among the general public. For instance, in the Religion and Diversity Survey, 55 percent of the public agreed that "Our democratic form of government is based on Christianity," and nearly four Americans in five agreed that "The United States was founded on Christian principles" (78 percent) and that "America has been strong because of its faith in God" (79 percent).

The contemporary candidate must strike a rhetorical balance that assuages fears about the moral fabric of our country while acknowledging a diverse religious electorate. Achieving this balance is made more challenging with the advent of post-9/11 fears regarding the Islamic faith. In the wake of 9/11, fundamental-ism and violence have been associated with one another, making it difficult for many to embrace religious diversity in the United States (Griffith & McAlister, 2007). Additionally, the Christian "just-war theory," which uses religious justification for military action, was the subject of much discussion among the electorate after 9/11 and reached the height of national discussion just prior to the 2004 election (Suarez, 2006). Many candidates seeking election in 2004 utilized such rhetorical strategies and were effective in winning their offices, thus further widening the chasm between Christians and Muslims.

Regardless of religious affiliation, for many American citizens religion and civic engagement are mutually inclusive. As Wald and Calhoun-Brown (2007) explain,

> In many minority communities, it is difficult to separate religious culture from the culture of a minority group. Religion is of course a major way that a group communicates its culture. Because places of worship are the most common civic associations to which people belong, minority religious institutions—churches, synagogues, temples, and mosques—can reflect the heartbeat and aspirations of an entire community. (pp. 283–284)

Due to the integration of religion and civic engagement, in the years to come presidential candidates will be challenged with the task of keeping a pulse on how religion informs and influences the American voter. The challenge will be especially salient to Democrats if they are to shake the label of the "secular party" and appeal to those voters who identify with religious values as the foundation for civic involvement. It will be a strategic imperative for Democratic candidates to find a balance between striking a chord that resonates with religious identity while at the same time avoiding the appearance of zealotry.

CONCLUSION

American politics boasts a rich history of religious underpinnings; these have been key components of political decision making from the country's infancy. Prior to the middle of the 20th century such connections between religion and politics were assumed and understated in, if not entirely absent from, campaign rhetoric. Campaigns in the latter half of the 20th century and the beginning of the 21st century suggest that the electorate has become more comfortable with public discussions of faith, and candidates have become more vocal about religious beliefs and values than they once were. Along with the rhetorical revival of "God language," American culture is beginning to feel the effects of religious diversity; gone are the days of assuming that national political voices will espouse solely Christian values. In this post-secular era, scholars of presidential campaigns must address how religion plays a role in electoral decision making. The 2008 presidential campaign, which embodied the reality of 21st-century politics and its relationship with religion, serves as an excellent subject for continued scholarly inquiry. As we saw in that election year, Democrats will need to be more cognizant of the rhetorical exigencies that may arise due to the electorate's need to legitimize their candidates through a religious filter. The Democratic Party has historically been associated (although not always accurately) with the secular voter. As religion continues to become more important to all voters, it is important that Democratic candidates find a way to communicate their own religious identity to the electorate without alienating significant voting blocs.

REFERENCES

Bauer, G. (2008, January 4). Democrats and religion; Will secularists fight to remain dominant? *Washington Times*, p. A21.

Bellah, R. N. (1967). Civil religion in America. *Journal of the American Academy of Arts and Sciences, 96,* 1–21.

Benoit, W. L., Blaney, J. R., & Pier, P. M. (1998). *Campaign '96: A functional analysis of acclaiming, attacking, and defending.* New York: Praeger.

Benoit, W. L., McHale, J. P, Hansen, G. J., Pier, P. M., & McGuire, J. P. (2003). *Campaign 2000: A functional analysis of presidential campaign discourse.* Lanham, MD: Rowman & Littlefield.

Bolce, L., & DeMaio, G. (2006). American politics is dominated by battles between religious and secular voters. In J. D. Torr (Ed.), *How does religion influence politics?* (pp. 48–57). Detroit: Thomson/Gale.

Bottum, J. (2010). American exceptionalism and American religion. *First Things: A Monthly Journal of Religion & Public Life, 199,* 63–67.

Brinton, H. G. (2008, August 11). The race for the religious center: John McCain and Barack Obama both realize that when it comes to faith and the American voter, the sweet spot is right down the middle. *USA Today*, p. 1A.

Butler, J. (2004). Jack-in-the-box faith: The religion problem in modern American history. *The Journal of American History, 90,* 1357–1378.

Button, M. (2006). Religion on Main Street: Toward a new politics of the sacred and secular. In D. Gutterman & A. Murphey (Eds.), *Religion, politics, and American identity* (pp. 129–150). Lanham, MD: Rowman & Littlefield Publishers.

Caprara, G. V., Schwartz, S., Capanna, C., Vecchione, M., & Barbaranelli, C. (2006). Personality and politics: Values, traits, and political choice. *Political Psychology, 27,* 1–28.

Cladis, M. S. (2008). Painting landscapes of religion in America: Four models of religion in democracy. *Journal of the Academy of Religion, 76,* 874–904.

Democrats hibernated, McMurry says. (2009, January 24). *Washington Post*, p. B8.

Domke, D., & Coe, K. (2007). The God strategy: The rise of religious politics in America. *Journal of Ecumenical Studies, 42,* 53–75.

Eisenstein, M. A. (2006). Religious motivation vs. traditional religiousness: Bridging the gap between religion and politics and the psychology of religion. *Interdisciplinary Journal of Research on Religion, 2*(2), 1–30.

Gangle, R., & Smick, J. (2009). Political phenomenology: Radical democracy and truth. *Political Theology, 10,* 341–363.

Gentile, E. (2006). *Politics as religion.* Princeton: Princeton University Press.

Goff, P. (2004). Diversity and religion. In P. Goff & P. Harvey (Eds.), *Themes in religion and American culture* (pp. 327–360). Chapel Hill: University of North Carolina Press.

Goodheart, E. (2009). Religion as a form of hope. *Dissent, 56,* 92–96.

Griffith, R. M., & McAlister, M. (2007). Is the public square still naked? *American Quarterly, 59,* 527–563.

Hart, D. G. (2001). Mainstream Protestantism, "conservative" religion, and civil society. *Journal of Policy History, 13,* 19–46.

Healy, P., & Luo, M. (2007, June 5). Edwards, Clinton and Obama describe journeys of faith. *New York Times.* Retrieved from http://www.nytimes.com

Holmes, D. L. (2006). *The faiths of the founding fathers.* New York: Oxford University Press.

Krieger, H. L. (2008, August 27). Democrats' new focus on faith has some but not all saying amen. *Jerusalem Post,* p. 1.

Laidlaw, S. (2008a, November 8). R.I.P. to the religious right: A faith movement that defined and polarized U.S. politics for decades may have been dealt a death blow this week. *Toronto Star,* p. ID07.

Laidlaw, S. (2008b, September 27). Jesus shuffles to the left: After years of wishful thinking, U.S. Democrats are finally winning over some evangelicals. *Toronto Star,* p. ID07.

Lindsay, D. M. (2007). Ties that bind and divisions that persist: Evangelical faith and the political spectrum. *American Quarterly, 59,* 883–909.

Mitchell, J. (2007). Religion is not a preference. *Journal of Politics, 69,* 351–362.

Murphy, J. M. (2005). To form a more perfect union: Bill Clinton and the art of deliberation. *Rhetoric & Public Affairs, 8,* 657–678.

Patrikios, S. (2008). American Republican religion? Disentangling the causal link between religion and politics in the US. *Political Behavior, 30,* 367–389.

Prothero, S. (2006). *A nation of religions: The politics of pluralism in multireligious America.* Chapel Hill: University of North Carolina Press.

Reichley, A. J. (2001). Faith in politics. *Journal of Policy History, 13,* 157–180.

Seymour, R. (2008, February 22). Democrats react to media stereotype. *Chapel Hill Herald,* p. 2.

Shelley, F. M., Zerr, K. J., & Proffer, A. M. (2007). The civil rights movement and recent electoral realignment in the South. *Southeastern Geographer, 41,* 13–26.

Spielvogel, C. (2005). "You know where I stand": Moral framing of the war on terrorism and the Iraq War in the 2004 presidential campaign. *Rhetoric & Public Affairs, 8,* 549–570.

Stuckey, M. E. (2005). One nation (pretty darn) divisible: National identity in the 2004 campaigns. *Rhetoric & Public Affairs, 8,* 639–656.

Suarez, R. (2006). *The holy vote: The politics of faith in America.* New York: Harper Collins.

Winston, D. (2007). Back to the future: Religion, politics, and the media. *The American Quarterly, 59,* 696–989.

Part II

Past Presidents and Presidential Hopefuls

Chapter 3

The Three Faces of John

Mutable Religious Personae in the 2004 Presidential Race

David Weiss

The 2004 presidential race has been described as the most religion-dominated—and religion-decided—in the history of the United States. Incumbent George W. Bush, an Evangelical Methodist who during his prior bid for the presidency had (in)famously declared his favorite philosopher to be "Christ . . . because He changed my heart" and who uniformly was characterized by both supporters and detractors as the most religious person ever to occupy the Oval Office, faced off against U.S. Senator John Kerry of Massachusetts. Kerry was only the third major-party presidential candidate in U.S. history to have been raised in the Catholic Church and the first to go on record as supporting the constitutional right to abortion.

During the months leading up to the election, the Republican Party mailed brochures to voters in Arkansas and West Virginia warning that a Kerry victory would lead to indiscriminate Bible-banning and rampant same-sex marriage, while campaign rhetoric supporting the Democrats described a Bush reelection as tantamount to the end of the separation of church and state. Meanwhile, media outlets spanning the sociopolitical spectrum from *The Nation* to the *National Review* trumpeted the claim that the "God Gap" would determine which candidate would win the White House. Where any given voter stood relative to that gap, the pundits pontificated, would determine for which candidate he or she would vote.[1]

At the same time, voters' own sense that religion was playing a larger part in the 2004 campaign than it had in previous contests, and the feeling that such a change was not only palpable but acceptable, was not without substantiation. A *New York Times* poll conducted in June 2004 found that 42 percent of Americans surveyed "welcomed candidates discussing the role of religion in their lives," while 53 percent said that religion "should not be part of a presidential campaign" (Goodstein, 2004, p. D2). By contrast, when the same question was put to Americans in 1984, only 22 percent of those surveyed felt that presidential candidates should discuss religion, while 75 percent disapproved of such communication in presidential campaigns (Goodstein, 2004). Religion scholar Mark Silk explained the change in attitude revealed by the *Times* poll numbers as a "clear social trend" (quoted in Goodstein, 2004, p. D2). In Silk's words, "it is the extent to which the evangelical voice has come back to American national politics, and the expectation since the 1980s that somehow it's a normal thing to talk about religion" (quoted in Goodstein, 2004, p. D2). Indeed, by the end of the 2004 campaign, hearing the major-party candidates talk about religion during their stump speeches, debates, and media interviews did come to seem "normal," if not necessarily always welcome.

While the overt religiosity of then incumbent President Bush undoubtedly was the driving force in the "normalization" of God talk in the White House and on the campaign trail, Bush's opponent John Kerry also contributed to this change, an ironic twist given that Kerry had frequently described himself as a fierce advocate for the metaphorical wall of separation between church and state and repeatedly criticized the Bush administration for dismantling that wall. However, once he declared his own presidential candidacy and won his party's nomination, Kerry clearly recognized that as a contender for the White House in 2004, he could no longer hold such a position, however principled and sincere it may have been. As a result, Kerry began to articulate rather different viewpoints on the campaign trail. Ironically, this may have led to his downfall, since those viewpoints, whose manifestations I have come to think of as The Three Faces of John, were multiple and inconsistent, both with each other and with the stands he had taken during his long pre-2004 Senate career. While perhaps not the most obvious or most highly publicized of the various "flip-flops" his detractors were so fond of pointing out, Kerry's rhetorical vacillations regarding religion did not help him—and may well have contributed to his failure to win the presidency.

RELIGIOUS RHETORIC IN PRESIDENTIAL CAMPAIGNS: 1960–2000

While the 2004 election may have been the most religion-infused in recent memory, it was by no means the first in which religion played a part. Indeed, as Paul Boase has observed, "religion . . . has often dogged the presidential campaign trail, even invading the White House" (1989, p. 1).

Of particular relevance to the present chapter is John F. Kennedy's 1960 campaign, one in which religion attracted a great deal of public attention—and, subsequently, scholarly attention—even though Kennedy's ostensible religious rhetoric was not particularly religious at all. As a number of historians have demonstrated, candidate Kennedy's references to religion were primarily defensive, attempts to rebut accusations leveled by his political opponents and by the media that his Catholicism would be an obstacle to the proper execution of his duties as president (Boase, 1989; Hutcheson, 1988; Massa, 1997; Pierard & Linder, 1988). Kennedy would have preferred not to discuss religion on the campaign trail at all, but did so only "after 150 Protestant ministers and laymen of Houston, Texas, suggested that John F. Kennedy's religion would color his political decisions" (Boase, 1989, p. 1). As a result, "the young Irish Catholic felt compelled to ply the Protestants with conciliatory rhetoric, vowing to make his decisions 'in the national interest, and without regard to outside religious pressure or dictates'" (Boase, 1989, p. 1). Kennedy's handling of the accusation that, if elected, he would be the servant of the Vatican and not the American people successfully demonstrated his commitment to First Amendment principles, the Jeffersonian wall of separation between church and state, and the tenets of what would later be identified by Bellah (1967) as the American civil religion (Massa, 1997; Pierard & Linder, 1988).

Taking a similar approach, 1972 Democratic candidate George McGovern of South Dakota "took great pains to hide the fact (and ban the photo) of himself as pastor of a Methodist church, even though he did, of course, make occasional theological allusions in his speeches" (Hart & Pauley, 2005, p. 57). Four years later, however, Georgia Democrat and born-again Baptist Jimmy Carter took campaign-trail religious communication in a completely new direction, offering rhetoric that has been described as a blend of "private and civic piety" as it was marked by "non-denominational spiritual terms and expressions acceptable to Jew, Catholic, and Protestant alike [alongside of] spiritual allusions, devotional language, and biblical quotations" (Erickson, 1980, pp. 221, 224). Still, the sincerity of Carter's religious communication, at least during his first (1976) run for the White House, was not called into question by most voters. If anything, Carter's God-talk on the campaign trail "demonstrated that Carter was not inconsistent in his religious messages, and suggested that [his] religion was deeply ingrained rather than added on for electoral advantage" (Hahn, 1984, p. 280).

As it turned out, neither Carter's campaign trail confessions nor his actions while in office endeared him to the increasingly important evangelical Christian voting bloc, a weakness Ronald Reagan exploited during his own 1980 run for the White House against Carter. Reagan, the first candidate to purposely and consciously court the burgeoning religious right, swept into office easily, carrying 44 of the 50 states and winning 50.7 percent of the popular vote, a margin of almost 10 percentage points above Carter. Along the way, he told his campaign-trail audiences that the nation's problems could be solved "by using our own powers, while trusting in a power greater than ours," lamenting the nation's loss of the "old time Constitution" and the "old time religion," and urging newly fired-up evangelicals "to come out of the closet . . . for the country's sake" (quoted in Boase, 1989, p. 5). Not surprisingly, Reagan used similar rhetorical tactics in his 1984 reelection campaign, "string[ing] together garbled Bible verses until . . . they [came] close to code-language and gibberish [and offering] invective against abortion and his plea for voluntary prayer in public schools" (Marty, 1984, p. 187). Reagan's God-talk may have been garbled gibberish, but it did not prevent him from winning reelection.

While religious rhetoric did not play an important role in the campaigns of 1988 (George H. W. Bush vs. Michael Dukakis), 1992 (Bill Clinton vs. George H. W. Bush), or 1996 (Bill Clinton vs. Bob Dole), the 2000 race was remarkable for the centrality of religion in the campaigns of the Republicans as well as the Democrats (Pauley, 2002). Indeed, in the 2000 contest, both major-party presidential candidates "publicly articulated a compelling portrait of how faith's place in the public square [had] been devalued, and . . . made thoughtful statements suggesting a better approach" (Treene, 2001, p. 577). Perhaps the most famous of those statements was the one offered by George W. Bush during a primary debate, namely, his comment that Jesus Christ was his favorite philosopher and that "when you turn your heart and your life over to Christ, when you accept Christ as the savior, it changes your heart and changes your life, and that's what happened to me" (quoted in Medhurst, 2002, p. 93). However, Bush was not the only 2000 hopeful to express his religious views openly. His Democratic opponent Al Gore "claimed to be a 'born-again Christian' and endorsed 'faith-based organizations' as conduits for distributing social services to the poor and needy" (Medhurst, 2002, p. 94). At various points along the campaign trail, Gore told audiences that "I believe in keeping my faith as the center of my life and everything I do" and that "I believe that the purpose of life is to glorify God" (quoted in Medhurst, 2002, p. 94). Even Gore's Web site "derided the 'hollow secularism' of the Left while also criticizing 'some on the Right who have said for too long that a specific set of religious values should be imposed'" (Treene, 2001, p. 577).

Gore's running mate Joseph Lieberman also addressed faith issues head-on while campaigning, offering rhetoric that exemplified "a newer 'personalized' religious language" that went "far beyond the typical 'God Bless America' tag line of campaign oratory" (Hostetler, 2002, pp. 151, 149). For example, in a speech given at the Detroit Fellowship Chapel, Lieberman called on Americans to renew their national commitment "to God and God's purposes" and punctuated his remarks with comments such as "I stand before you today as a witness of the goodness of God"; "for me, like you, and like my running mate, Al Gore, faith has provided a foundation, order, and purpose to my life"; and "I was taught to serve God with gladness by living as best I could according to the laws and values that God gave Moses on Mount Sinai" (quoted in Hostetler, 2002, p. 149). In Lieberman's rhetoric, American history, too, was framed within a religious context, as exemplified by the vice presidential candidate's remark that the Constitution "guarantees freedom of religion, not freedom from religion. So I say that there must be and can be a constitutional place for faith in our public life" (quoted in Hostetler, 2002, p. 160).

This was certainly not an idea that had to be impressed on George W. Bush in either of his runs for the White House. As other scholars and I have discussed elsewhere (Domke & Coe, 2004, 2007; Weiss, 2005, 2008), on the 2004 presidential campaign trail, Bush continued to bring expressions of faith into his public communication. Indeed, Bush's religious rhetoric as a candidate in 2004 appeared to be a seamless extension—and even an amplification—of that of his 2000 campaign and his first term in office, all befitting that of the man who had established the first-ever White House Office of Faith-Based and Community Initiatives. John Kerry, however, was a different story.

KERRY'S RELIGIOUS PERSONAE

Unlike his opponent George W. Bush, whose 2004 religion-related rhetoric was remarkably consistent for the duration of his campaign (Weiss, 2005) just as it had been in 2000, candidate John Kerry presented to voters radically differing visions of his faith, his relationship to his (Catholic) church, his positions on church-state issues and, perhaps most important, his identity as a religious individual. Indeed, what emerges from an analysis of Kerry's 2004 campaign-trail communication is a picture of a candidate who talked about himself relative to religion in ways that varied from speech to speech, from interview to interview, and from debate to debate.

However, as I will show here, these variations were not completely without pattern or motivation, nor were they unlimited. I have found that for any given political communication event (i.e., stump speech, media interview, or debate), Kerry selected from among precisely three different personae: Advocate of the Separation of Church and State; Devout Person

of (Unspecified) Faith; and Respectfully Dissenting Catholic. I have come to
think of these personae as "The Three Faces of John."

Face #1: Advocate of the Separation of Church and State

The first Kerry face of the 2004 race actually emerged well before the
campaign began, predating not only the Democratic Party primaries, but
even Kerry's preprimary indications of his intention to seek the presidency.
Significantly, this persona, the one most distinctly different from that of his
ultimate rival George W. Bush, was the *only* Kerry face visible before "Super
Tuesday" (March 2, 2004, the day Kerry clinched his party's nomination) and
yet the one least likely to be on display after that date. However, since this
first persona emerged well before 2004, it served to set the tone for the early
days of the campaign and, more important, to shape public expectations and
perceptions about Kerry's faith identity and his campaign position relative to
religion.

A review of John Kerry's public addresses delivered during 2001, 2002,
and the first eight months of 2003 reveals that the Senator spoke only rarely
about religious issues (including his own Catholic upbringing) before he
made public his intention to seek the presidency.[2] Unlike George W. Bush,
in whose speeches God was a more frequently appearing character than Dick
Cheney, Kerry almost never uttered the word "God" in public addresses—
and when he did do so, it was virtually always as part of a perfunctory
"God bless America" sign-off. Similarly, when the word *faith* appeared in a
Kerry speech, it usually had the generic connotation of *trust* rather than any
religion-related shading.

This is not to say that Kerry failed to speak publicly about socioreligious
and politico-religious issues prior to his September 2003 declaration of
candidacy. Indeed, as amply detailed on "Kerry Wrong for Catholics," a
Web site constructed by the Republican National Committee (2004) that
was visible for the duration of the 2004 campaign, during his Senate career
Kerry had publicly spoken out on a number of "culture war" topics such as
abortion, stem cell research, and gay marriage and adoption—and in doing
so had, in fact, consistently opposed many of the official stands taken by the
Vatican and/or U.S. Catholic Church leadership on such issues (Republican
National Committee, 2004; see also Kranish, 2004). In 1994, for example,
Kerry had "called on the Catholic Church to 'not be a barrier' to birth control
worldwide," according to a report in the *Boston Globe* (Flint, 1994), while
in 1995, he had joined three fellow Catholic legislators from Massachusetts
in a denunciation of Pope John Paul II's encyclical opposing abortion laws
(Page, 1995). Even as late as August 2003, just weeks before declaring

his presidential candidacy, Kerry expressed what the *Boston Herald* called "moral outrage" over the Vatican's condemnation of proposed gay marriage legislation in the United States (Guarino, 2003).

The consistent theme running through these preprimary statements was a call for clear and strong separation of church and state. Characteristically, in his critique of the Vatican's statement, Kerry said that the call for Catholic politicians to fight gay marriage was

> an inappropriate violation of the separation of church and state in America. . . . This is an inappropriate crossing of the line in America. . . . Our founding fathers separated church and state in America . . . and we need to honor that as we go forward and I'm going to fight to do that. (quoted in Guarino, 2003)

Thus, even before officially announcing his candidacy, Kerry had not only identified a position on church-state relations but also directly linked it to his own campaign's mission.

In his 2003–2004 Democratic primary debate comments, Kerry underscored this position by taking jabs at the Bush administration's handling of church-state issues. During a December 2003 debate in New Hampshire, for example, Kerry (2003b) answered a moderator's question about his party's handling of politics-and-religion issues by saying:

> I think that we [Democrats] can be people of faith, and we are. But as President Kennedy made clear to the nation in Houston in 1960, we cherish as a country the separation of church and state. . . . And in fact, there is nothing conservative or traditionally Republican about this administration. It is radical in the way that it has trampled on that fine line drawn between church and state and in the way that it has trampled . . . on the civil rights of Americans. (2003b)

As the debate continued, Kerry further clarified his position on the place of religious belief in American public and political life:

> I think that many of us turn to God in our private moments and also when we go to church or mosque or synagogue. But we recognize that the beauty of America respects the divisions. And I think it is critical to have an administration that honors that tradition in our country. (Kerry, 2003b)

Similarly, in late February 2004, during the final Democratic primary debate, when confronted with a question about his own beliefs concerning God and God's relationship with America, Kerry said "I believe in God [but] I don't believe, the way President Bush does, in invoking it all the time in that way. I think it is—we pray that God is on our side and we pray hard. And God has been on our side through most of our existence" (2004a).

Among the clearest, most consistent, most detailed, and most persuasively argued of explanations of Kerry's positions on politico-religious issues—at any point before or during his bid for the presidency—were to be found in a mid-December 2003 interview conducted by the Interfaith Alliance. At the very start of the interview, in response to a question about the relationships among his faith, his politics, and his policies, Kerry said, "well, if you're a person of faith, as I am, it's your guidepost, your sort of moral compass, your sustaining force if you will, in everything you do" (2003c). Indeed, Kerry even argued that being a religious person was central to his own morality: "There is always a sense of what's right and what's wrong, and there are all the lessons of a lifetime of my relationship as a person of faith." However, as the interview continued, Kerry quickly drew a line between the place of religion in his private life and its place in the public role that he hoped to play as president. While he stated that his personal faith served as his moral compass, he also felt it necessary to qualify that statement:

> Even as that is true, I've always—maybe it's a little bit the New Englander in me or something—you wear it in your heart and in your soul, not necessarily on your sleeve . . . [faith] is not something that I think you ought to push at people every single day in the secular world . . . You can go where you go privately for your sustenance, but at the same time you go where you need to go publicly as a leader. . . . Affairs of state are affairs of state and they ought to be based on the discussion we have day to day about how we fund education or how big the military ought to be. And affairs of faith are affairs of faith. And they're separated. (2003c)

Kerry made clear throughout the interview that Republican politicians were not seeking such a separation. In response to the question "Why do you think the Republican Party is perceived as being the party of faith and morality?" Kerry responded that he felt that the GOP "throws [faith and morality] at people so overtly" and "uses it as a wedge in American politics . . . in a way that I think contradicts the Constitution itself." In Kerry's view this was done cynically, in order to gain political advantage: "Some of the work of certain groups in this country [is] really specifically designed towards building an electoral majority around their faith, so that they can implement certain programs that their particular faith believes in."

However, once Super Tuesday had come and gone and the general election campaign began in earnest, such statements by Kerry were few and far between. Among the rare occasions that did see the appearance of the Advocate of the Separation of Church and State persona were the Democratic National Convention in late July, at which Kerry declared, "I don't wear my religion on my sleeve," and "I don't want to claim that God is on our side.

As Abraham Lincoln told us, I want to pray humbly that we are on God's side" (2004b); his October 13 debate against George W. Bush, where he said, "The president and I have a difference of opinion about how we live out our sense of our faith. . . . As president I will always respect everybody's right to practice religion as they choose or not to practice, because that's part of America" (Kerry, 2004c); and the October 8 debate, where in response to a moderator's question about abortion he said, "I can't take what is an article of faith for me and legislate it for someone who doesn't share that article of faith, whether they be agnostic, atheist, Jew, Protestant, whatever. . . . As a president, I have to represent all the people in the nation" (Kerry, 2004d). For the most part, however, such statements became increasingly anomalous as Election Day neared.

Face #2: Devout Person of (Unspecified) Faith

March 2004's Super Tuesday not only marked Kerry's status change from primary hopeful to primary winner, but also catalyzed a distinct change in the way Kerry talked about religion—and thus the emergence of the second of the three faces of John. These changes were likely motivated by Kerry's realization that he was no longer competing against fellow Democrats John Edwards, Howard Dean, Wesley Clark, Dennis Kucinich, and Al Sharpton, and that the only rival he needed to concern himself with was George W. Bush, a politician who consistently and convincingly incorporated religious language and references to his own beliefs into his public communication (Weiss, 2005, 2008). Just five days after Super Tuesday, Kerry delivered a speech markedly different in both style and content than any he had given to that point—and one that set the tone for much of the religious rhetoric that Kerry displayed during the eight months of the general election campaign.

This speech, given on the morning of Sunday, March 7, was addressed to the Greater Bethlehem Temple Apostolic Faith Church, a predominantly black Pentecostal congregation in Jackson, Mississippi. Anyone reading the transcript of the speech without knowing who delivered it might reasonably mistake its speaker—a white, Catholic, New England-raised senator and self-proclaimed champion of the secular state—for a Southern black preacher giving a Sunday sermon or, possibly, for George W. Bush addressing a conference organized by his controversial White House Office of Faith-Based and Community Initiatives. During the speech, Kerry (2004e) referred to the church as "this house of God and home of good works," called its pastor "the rock upon which this community of worship was built," and addressed the congregants as "my brothers and sisters." He encapsulated the themes of the speech—delivered on the 39th anniversary of Bloody Sunday, the day of horrific violence against

civil-rights activists in Alabama which ultimately inspired the passage of the
Voting Rights Act of 1965—in the following sentences:

> If anyone ever asks you what it means to match words with deeds, tell them
> about Bloody Sunday—a day when faith was lived by the people who held it.
> A day when prayers were spoken with feet. And brothers and sisters, when they
> ask you if we can change America, if we can march forward for the vision we
> hold true today, just make it clear: if they could do that, if they could stand on
> that bridge,[3] surely we know we can do this.

No prior Kerry speech, interview, or debate had incorporated these stylistic
or lexical elements.

As the speech continued, its distinctions from its predecessors became
even sharper. Using language similar to that found in George W. Bush's 2004
State of the Union address (Bush, 2004a), Kerry predicted "we're going to be
tested . . . tested in our faith, tested in our commitment to something bigger
than ourselves." Later still, paraphrasing a famous line from the New Testament book of James, as he would do on so many subsequent occasions, Kerry
offered this thinly veiled criticism of the incumbent president:

> We'll be tested to see how much we really remember the words of the scripture,
> 'What good is it, my brothers, if a man claims to have faith but has no deeds?'[4]
> We need to remember those words as we march forward against a sorry politics
> where too often words suffice where deeds are demanded. . . . We have to march
> against cynicism and disaffection, so we can show those who've stopped believ-
> ing in our nation's common cause that we're different, that we will match our
> faith with our deeds. . . . We're marching with faith. (Kerry, 2004e)

Although his talking points echoed classic populist Democratic rhetorical
themes—"we will restore a government that is a provider of opportunity
instead of a tool of the privileged"; "we will honor hard work and mainstream
values"; "we will make sure that your family's check-up doesn't empty the
family checkbook"—what distinguished Kerry's speech was the fact that it
delivered an anti-Bush message using some of the very cadences and content
more regularly associated with Bush himself: "We will walk towards a
brighter tomorrow together because we will *answer the call* that President
Kennedy spoke so long ago—that here on Earth, *God's work* must truly be
our own. . . . My brothers and sisters, our time has arrived: we can bring
change to America. And if we *live by our faith* and pray with our feet, no
one's going to stop us now."

In this speech—delivered just seven days after stating in the final Democratic
primary debate that "I believe in God [but] I don't believe, the way President

Bush does, in invoking it all the time in that way" (2004a)—John Kerry set a new tone for his rhetoric around religion, establishing narrative and stylistic elements that he would repeat and embellish throughout his campaign against Bush. Few of these new elements, however, reflected any consistency with his preprimary speeches, primary debate remarks, and Interfaith Alliance interview answers, all of which had established a fairly clear, unambiguous picture of Kerry's vision of himself, his country, and the respective—and distinct—roles of religion, private life, and political leadership in the United States. Rather than John "Separation Advocate" Kerry, the face that emerged in a black church in Mississippi was that of John "Devout Person of Faith" Kerry. And as the race for the White House continued, this was the face that Kerry put on most frequently.

Beginning with the March 7 speech in Jackson, this Kerry face was on view on at least ten different occasions, at events ranging from addresses given at church conventions to remarks made during the presidential debates. This version of Kerry was first and foremost that of a religious believer: Someone who believes in God and sees the world through the eyes of one who recognizes that God has created it. When wearing this face, Kerry used language frequently associated with Christian believers, including George W. Bush, to reflect that recognition. In July 2004, for example, Kerry told the African Methodist Episcopal Convention, "I am running for president because it is time to turn the words into deeds, and faith into action. . . . There are so many issues that call us to put our faith into action" (Kerry, 2004f). While addressing the Anti-Defamation League in May, he referred to the group's efforts to eradicate inter-ethnic hostility as "not just the calling of the ADL. This is the calling of all Americans and all those who believe in our common humanity across this planet. I believe we can harness that spirit to lift our own land and the life of the world. I believe that spirit is alive" (Kerry, 2004g). And while speaking during the 124th annual session of the predominantly black National Baptist Convention in September,[5] Kerry (2004h) opened his remarks with two lines from the hymn "Amazing Grace"; talked about his audience's and his own "seek[ing] the America of our dreams"; commented that "I know, as you do, that we cannot finish that journey and reach the mountaintop without the blessings of amazing grace"; and then cited James 2:14 ("faith without works is dead"), 2 Corinthians 5:7 ("as you know, my friends, we are taught to walk by faith, not by sight"), Hebrews 11:1 ("faith is the substance of things hoped for, evidence of things not seen"), and Luke 10's story of the Good Samaritan, all as parts of his criticism of George W. Bush's so-called compassionate conservatism. Kerry also alluded to a New Testament verse in order to critique what he saw as Bush's predilection for issue obfuscation: "On issue after issue," Kerry declared, "the other side has been trying to muddy the waters to keep you from seeing the real differences and the real choices in this election. The Bible tells us that we must sometimes see through a glass darkly.[6] But on every issue . . . the choice is clear" (2004h).

Such allusions might not seem remarkable in a speech delivered at a church group's convention. However, throughout the March–November 2004 general election campaign period, Kerry used religion-inflected language even when addressing nonreligious groups and speaking about ostensibly secular issues. While addressing the National Conference of Black Mayors about environmental issues, for example, Kerry said that the nature walks he took as a child "instill[ed] a value to honor God's gift and pass on something better to our children and theirs" (2004i). While speaking to the Democratic Leadership Council, Kerry talked about "America's higher promise," explaining that "I am running for President to renew that idea and spirit again. With God's blessing, America will stand as strong and reach as high as we're willing to ask of ourselves and hold ourselves accountable" (Kerry, 2004j). And during his nomination acceptance speech at the Democratic National Convention, Kerry explained his support for taxpayer-supported Social Security by saying "we believe in the family value expressed in one of the oldest Commandments: 'Honor thy father and thy mother.' As president, I will not privatize Social Security" (2004b).

Kerry made similar statements during his debates against George W. Bush in order to bolster his own policy positions. During the third debate, for example, Kerry (2004c) noted that:

> My faith affects everything I do, in truth. There's a great passage of the Bible that says "What does it mean, my brother, to say you have faith if there are no deeds? Faith without works is dead." And I think that everything you do in public life has to be guided by your faith, affected by your faith. . . . That's why I fight against poverty. That's why I fight to clean up the environment and protect this earth. That's why I fight for equality and justice. All of those things come out of that fundamental teaching and belief of faith. (2004c)

Later in that debate, Kerry pointedly used his religious beliefs to contrast his positions and persona with those of his opponent, although he opened his comments with an apparent capitulation to something Bush had said about his own religious views:

> I respect everything the president has said and certainly respect his faith. I think it's important and I share it. I think that he just said that freedom is a gift from the Almighty. Everything is a gift from the Almighty . . . I went to a church school and I was taught that the two greatest commandments are: Love the Lord

your God with all your mind, your body, and your soul, and love your neighbor as yourself. And frankly, I think we have a lot more loving of our neighbor to do in this country and on this planet. (2004c)

Kerry even linked his "Devout Person of Faith" face to his own active-duty military experience, an item not found on his opponent's résumé: "I fought for our country as a young man, with the same passion I will fight to defend this nation that I love. And with faith in God and with conviction in the mission of America, I believe that we can reach higher. I believe that we can do better" (2004c).

The event at which Kerry displayed his "Devout Person of Faith" persona in its fullest glory was a Florida stump speech given in the final days of the campaign. On Sunday, October 24, at an ostensibly secular setting—the Broward Center for the Performing Arts in Fort Lauderdale—Kerry delivered a remarkably religion-packed oration, opening with this comment: "Today I want to talk about the foundations of belief and commitment that brought me to public service, that have sustained me in the best and worst of times, and that I will carry with me every day as president" (2004k).[7] And, in fact, he did just that.

Kerry started by speaking about his childhood: "It all began with my parents who, in addition to making sure I learned and lived my faith, also taught me at an early age that we are all put on this earth for something greater than ourselves" (2004k). He connected his faith to his Vietnam War experiences: "Faith was as much a part of our daily lives as the battle itself. Some of my closest friends were killed. I prayed. I even questioned how all the terrible things I'd seen fit into God's plan. But . . . I came home with a sense of hope and a belief in a higher purpose" (2004k). And most important, Kerry drew connections between his beliefs, his religious identity, and his vision for manifesting his religious persona in his presidency:

> As children of the same God, we share a common destiny. We express our humanity by reaching out to our fellow citizens, and indeed, to all our brothers and sisters in this country and on this earth . . . These values will guide me as president. I will put middle class families and those struggling to join them ahead of the interests of the well-to-do and the well-connected. (2004k)

As the speech continued, Kerry incorporated more frequent and more elaborate New Testament allusions into his comments:

> My faith, and the faith I have seen in the lives of so many Americans, also teaches me that "whatever you do to the least of these, you do unto me."[8] That means we have a moral obligation to one another, to the forgotten, and to those

who live in the shadows . . . The Bible tells us that in others we encounter the face of God: "I was hungry and you fed me; thirsty and you gave me a drink. I was a stranger and you received me in your homes; naked and you clothed me. I was sick and you took care of me. I was in prison and you visited me."[9] (2004k)

Kerry then linked these ideas from the Gospel of Matthew to his own political agenda, sounding increasingly Bush-like as he did so: "This is the final judgment of who we are and what our life will mean," he told his Fort Lauderdale audience; "I believe we must keep faith, not only with the Creator, but also with present and future generations" (2004k).

Perhaps even more remarkable, Kerry portrayed himself as the leader of a mission not secular, but spiritual; not terrestrial, but heavenly: "We will never fully finish [our] journey—not on this earth. But let us move forward with a strong and active faith" (2004k). In doing so, Kerry manifested not merely a Devout Person of Faith persona, but that of a priest or prophet who would lead *his* people in prayer toward this lofty goal and who would need prayers himself. To achieve his rhetorical goal, Kerry incorporated yet another New Testament reference into his exhortation:

So I ask all of you—Republicans and Democrats, progressives and conservatives, faithful and less faithful—to pray together that God guide this nation in the decision we make nine days from now. We will elect a president. Whether it is me or George Bush, we will both be in need of your prayers and your support. And pray also that our president will make this a more secure and peaceful world and lead us on our next step in America's journey to that shining city on a hill.[10] (2004k)

In this speech, John "Separation Advocate" Kerry—who less than a year earlier had declared that faith "is not something that I think you ought to push at people" (2003c)—was nowhere to be found, having been replaced almost entirely by John "Devout Person of Faith" Kerry.

Face #3: Respectfully Dissenting Catholic

While both John Kerry and George W. Bush presented themselves as "people of faith" during the 2004 race, the defining characteristics of Kerry's faith— that is, both his set of personal beliefs and the religious tradition with which he associated himself—were in many ways different from those of his opponent, a point that Kerry wanted and needed to convey to potential voters during the 2004 race. While Bush was a born-again Methodist, and thus a member of a mainline Protestant denomination to which many previous presidents also belonged, Kerry was a Roman Catholic, a fact that, as was the case for John F. Kennedy in 1960, he might have been perfectly content not turning into a campaign issue. However, like Kennedy, Kerry found himself having to defend his Catholicism to the American people. As a result, over the course of the 2004 general election campaign, a third face also made appearances— "(Respectfully Dissenting) Catholic Kerry." This persona manifested qualities not seen in earlier stages of the race.

While both Kennedy and Kerry found themselves reluctantly and defensively dealing with their own Catholicism as a campaign issue, where Kerry differed from Kennedy was in the way he constructed his defense. In 1960, Kennedy was under pressure from a vocally anti-Catholic press to convince voters he would not let his upbringing—or the Vatican—interfere with the execution of his duties as president; Kennedy, in other words, was put in the position of having to argue that he wouldn't be *too* Catholic for the American people (Boase, 1989; Hutcheson, 1988; Kranish, 2004; Massa, 1997; Pierard & Linder, 1988). By contrast, in 2004, Kerry had to convince conservative Catholics and like-minded fundamentalist Protestants and Jews that he would be *sufficiently* Catholic; that is, that as president he would *not* stray far from his church's dogma on sociocultural concerns.

What mitigated Kerry's success in making this case, however, was something well established and long acknowledged by both the Senator himself and his opponents (not to mention the secular and religious media): the fact that John Kerry did *not* endorse all of the positions taken by the Catholic Church on certain "hot-button" issues. Indeed, as noted earlier, Kerry had publicly contradicted the church's stands on culture-war concerns such as abortion and gay rights for more than a decade—contradictions exploited during the 2004 campaign by the Republican National Committee on its "Kerry Wrong for Catholics" Web site and elsewhere. Kerry therefore had to figure out precisely how to construct his "(Respectfully Dissenting) Catholic" persona for his presidential campaign.

One component of this persona drew upon the simple facts of Kerry's biography. As he declared during his second debate against George Bush, "I'm a Catholic, raised a Catholic. I was an altar boy. Religion has been a huge part of my life. It helped lead me through a war, leads me today" (2004d). And as *Time* Magazine reported in "A Test of Kerry's Faith," an April article built around an interview with the candidate, "his faith was instilled in him in childhood and . . . in Vietnam he wore a rosary around his neck" (Tumulty & Bacon, 2004). But (Respectfully Dissenting) Catholic Kerry was not simply a character who had been Catholic in some distant past. Throughout the 2004 campaign, Kerry called himself "a believing and practicing Catholic, married to another believing and practicing Catholic" (2004l). According to the *Time* article, Kerry complained when his campaign schedule required him to miss Sunday Mass, he took Communion regularly, and he made a point of letting the media know that he chose to annul his first marriage rather than defy Catholic tradition by ending it in divorce (Tumulty & Bacon, 2004).

On several occasions during the 2004 campaign, Kerry talked about his warm feelings for his church and its positive effect on his own identity. He told his *Time* interviewers that the Catholic Church was his "bedrock of values, of sureness about who I am" (2004l). During his Fort Lauderdale speech in October, Kerry said that much of the effort he had put into making America a better place "has been nourished by my faith. . . . I love my Church" (2004k). And yet, despite—or perhaps because of—his stated devotion to his Catholicism, Kerry did not wish to be classified *solely* on the basis of his religion. During a preconvention interview on CNN's *Larry King Live* program, Kerry told King, "as President Kennedy said, when confronted with this same question . . . I'm running to be a president who happens to be Catholic, not a Catholic president" (2004m).

The drawback to Kerry focusing attention on his Catholic background and his ongoing involvement in and respect for the Catholic Church was that it gave his political opponents a regular source of ammunition. During presidential debates and elsewhere on the campaign trail, Kerry was regularly called to account for the apparent discrepancy between his professed love for his Church and his frequent acknowledgments of his points of disagreement with its teachings and practices. This led to proclamations like this one during the final debate against George W. Bush, in response to a question about Catholic archbishops telling church members that voting for Kerry would be a sin since he supported a woman's right to choose an abortion:

> I respect their views. I completely respect their views. I am a Catholic. And I grew up learning how to respect those views. But I disagree with them, as do many. . . . I believe that choice is a woman's choice. It's between a woman, God, and her doctor. (2004c)

Similarly, in his *Time* interview, Kerry made a slightly less nuanced comment with the same subtext: "I don't tell church officials what to do, and church officials shouldn't tell American politicians what to do" (2004l). At such moments, Kerry portrayed himself as an independent thinker who disagreed, usually respectfully, with his Church—and, as such, as a Catholic having much in common with many other 21st-century U.S. Catholics.

The senator offered additional insight into his (Respectfully Dissenting) Catholic persona—and the tensions he faced as not merely a "person of faith" but, specifically, as a practicing *Catholic* seeking to be the president of the entire United States—during two other October 2004 speech events. At one point during the second presidential debate, Kerry fielded a question about taxpayer-supported abortion as follows:

> I cannot tell you how deeply I respect the belief about life and when it begins. I'm a Catholic. . . . But I can't take what is an article of faith for me and leg- islate it for someone who doesn't share that article of faith, whether they be agnostic, atheist, Jew, Protestant, whatever. I can't do that. . . . As a president, I have to represent all the people in the nation. And I have to make that judg- ment. (2004d)

Kerry's (Respectfully Dissenting) Catholic persona, then, was one who was knowledgeable about and respectful of his church's particular teachings but felt he could not incorporate (all of) them into law or policy as a political leader.

Just two weeks later, in his October 24 Fort Lauderdale speech, Kerry directly addressed the fact that certain Catholic Church officials had criticized such positions:

> I know there are some bishops who have suggested that as a public official I must cast votes or take public positions—on issues like a woman's right to choose and stem-cell research—that carry out the tenets of the Catholic Church. I love my Church, I respect the bishops, but I respectfully disagree. (2004k)

Kerry located the justification for this position in the nature of American society and its system of government, and in doing so, further clarified the nature of his Respectfully Dissenting Catholic persona: "My task, as I see it, is not to write every doctrine into law. That is not possible or right in a pluralistic society. But my faith does give me values to live by and apply to the decisions I make" (2004k).

CONCLUSION

Before and during his 2004 run for the presidency, John Kerry created for himself three personae relative to religion. While it may be hypothetically possible for one person to simultaneously occupy three personal, profes- sional, or social roles, Kerry rarely, if ever, showed how his own three cam- paign faces complemented one another. Rather, his choice of persona varied from speech event to speech event, often in anticipation of, or in response to, the specific audience he was addressing or the specific venue in which he was speaking. Moreover, two of his faces appeared to be not only incompatible but also mutually exclusive: (1) Kerry the advocate of church-state separation who also happened to be a discreet New Englander uncomfortable with public confessions of private faith; and (2) Kerry the devout person of (unspecified) faith who quoted Bible verses, talked about praying, and criticized the incumbent president's empty professions of religious belief. The third face of John, that of the respectfully dissenting Catholic, could be seen as serving as an overlay to either or both of the other two.

While Kerry's personae were variable and inconsistent, each face individually—and the aggregate coexistence of the three—showed that it was virtually mandatory to take a position (any position!) on issues of faith, church-state relations, and personal religious identity during the 2004 race. For good or bad, it appears that in a post-Carter, post-Reagan, post-Clinton presidential campaign, the minimization of God and the maximization of church-state and private-public separation may simply no longer play. George W. Bush certainly knew that—and, as Kerry eventually discovered or decided, Bush could not be allowed to have a monopoly on faith-talk in the election. Kerry, too, had staked out a religious position of his own.

However, while religion and its personal profession had been seen before on the presidential campaign trail, in 2004 Bush raised the stakes, foregrounding religion to an extent previously unseen and to a degree that Kerry was perhaps unprepared for and most likely uncomfortable with. Try as he might, Kerry could not strike the right tone, but he realized he had to strike *some* tone, put some face—or three faces—on his own position(s) regarding religion, its place in American public life, and its connection to his political and policy positions.

Having reviewed John Kerry's varying personae relative to religion before and during his bid for the presidency, I am put in mind of a New Testament passage. In his first letter to the Corinthians, Paul made the following confession:

> For though I am free from all, I have made myself a servant to all, that I might win more of them. To the Jews I became as a Jew, in order to win Jews. To those under the law I became as one under the law (though not being myself under the law) that I might win those under the law. To those outside the law I became as one outside the law (not being outside the law of God but under the law of Christ) that I might win those outside the law. To the weak I became weak, that I might win the weak. I have become all things to all people, that by all means I might save some. (1 Corinthians 9:19–22; English Standard Version)

It seems that in regard to his own religion, his views on the proper relationship between private faith and public life, and his attempts at developing a genuine and convincing personal politico-religious rhetoric, Kerry in his 2004 campaign narrative made of himself all things to all people—and as a result, like Paul, could win only some.

NOTES

1. A postelection study commissioned by the Pew Forum on Religion and Public Life (Green, Smidt, Guth, & Kellstedt, 2005) confirmed many of the pundits' preelection predictions. As telegraphed by the report's title, "The American Religious Landscape and the 2004 Presidential Vote: Increased Polarization," a sharp divide along religious ideological lines did in fact characterize voting behavior more than any other.

2. Kerry (2003a) formally announced his candidacy on September 2, 2003, although he had made clear during numerous speeches earlier that year his intention to seek his party's nomination.

3. The bridge Kerry refers to is the Edmund Pettis Bridge near Selma, Alabama, over which 600 civil rights activists marched before being attacked en route to Montgomery.

4. The Revised Standard Version of the New Testament, James 2:14, is rendered as follows: "What does it profit, my brethren, if a man says he has faith, but has not works?"

5. Not to be confused with the *Southern* Baptist Convention, the predominantly white and far more conservative denomination, whose annual conference featured George W. Bush (2004b), not John Kerry, as its keynote speaker.

6. "When I was a child, I spake as a child, I understood as a child, I thought as a child: but when I became a man, I put away childish things. For now we see through a glass, darkly; but then face to face: now I know in part; but then shall I know even as also I am known" (1 Corinthians 13: 11–12; King James Version).

7. The speech was "crafted with input from such Catholics as Jesuit priest and former Georgetown University president Leo O'Donovan, Jesuit Fr. Robert Drinan, former Hillary Clinton chief of staff Melanne Verveer, former Clinton administration ambassador to Portugal Elizabeth Bagely, and Victoria Reggie, wife of Sen. Edward Kennedy [in] an attempt 'to fill in the blanks' about Kerry's faith for undecided voters, said [Kerry spokesman Mike] McCurry. It is 'relevant' and 'appropriate,' McCurry [said], for voters to want to understand the 'quality of the character' of a potential president" (quoted in Feuerherd, 2004).

8. Matthew 25:40 (New International Version).

9. Matthew 25:35–36 (New International Version).

10. In Matthew 5:14 (New International Version), Jesus tells his followers: "You are the light of the world. A city on a hill cannot be hidden."

REFERENCES

Bellah, R. (1967). Civil religion in America. *Daedalus, 96,* 1–21.

Boase, P. H. (1989). Moving the mercy seat into the White House: An exegesis of the Carter/Reagan religious rhetoric. *Journal of Communication and Religion, 12,* 1–9.

Bush, G. W. (2004a, January 20). State of the Union address (Washington, DC). Retrieved from http://www.whitehouse.gov

Bush, G. W. (2004b, June 15). President's remarks via satellite to the Southern Baptist Convention (Washington, DC, and Indianapolis, IN). Retrieved from http://www.whitehouse.gov

Domke, D., & Coe, K. (2004, October 11). President or prophet? An analysis of 70 years of presidential rhetoric reveals the radicalism of Bush's religion. *The Revealer.* Retrieved from http://www.therevealer.org/archives/timely_000998.php

Domke, D., & Coe, K. (2007). *The God strategy: How religion became a political weapon in America.* New York: Oxford University Press.

Erickson, K. V. (1980). Jimmy Carter: The rhetoric of private and civic piety. *Western Journal of Speech Communication, 44,* 221–235.

Feuerherd, J. (2004, October 26). "Respectful disagreement" could be key to Kerry Catholic vote. *National Catholic Reporter.* Retrieved from http://www.nationalcatholicreporter.org/washington/wnb102604.htm

Flint, A. (1994, March 5). U.S. plans key role on population: Aim is to make birth control globally available, official says. *Boston Globe.* Retrieved from http://www.boston.com/news/globe

Goodstein, L. (2004, July 4). Politicians talk more about religion, and people expect them to. *New York Times,* p. D2.

Green, J. C., Smidt, C. E., Guth, J. L, & Kellstedt, L. A. (2005). The American religious landscape and the 2004 presidential vote: Increased polarization. Retrieved from http://pewforum.org/publications/surveys/postelection.pdf

Guarino, D. R. (2003, August 2). Kerry raps pope: Senator fuming over gay marriage order. *Boston Herald,* p. 1.

Hahn, D. F. (1984). The rhetoric of Jimmy Carter, 1976–1980. *Presidential Studies Quarterly, 14,* 265–288.

Hart, R. P., & Pauley, J. L. (2005). *The political pulpit revisited.* West Lafayette, IN: Purdue University Press.

Hostetler, M. J. (2002). Joe Lieberman at Fellowship Chapel: Civil religion meets self-disclosure. *Journal of Communication and Religion, 25,* 148–165.

Hutcheson, R. G., Jr. (1988). *God in the White House: How religion has changed the modern presidency.* New York: Collier Books.

Kerry, J. (2003a, September 2). Announcement speech (Patriot's Point, SC). Retrieved from http://www.vote-smart.org

Kerry, J. (2003b, December 9). Democratic presidential candidates' debate. (Durham, NH). Retrieved from http://www.vote-smart.org

Kerry, J. (2003c, December 16). In their own words: Interview with the Interfaith Alliance. Retrieved from http://www.interfaithalliance.org/pressroom/speeches/spc_2004_0503.html

Kerry, J. (2004a, February 29). Democratic presidential candidates' debate (New York). Retrieved from http://www.vote-smart.org

Kerry, J. (2004b, July 29). Nomination acceptance address, 2004 Democratic National Convention (Boston). Retrieved from http://www.presidentialrhetoric.com

Kerry, J. (2004c, October 13). Debate transcript: The third Bush-Kerry presidential debate (Tempe, AZ). Commission on Presidential Debates. Retrieved from http://www.debates.org

Kerry, J. (2004d, October 8). Debate transcript: The second Bush-Kerry presidential debate (St. Louis, MO). Commission on Presidential Debates. Retrieved from http://www.debates.org

Kerry, J. (2004e, March 7). Speech before the Greater Bethlehem Temple Apostolic Faith Church (Jackson, MS). Retrieved from http://www.johnkerry.com/pressroom/speeches/spc_2004_0302.html

Kerry, J. (2004f, July 6). Speech before the African Methodist Episcopal convention (Indianapolis, IN). Retrieved from http://www.johnkerry.com/pressroom/releases/pr_2004_0706a.html

Kerry, J. (2004g, May 3). Speech before the Anti-Defamation League (Washington, DC). Retrieved from http://www.johnkerry.com/

Kerry, J. (2004h, September 9). Remarks to the 124th annual session of the National Baptist Convention (New Orleans, LA). Retrieved from http://www.johnkerry.com/pressroom/releases/pr_2004_0909.html

Kerry, J. (2004i, April 29). Speech before the National Conference of Black Mayors (Philadelphia, PA). Retrieved from http://www.johnkerry.com/pressroom/speeches/spc_2004_0429.html

Kerry, J. (2004j, May 7). Remarks of Senator John Kerry at the Democratic Leadership Council (Phoenix, AZ). Retrieved from http://www.vote-smart.org

Kerry, J. (2004k, October 24). Speech at the Broward Center for the Performing Arts (Fort Lauderdale, FL). Retrieved from http://www.johnkerry.com/pressroom/speeches/spc_2004_1024.html

Kerry, J. (2004l, April 5). A test of Kerry's faith: Interview with *Time*. Retrieved from http://www.time.com

Kerry, J. (2004m, July 10). Interview. *Larry King Live*. [Television broadcast.] New York: CNN. Retrieved from http://www.vote-smart.org

Kranish, M. (2004, September 26). GOP urges Catholics to shun Kerry. *Boston Globe*. Retrieved from http://www.boston.com

Marty, M. (1984, February 22). Presidential piety: Must it be private? *Christian Century*, pp. 187–188.

Massa, M. S. (1997). A Catholic for president? John F. Kennedy and the "secular" theology of the Houston speech, 1960. *Journal of Church and State, 39,* 307–327.

Medhurst, M. J. (2002). Forging a civil-religious construct for the 21st century: Should Hart's "contract" be renewed? *Journal of Communication and Religion, 25,* 86–101.

Page, C. (1995, March 31). Vatican targets lawmakers on abortion. *Boston Herald*, p. 1.

Pauley. J. (2002). Religion, politics, and rhetoric: Twenty-five years after *The Political Pulpit. Journal of Communication and Religion, 25,* 1–5.

Pierard, R. V., & Linder, R. D. (1988). *Civil religion and the presidency.* Grand Rapids, MI: Academie Books.

Republican National Committee (2004). Kerry wrong for Catholics. Retrieved from http://www.kerrywrongforcatholics.org

Treene, E. W. (2001). Religion, the public square, and the presidency. *Harvard Journal of Law and Public Policy, 24,* 573–621.

Tumulty, K., & Bacon, P. (2004, April 5). A test of Kerry's faith. *Time.* Retrieved from http://www.time.com

Weiss, D. (2005). *Losing my (civil) religion: George W. Bush, John Kerry, and the ascendance of personal politico-religious rhetoric* (Unpublished doctoral dissertation). University of New Mexico, Albuquerque.

Weiss, D. (2008). George W. Bush and the language of faith: An Althusserian interpretation. *Queen: A Journal of Rhetoric and Power, 5.1.*

Chapter 4

Bill Clinton's Looking Glass

A Metaphorical Analogy for the Faith and Values of the Democratic Party

Paul R. Raptis, C. Thomas Preston, Jr., Allison J. Ainsworth, and David Weiss

On Sunday, August 29, 2004, just before the start of the Republican National Convention, former President Bill Clinton addressed the congregation of the Riverside Church in New York. In a speech titled "All of Us See through a Glass Darkly," Clinton (2004a) criticized what he saw as inconsistency between the rhetoric and the actual behavior of Republicans, most notably that of then President George W. Bush, during the 2004 presidential campaign. According to Hernandez (2004), Clinton was especially angered by distortions of the Vietnam War record of Senator John Kerry, the Democratic presidential candidate.

To show his support for Kerry and the Democratic Party and encourage potential voters, Clinton spoke on many occasions, including at the 2004 Democratic National Convention. What makes the Riverside speech remarkable, however, is not only the time and place of its delivery—in a church on a Sunday morning—but also the fact that it involved Bill Clinton, addressing a congregation from behind a pulpit on the topic of faith and values, speaking from the perspective of a sinner admitting his fallibility and seeking redemption. In his message, Clinton noted that all humans, as imperfect beings, "see through a glass darkly" when it comes to issues in the spiritual realm. Even beyond the point regarding human imperfection Clinton made, the notion that Clinton delved into religion at all likely surprised many who considered the Monica Lewinsky scandal the defining issue of the Clinton presidency.

Interestingly, however, the theme of seeing through a glass darkly recurred repeatedly throughout Clinton's rhetorical discourse. For example, as early as February 1, 1996, at the annual National Prayer Breakfast, Clinton stated:

> I would ask you to remember, all of you, how that passage [1 Corinthians 13:12] is worded in the King James Bible: "Now we see through a glass darkly. Now I know in part." Every one of us is subject to error in judgment as part of the human condition. And that is why the last chapter of that magnificent verse says, "Now abideth these three—faith, hope and charity—and the greatest of these is charity." We need a charitable outlook in our feelings and our dealings toward those with whom we disagree, because we do not know as we are known by God. (Clinton, 1996, para. 20)

Three years later, in a May 1999 address to the Columbine High School community in the wake of the Colorado shooting, Clinton commented that "in the Scriptures, St. Paul says that all of us in this life see through a glass darkly. So we must walk by faith, not by sight. We cannot lean on our own wisdom. None of this can be fully, satisfactorily explained to any of you. But you cannot lose your faith" (para. 40). And in remarks made on May 28, 2003, at the JFK Distinguished Awards Ceremony, Clinton noted:

> I have no doubt that I am not right about everything. It never occurred to me that I was in sole possession of the truth. The Bible that I read said that I wasn't. It said that we all see through a glass darkly, and know in part. And only after this life is over, we will know even as we are known. (2003, para. 90)

Thus, Clinton's decisions in August 2004 to speak in a church and to base his speech on the "glass darkly" theme were not unprecedented. In making these decisions, he illustrated an observation by E. J. Dionne, Jr., that political parties often "use the votes of religious people for purposes having nothing to do with a religious agenda—and, often enough, for causes that may contradict the values such voters prize most" (2008, p. 3). What *was* noteworthy about the 2004 speech was the fact that Clinton used it to point out the Republican Party's inconsistencies between walking the walk and talking the talk.

Moreover, through the use of Christian principles cited in the Bible and, specifically, the reference to seeing through a glass darkly, Clinton sought to recapture the moral high ground for the Democratic Party. Echoing an assertion made by Jim Wallis (2005, p. 8) that "God is not a Republican or a Democrat," Clinton in his August 2004 Riverside Church address made the claim that faith and values are not determined by one's affiliation with a particular political party. As he put it,

> I remember how I felt the first time I read the promise of the scriptures in Isaiah, where God says to Isaiah, "Fear not, for I have redeemed thee. I call thee by thy

name. Thou art mine." I didn't read that I had to join one party or another to get that promise. (2004a, para. 38)

EARLIER CLINTON SPEECHES WITH
RELIGIOUS CONTENT

As noted earlier, speaking openly about faith and values was not new to Bill Clinton. During his terms as Arkansas governor and U.S. president, Clinton, a Southern Baptist, often quoted scripture, spoke to religious groups, delivered speeches in churches, held prayer breakfasts at the White House, and established connections between himself and religious leaders as diverse as Billy Graham, Mother Teresa, Pope John Paul II, Jesse Jackson, and the Dalai Lama (Clinton, 2004b; Sullivan, 2008). Allusions to religious texts and themes that occurred could be found in many of those other speeches.

While the Democratic Party in general may have once distanced itself from talking about faith, Clinton in particular sought to make religion an essential element of his rhetoric. As journalist Amy Sullivan (2008) pointed out, within the first six months of his presidency,

> [Clinton] made religion a prominent part of his political and personal life. He had chosen the label "The New Covenant"—a richly significant biblical phrase—for his 1992 campaign reform. Just a few weeks after moving into the White House, he had hosted a private dinner for Billy Graham, whose preaching he credited for "the come to Jesus" moment he had experienced as a young boy in Arkansas. When it came to religion, Clinton could go toe-to-toe with anyone—whether over Scripture quotations, Catholic doctrine, or Jewish teaching. (p. 81)

At the National Prayer Breakfast in 1998, Clinton used religious language when speaking about the nature of sin, redemption, and reconciliation about the Lewinsky affair (Kramer & Olson, 2002; Lee, 2002; Ofulue, 2002). In his remarks to the Ministers' Leadership Conference at the Willow Creek Community Church on August 10, 2000, Clinton identified I Corinthians as one of his favorite Bible chapters (Clinton, 2000). Even after leaving office in 2001, he continued to speak out on issues related to faith and values, and in his autobiography *My Life,* reflecting the comments he had made at Columbine some five years earlier, Clinton stated, "I think Saint Paul had it right when he said that in this life we 'see through a glass darkly' and 'know in part.' That's why he extolled the virtues of 'faith, hope, and love'" (2004b, p. 957).

METAPHOR: DEFINITIONS AND USES IN
RHETORICAL ANALYSIS

Many rhetorical scholars (Burke, 1969; Foss, 1996; Hart & Daughton, 2005; Lakoff & Johnson, 1981; Osborn, 1976; and Preston, 1992; among others) have employed metaphorical analysis to extract the deeper meaning hidden in rhetorical artifacts. We will quickly review here just a few of metaphor's many theoretical underpinnings and analytical applications.

A simplistic definition of metaphor is the abstract use of a word or phrase to represent a concrete object or source. Hart and Daughton (2005) explained metaphor as a type of imagery. They noted that speeches, especially political speeches, are often rife with metaphors and analogies, pointing out that metaphors are used to make a connection or bond between the rhetor and the audience by demonstrating that both are a part of the same speech community. This use of metaphor creates an imagery map, which includes a shared understanding of life-as-given. Additionally, Hart and Daughton explained that metaphors can be "treated as a kind of depiction equating one thing with another" (p. 141).

According to Osborn (1976, p. 16), metaphors can be grouped into 11 metaphorical patterns based on human experience: (1) water and sea; (2) light and dark; (3) the human body; (4) war; (5) structures; (6) animals; (7) the family; (8) above and below; (9) forward and backward; (10) natural phenomena; and (11) sexuality. (As we will argue, below, Clinton used many of these patterns in his 2004 Riverside Church speech.)

Foss (1996, p. 358) defined metaphor as "a basic way by which the process of using symbols to know reality occurs," a definition rooted in Lakoff and Johnson's (1981) argument that "metaphor is pervasive in everyday life, not just in language, but in thought and action" (p. 287). Preston (1992, p. 185) describes metaphors as "indirect comparisons to conceptualize and respond to reality." Burke (1969) defined metaphor as "a device for seeing something in terms of something else" (p. 503), suggesting also that the term *perspective* could be substituted for metaphor. He argued, moreover, that metaphor "tells us something about one character as considered from the point of view of another character. And to consider A from the point of view of B is, of course, to use B as a *perspective* upon A" (Burke, 1969, pp. 503–504).

Lakoff and Johnson (1980) asserted that metaphors serve as a framework to establish a generative function for the text. This generative function further speaks to how metaphor not only shapes action and thought, but also helps to create the understandings that lead to both action and thought. Schon (1993) expanded on the notion of generative metaphor, succinctly summarized by

Haw (2006, p. 341) as "one that in a sense exists already but as it is taken up, combined with other factors and then applied to a new area where it has not previously been used, it generates different insights and understandings."

PURPOSE

In this section we will examine Bill Clinton's use of metaphor and religious allusion in his August 2004 speech, "All of Us See through a Glass Darkly," in order to illuminate the former president's views on the subject of faith and values in connection with political party affiliation. During his address, Clinton made a variety of claims, all of which were rhetorically connected via the metaphor of seeing through a glass darkly: (1) no one person or political party can or should claim to have an absolute understanding of God or of the Truth; (2) disagreeing with the political views of a political party does not diminish one's Christianity or concern with faith and values; and (3) human beings are imperfect and know only in part; we all, in other words, see through a glass darkly.

Because this speech constitutes a metaphor in and of itself and uses rich metaphors throughout, its analysis provides fertile ground for both the application and evaluation of a variety of theories regarding metaphor's use. Therefore, this analysis will identify the metaphorical families and functions that establish a systematic pattern of metaphorical usage, explain the meaning behind Clinton's use of scripture as metaphor, and discuss the impact of using metaphors on religious voters. Specifically, we seek to ask and answer the following questions about the August 2004 Riverside Church speech:

1. How does Clinton's use of the "seeing through a glass darkly" metaphor equip him to make a connection to (and reflect shared experiences with) his audience as fellow members of the same speech community?
2. How does the use of metaphor shape thought and action on the part of the audience?
3. Ultimately, what sorts of understanding does Clinton's metaphor generate in order to get his message across?

ANALYSIS

Clinton's usage of the "seeing through a glass darkly" metaphor allowed him to forge connections to his audience in several ways. First, he chose a church community closely associated with social doctrine as well as the doctrine of spreading the good news. In the Riverside Church, the congregation could relate to Clinton's message. At the same time, the complexity yet consistency of Clinton's use of metaphor allowed him to appeal to the wider and more diverse audience that might experience the speech through the media.

The metaphorical patterns in Clinton's speech can be understood by considering Osborn's (1976) work on metaphorical patterns or families. In his August 2004 address, Clinton employed six of Osborn's metaphorical families—namely, references to light and darkness, war, the human body, structures, animals, and family. This allowed Clinton to appeal to a broad speech community. However, the specific metaphor family Clinton used most frequently in "All of Us See through a Glass Darkly" was that of the human body. As a result, Clinton's language served the rhetorical purpose of reflecting shared experiences—some religious, others not—with a wide audience. For example, Clinton made many references to human actions, such as *"embrace"* ("If only we could embrace a clean energy future we could liberate ourselves"; para. 17); *"kicked"* ("it bothers me that 300,000 poor kids were kicked out of school"; para. 20); *"put a uniform on"* ("when Charlie Rangel fought in Korea and John Kerry fought in Vietnam, they did not ask what their political party was before they let them put a uniform on"; para. 50) or *"men and women in uniform"* (a reference to soldiers in Iraq in para. 23); *"cut"* ("it bothers me that we . . . cut down trees that shouldn't be cut; para. 17); *"talk"* (about John Kerry's service in para. 15; about the environment in para. 17; about national defense in para. 25; about the Republican Party in para. 30); *"running"* ("Why are we all running to the head table?"; para. 34); *"whip"* ("we plainly can't whip everyone who might ever disagree with us"; para. 34); and, most directly revealing in a speech delivered in a religious context, *"see"* and *"seeing"* ("I will see your faith through your works" in para. 21; "When did we ever see you hungry and not feed you?" in para. 21; and "see[ing] through a glass darkly" in para. 12, 13, 15, 22, and 37).

Of particular interest, Clinton grouped his human body metaphors into three categories: Democrats, Republicans, and human beings. The metaphors referring to Democrats allowed Clinton to express his opinion about how Republicans defined Democrats; for example, "on the security issues, I'm so sick and tired [Republicans say] Democrats are weak" (para. 23). Clinton's metaphors referring to Republicans showed how he, a Democrat, viewed the GOP: "I was raised a Southern Baptist. I used to wonder why the Republicans hated me so much. I'm kind of nice and accommodating. I even go duck hunting once a year. I think it's because I'm supposed to be some sort of apostate—a white, southern, Protestant. Why am I not a Republican, especially now that they've given me all those tax cuts?" (para. 5).

Most revealing, though, were Clinton's human-beings metaphors, which he used to create associations that would allow his audience to consider and judge the differences in morality between Republicans and Democrats. Speaking specifically about tensions between the two major political parties, Clinton claimed that the (Republican) members of the religious right, in their persecution of Democrats, have "tried to turn all who disagree with them into two-dimensional cartoons" (para. 3) and have implied that "all who disagree with them are somehow almost nonhuman, certainly not deserving of basic consideration" (para. 8). While Clinton was clearly critical of this Republican/religious-right treatment of Democrats, he expressed his criticism of Democrats returning the favor, stating a bit later in his speech that "we have no choice but to have a charitable attitude toward one another. It is wrong to demonize and cartoonize one another" (para. 12–13). Still, there was no question that Clinton was angrier at Republican human beings than Democratic human beings:

> It is wrong to demonize and cartoonize one another and ignore evidence and to make false charges and to bear false witness. Sometimes I think our friends on the other side have become the people of the Nine Commandments. It is wrong to bear false witness because we all see through [the] glass darkly. (para. 13)

However, while this line of argument contributed to a pattern of opposition between the parties, Clinton subsequently attempted to show how Democrats and Republicans, as fellow members of the same human race and as fellow citizens of the same nation, are actually more similar than different:

> [M]ost of the time we do the right thing if we've got enough information and enough time to think about it. We have never been perfect but we keep getting more perfect which is what the founders told us to do, and which the Bible says is all we can do in this life. We can't be perfect, we can just be more perfect. (para. 31)

Not surprisingly, given the church setting for this speech, these references to (im)perfection also alluded to the Christian belief that Christ is perfect while human beings are not. Indeed, a bit later in his speech Clinton noted that "all have sinned and fallen short of God's glory and all of us see through the glass darkly" (para. 37), a reference to Romans 3:23 ("We have all fallen short of the Glory of God"; Revised Standard Version) as well as to 1 Corinthians 13:12. In other words, Clinton was saying, human beings can never attain glory on their own but will achieve certainty and perfection only when they are face-to-face with God. At the same time, however, Clinton linked the Christian notion of (im)perfectibility to a secular concept fundamental to

America, as the Preamble to the United States Constitution calls on us to create a "more perfect Union." Clinton's metaphorical call to strive for perfection, then, was able to reach the religious believers in his immediate audience as well as the nonbelievers who might have read or heard a mass-mediated version of the speech.

Goffman's facework theory (1955, 1959, 1967), although not expressly concerned with metaphor, can also help us understand how metaphors shape the thought and action of the audience. As Goffman (1967) notes, face is a mask that changes depending on the audience and the social interaction. With respect to political communication, rhetors appear to be wearing different masks in the eyes of different persons, who, as audience members, control the face of the speaker just as they would the face of a person communicating on a face-to-face level. Therein lies the challenge to politicians' self-presentation in general, as well as their specific attempts to mask themselves. However, it is the variability of audience control over face that not only challenges but also presents opportunities for those speakers who use metaphor to try to influence the face assigned by various audiences. Goffman (1955) pointed out that we often present a certain type of face whenever we communicate in public with others. The face we present to the world is one we create for others to see. The faces we show can change with the various roles we play, such as husband or wife, parent, friend, teacher, or student. Goffman (1959) also noted that the face we show to others could also serve as a mask we show in public that serves to hide our private self.

Goffman's (1955, 1959) facework theory further illuminates the ways in which Clinton's use of the "seeing through the glass darkly" metaphor shapes the thoughts and actions of his audience. In his references to Republicans, Clinton used metaphors based on the importance of the face as representative of one's essence. He noted, sarcastically, that the GOP, on the verge of its 2004 national convention, was "about to convene here, putting on its once-every-four-years compassionate face" (para. 6), and that while "these people really do believe they are in possession of absolute truths, you won't hear about it during this convention. They'll put up their other face" (para. 8). Yet in a more compassionate moment, after reciting the "glass darkly" verse from 1 Corinthians, he asserted that if Republicans will look, then they will see God "face to face," concluding that "we have no choice but to have a charitable attitude toward each other" (para. 12). Still, the impression left by Clinton's use of face metaphors was that, during the 2004 election campaign period, Republicans were still merely putting on and taking off a variety of faces that served primarily to mask who they really were.

At the same time, in using the human body metaphor (Osborn, 1976), Clinton asserted that Republicans portrayed themselves as having a monopoly on knowing the Truth and "claim[ing] the exclusive allegiance of America's 'real Christians'" (para. 6). Yet the irony is that in portraying itself as perfect, the GOP in and of itself had erred ("these people really do believe they are in possession of absolute truths"; para. 8). As Clinton went on to argue, as imperfect human beings, none of us can ever know the absolute truth. Clinton underlined his point by talking about then President Bush and Bush's opponent in the 2004 race, John Kerry:

> I believe President Bush is a committed Christian. I believe that his faith in Jesus saved him. I believe it gave him a purpose and direction to his life. But that doesn't mean that he doesn't see through a glass darkly and knowing parts just like the rest of us. That doesn't mean that their positions are not subject to evidence and argument and doesn't mean that you can have a bunch of people act on your behalf and pretend like you don't know 'em to say that the seven people who were on John Kerry's swift boat don't know what they're talking about when they say John Kerry deserved the silver star, the bronze star, and three purple hearts. (para. 15)

Thus, even Bush, "a committed Christian," a man saved by "his faith in Jesus," did not have an absolute understanding of the truth. Bush, like all humans, could only see through a glass darkly and know only in part. However, Bush did not acknowledge his own human weaknesses. Clinton, then, seemed to be challenging Bush and other Republicans not only to acknowledge their human weaknesses but also to refrain from both passing judgment on others (Democrats) and from bearing false witness against them.

While others might have pretended to be unaware of the types of deception practiced by Bush (and, by extension, by other Republicans), Clinton's speech suggested that he could and did see what was truly happening in the 2004 race. He called on Republicans to be aware of their own deceptions and acknowledge that they neither had all the answers nor had a right to monopolize the moral high ground; as he put it, "we [Democrats] have values too . . . and we believe God redeemed us too" (para. 30). Since Clinton as an individual human could admit that he was a sinner and therefore imperfect, he stated his belief that his fellow Democrats, too, could recognize that they are imperfect and, at the same time, voice their disagreements with the GOP in a positive, constructive, charitable manner that would challenge Republicans to follow suit:

> [W]e have values too, those of us who respectfully disagree. And we believe God redeemed us too. I ask you [Democrats] not to talk about [the Republicans] the way they so often talk about us. Don't say they're weak and don't say they're bad. It's wrong. It's wrong when they do it to us and we don't want to do the same to them. But say we think they're wrong. We just disagree and our

values lead us to a different place. We want Americans to know the truth and we want Americans to understand the consequences of their choice. (para. 30)

Taken in the aggregate, all of Clinton's metaphors—those regarding the human body, the face, and the imperfection of humanity—can be seen as creating a generative framework (Lakoff & Johnson, 1980; Schon, 1993). By alluding to 1 Corinthians 13:12 repeatedly in his speech, Clinton combined these metaphors to link faith and values to political action. The repetition of the ideas of lacking and attaining perfection created a shared code that was understood by members of the evangelical Christian community. Yet, at the same time, all human beings, regardless of faith tradition, could acknowledge their imperfections in thoughts, actions, and ways of knowing. As Clinton argued in his speech, "all have sinned and fallen short of God's glory and all of us see through a glass darkly and all of us know only in part" (para. 37). Thus, Clinton reminded us all of our human frailty. He contended that all of us must acknowledge our imperfection and admit our lack of knowledge and understanding of the Truth. It is not until we are face-to-face with God that we will truly see and truly understand.

CONCLUSION

By examining the metaphorical frameworks operating in Clinton's speech, we see that Clinton was sending a message to current and future presidential candidates (as well as current and future presidents) about their actions and rhetoric and how both could appeal to the religious voter. By grouping Democrats and Republicans together as human beings, Clinton created an understanding that the evangelical or religious voter sought a more "charitable attitude" (para. 12) in politics, one that was both less divisive and more honest about the fallibility inherent in being human. His references to Saint Paul, author of 1 Corinthians, made clear that Clinton believed there was no other choice but to act charitably toward one another.

Clinton's emphasis on finding constructive ways to discuss ideological differences holds particular relevance for communication scholars. Another implication for the practice of discourse comes from Clinton's consistent use of a metaphorical framework across a series of speech events. Because Clinton had used the "seeing through the glass darkly" metaphor on prior occasions, he was able to refine its use in a speech delivered at this critical juncture in the 2004 presidential contest.

The use of metaphorical criticism can also be particularly valuable when attempting to come to grips with a subject such as religion, a discursive field where metaphors prove so prominent. Further, the current study adds to the broader understanding of metaphor as an appreciation for the ways in which political communication can help an audience recognize the importance of its own uses of face and mask, as well as the uses of its political allies and adversaries, whether or not religious appeals are being used to shape political decisions. Both current and future presidential candidates can benefit by recognizing the importance of showing voters a more open, charitable face. However, candidates must remember that once they remove their masks, voters may be unwilling to allow them to put those masks back on, thus rejecting politicians' attempts to force them to see through a glass darkly.

REFERENCES

Burke, K. (1969). *A grammar of motives.* Berkeley: University of California Press.

Clinton, W. J. (1996, February 1). Remarks by the President at the National Prayer Breakfast. Retrieved from http://www.clintonfoundation.org/legacy/020196

Clinton, W. J. (1999, May 20). Remarks by the President and the First Lady to the Columbine High School community. Retrieved from http://www.clintonfoundation .org/legacy/052099

Clinton, W. J. (2000, August 10). Remarks at a discussion at the Ministers' Leadership Conference in South Barrington, Illinois. *The American Presidency Project* [online]. Santa Barbara, CA. Retrieved from http://www.presidency.ucsb.edu/ws/ index.php?pid=1485

Clinton, W. J. (2003, May 28). Remarks at the JFK Distinguished Award Ceremony. Retrieved from http://www.clintonfoundation.org/053803-sp-cf-gn-usa-remarks-at -the-john-f-kennedy-distinguished-awards-Ceremony

Clinton, W. J. (2004a, August 29). All of us see through the glass darkly [Transcript of speech delivered at Riverside Church, New York, NY]. Retrieved from http:// www.beliefnet.com/News/Politics/2004/09/All-Of-Us-See-Through-The-Glass -Darkly.aspx

Clinton, W. J. (2004b). *My life.* New York: Alfred A. Knopf.

Dionne, E .J., Jr. (2008). *Souled out: Reclaiming faith & politics after the religious right.* Princeton, NJ: Princeton University Press.

Foss, S. K. (1996). *Rhetorical criticism: Exploration and practice* (2nd ed.). Prospect Heights, IL: Waveland Press.

Goffman, E. (1955). On facework: An analysis of ritual elements of social interaction. *Psychiatry, 18,* 319–345.

Goffman, E. (1959). *The presentation of self in everyday life.* Garden City, NY: Doubleday Anchor Books.

Goffman, E. (1967). On facework: An analysis of ritual elements in social interaction. In A. Jaworski & N. Coupland (Eds.), *The discourse reader* (pp. 306–321). London: Routledge.

Hart, R. P., & Daughton, S. (2005). *Modern rhetorical criticism* (3rd ed.). Boston: Allyn and Bacon.

Haw, K. (2006). Risk factors and pathways into and out of crime, misleading, misinterpreted or mythic? From generative metaphor to professional myth. *The Australian and New Zealand Journal of Criminology, 39,* 339–353.

Hernandez, R. (2004, August 30). The Republicans: The convention in New York—The Clintons; after sharing the White House, sharing a critique of the G.O.P. Retrieved from http://www.nytimes.com/2004/08/30/us/republicans-convention -new-york-clintons-after-sharing-white-house-sharing.html

Kramer, M. R., & Olson, K. M. (2002). The strategic potential of sequencing apologiastases: President Clinton's self-defense in the Monica Lewinsky scandal. *Western Journal of Communication, 66,* 347–368.

Lakoff, G., & Johnson, M. (1980). *Metaphors we live by.* Chicago: University of Chicago Press.

Lakoff, G., & Johnson, M. (1981). Conceptual metaphor in everyday life. In M. Johnson (Ed.), *Philosophical perspectives on metaphor* (pp. 286–325). Minneapolis: University of Minnesota Press.

Lee, R. (2002). The force of religion in the public square. *Journal of Communication and Religion, 25,* 6–20.

Ofulue, N. I. (2002). President Clinton and the White House prayer breakfast. *Journal of Communication and Religion, 25,* 49–63.

Osborn, M. (1976). *Orientations to rhetorical style.* Chicago: Science Research Associates.

Preston, C. T., Jr. (1992). Characterizing the issue: Metaphor and contemporary impromptu discussions of gender. *Argumentation and Advocacy, 28,* 185–191.

Schon, D. A. (1993). Generative metaphor: A perspective on problem setting in social policy. In A. Ortony (Ed.), *Metaphor and thought* (2nd ed., pp. 137–163). Cambridge, UK: Cambridge University Press.

Sullivan, A. (2008). *The party faithful: How and why the Democrats are closing the God gap.* New York: Scribner.

Wallis, J. (2005). *God's politics: Why the right gets it wrong and the left doesn't get it.* New York: Harper Collins.

Chapter 5

The "Voice of God" in Democratic Political Rhetoric

Exploring the Social-Political Gospel of John Edwards

Brent S. Roberts and Daniel D. Gross

The only image of God is humanity.

—Terry Eagleton, commenting on Mosaic Law

Men never do evil so completely and cheerfully as when they do it from religious conviction.

—Blaise Pascal

During the 2004 and 2008 presidential elections, Republicans portrayed themselves as the party of family values and faith. They utilized this declaration to attract a large, religiously sensitive segment of American society, in particular self-identified Christian evangelicals, who constitute some 26 percent of the U.S. adult population (Pew Forum, 2008). As a result of their faith-based platform, Republicans left the Democrats with the task of combating claims that they had ignored religious values as well as those who espouse them (Gibbs & Duffy, 2007).

For the past quarter-century, Democrats have generally avoided addressing religious issues in political campaigns (Prothero, 2008). When Democrats began to explicitly express their "faith and values," it was perceived by some as an after-the-fact appeal, merely empty political rhetoric rather than the expression of true religious conviction. This state of affairs caused great frustration for Democrats of faith. As Janet Napolitano, Democratic governor of Arizona, lamented following her party's losses in 2004 races, "How did a party that is filled with people with values . . . get tagged as the party without values?" (quoted in Nagourney, 2004, para. 4).

Given this deserved or undeserved distinction, this chapter explores the religious convictions of leading Democrats by presenting the faith of one leading Democratic presidential contender—John Edwards. We will demonstrate that John Edwards maintained a clear and distinct declaration of religious faith, and that his faith statements formed the bedrock of a distinctive social gospel, which in turn influenced his fellow candidates. As Boston (2007) noted, Edwards's conference calls and multicity antipoverty tour were quickly followed by faith forums sponsored by the Obama campaign, and statements by Hillary Clinton regarding her belief in the resurrection of Jesus. Though he was ultimately unsuccessful as a presidential candidate, his relentless assertions of faith and his articulation of a vision of a "just society" (Edwards, 2006, p. 434) raised the bar for populist campaign rhetoric among Democratic contenders, particularly in the 2008 election cycle.

THE SOCIAL GOSPEL TRADITION IN AMERICAN RELIGION AND POLITICS

At the dawn of the 20th century, a unique American-Christian theological concept was born. One of the primary articulators of this concept, called the "social gospel," was Walter Rauschenbusch, who argued that the time had come for Christians to bring the negative forces of society—social problems such as poverty, crime, inadequate or unequal education, racism, and even war—under control. Rauschenbusch stated that the essential purpose of Christianity was to "transform society into the kingdom of God by regenerating all human relations and reconstituting them in accordance with the will of God" (1907, p. xiii). Rauschenbusch predicted that as Christians gained control over the negative forces in society, a new age would dawn—specifically, the "Millennium," the 1000-year rule of Christ on Earth referred to in the New Testament Book of Revelation. The Millennium, Rauschenbusch claimed, was the "social hope of Christianity" and would offer "a perfect social life, victory over all the evil that wounds and mars human intercourse, and satisfaction for the hunger and thirst after justice, equality, and love" (1907, pp. 106–107).

The social gospel sprang in part from scientific notions of the day, primarily those highlighted by the ongoing debate stimulated by Darwin's theory of evolution. The logic of those advocating the social gospel was that if the biological world evolved from a lower state, so too could society evolve, with the Kingdom of God being "the culmination of man's long upward climb" (Nixon, 1942, p. 348). The social gospel was the practical application of Darwin's theory of evolution to social concerns, its adherents seeking to alleviate inequities that had arisen in the United States due to rapid industrialization ("A New 'Social Gospel,'" 2004, p. B6).

A vocal and passionate spokesperson for the social gospel was Harry Emerson Fosdick, an influential preacher in early 20th-century America. He authored 40 books and delivered numerous sermons at Riverside Church in New York, preaching such ideas as "the Kingdom [of God] on earth, with God's will done here in heavenly fashion, is a social idea," and arguing that true character was based on "men living with genuine power of choice, fused into a fellowship of social life, living in a law-abiding and progressive world" (1917, pp. 296, 154).

The inherent optimism of the social gospel message as articulated theologically by Rauschenbusch and homiletically by Fosdick nonetheless garnered criticism. Fundamentalist theologians and preachers like John Gresham Machen (1923) claimed that the social gospel, unacceptably, threatened to replace the importance of a personal faith in Jesus. Yet perhaps the harshest counterpoint to the concept's optimistic tenets was the advent of World War II. The war, coupled with the intensive anti-Communist movement of the postwar years, brought an end to the central theological notion that the rule of Christ would be ushered in through the process of gaining control of social forces (Rossinow, 2005).

Similar criticism of social gospel principles can be seen today as evidenced by those evangelical strains of Christianity that focus on individual faith, repentance, and salvation, rather than on broader social issues, such as justice, service, love, and care for the disadvantaged (Nixon, 1942). In a warning against being overly persuaded by the social gospel, Battle warned against it as a "false gospel" (1999, p. 6). Claiming that greater emphasis should be given to personal faith and the cleansing of the individual's heart, many evangelicals and fundamentalists continue to assert that a purely social gospel is a misrepresentation of the New Testament gospel (Coleman, 1972) and that society's ills are merely symptomatic of each sinner's heart. At the same time, other self-identified evangelical denominations have begun to revisit the general tenets of earlier exponents of the social gospel. As early as 1974, Quebedeaux identified the rise of a new generation of evangelicals who saw treating social ills as the responsibility of all good Christians. Similarly, Price (1979) noted the emergence of a "fundamentalist social gospel . . . [the] not-so-hidden agenda [of which] was to make evangelical Christianity the spearhead for social reform" (p. 1183). Michael Gerson, a speechwriter in the George W. Bush administration, referred to a "head-snapping generational change among evangelicals" (2006, p. 40) committed to causes such as poverty, medical care, and AIDS research.

It was within this context of the revival of Christian social responsibility that John Edwards developed and articulated his own faith-based social and political agenda. Edwards's sense of shared responsibility for the poor and disadvantaged drove him to political activity (Zernike, 2007) and earned him the title of the "voice of the downtrodden" ("Advocates for the Poor," 2008, p. A8). In campaign appearances, he did not hesitate to characterize caring for the poor as a "moral responsibility" ("A New 'Social Gospel,'" 2004, p. B6).

JOHN EDWARDS'S BIOGRAPHICAL AND RELIGIOUS BACKGROUND

John Edwards was born in 1953 in Seneca, South Carolina, and was raised in Robbins, North Carolina. His father, Wallace, was a mill worker; his mother, Bobbie, held a number of jobs, including refinishing furniture and working at the local post office, in order to help put John through college (Edwards, 2004b). Of these early years, Edwards's mother said, "My children were well fed and well clothed, and we lived in a decent house, but we had to be very careful with money because there was no extra" (Sabar, 2007, para. 18). These early experiences had a deep impact on the young Edwards. As he said on the presidential campaign trail in 2004, "the values that I carry with me in my heart: faith, family, responsibility, and opportunity for everyone . . . that there's dignity and honor in a hard day's work . . . [and] that you look out for your neighbors, you never look down on anybody, and you treat everyone with respect" (Edwards, 2004b, pp. 615–616).

With a law degree and a Tom Cruise smile, Edwards soon made a name for himself by representing clients in personal injury cases. He specialized in confronting large corporations in cases involving car accidents, faulty products, and botched medical procedures (Sabar, 2007). Known for relentless preparation, Edwards was also a "natural courtroom showman," winning the trust of juries as well as record verdicts for his clients (Campo-Flores, Bailey, Alter, Clift, & Ramirez, 2007, para. 18).

On April 4, 1996, Edwards's world was shaken to the core when his son Wade died in a tragic one-car accident. Though the Edwardses had discussed John's possible entry into the world of politics prior to this event, Wade's death galvanized the couple, giving them a shared sense of purpose and a drive to serve. As John Edwards said, "We've been through the worst a couple can go through. . . . So long as there's something you can do that's positive, there's a chance. As long as there's a chance, there's something to hold on to" (quoted in Zernike, 2007, para. 7).

Edwards served one term in the U.S. Senate, from 1998 to 2004. He ran for president in 2004, sounding a frequent theme of "Two Americas"—"one for people who have lived the American Dream and don't have to worry, and another for most Americans who work hard and still struggle to make ends meet" (Edwards, 2004b, p. 616; see also Keen, 2007; Ross, 2004). He was tapped as the vice presidential running mate by John Kerry in the 2004 election in hopes that his Southern connections would improve the Massachusetts senator's chances to win the presidency.

In spite of—or perhaps because of—the Democrats' loss in 2004, Edwards continued his antipoverty crusade unabated. He founded the Center on Poverty, Work, and Opportunity at the University of North Carolina, chaired the Half in Ten campaign dedicated to reducing poverty by half within a decade, worked with college students in New Orleans following Hurricane Katrina, and sponsored several forums on poverty (Edwards, 2008c; Keen, 2007; Sabar, 2007).

Edwards ran for president again in 2008, continuing to campaign in spite of his wife's recurrent breast cancer (Connelly, 2007). Instead of withdrawing from the race, Edwards saw the diagnosis as a further motivation to press forward with the campaign, stating:

> If you are looking for heroes, don't look to me, look to Elizabeth. We have support, we have health care, we have the American people behind us. Look to them; they are the ones that we speak for. They are the ones that we stand up for. And Elizabeth and I decided in the quiet of a hospital room, after 12 hours of tests and after getting very bad news, what we were going to spend our lives doing. For all those that have no voice. We are not going to quietly go away. Instead we are going to go out and fight for what it is we believe in. It is time for our party, the Democratic Party, to show a little backbone, to have a little guts. Stand up for working men and women. If we are not their voice, they will never have a voice. (quoted in Hauser, 2007, para. 2)

However, after early successes, Edwards fell behind Obama, Clinton, and Gore (who was not even running) in the polls (Keen, 2007). He withdrew from the race abruptly in January 2008. A senior campaign adviser, Joe Trippi, claimed that Edwards "wanted to have a shot at being president. . . . He wanted to have a chance to change people's lives, not to be a spoiler or a kingmaker and not play political games" (quoted in Bosman & Zernike, 2008, para. 4).

In analyzing Edwards's social-political gospel, it is important to trace the roots of his faith, including his declarations of faith on the campaign trail. The son of a Southern Baptist deacon, Edwards said "[my] belief in Christ plays an enormous role in the way I view the world" (quoted in Burke, 2007,

p. 12), and "my faith informs everything I think and do" (quoted in Kennedy, 2007, para. 5).

Though he attended meetings and revivals with his parents as a child, he "drifted from [his] faith" during his college years, and after marrying Elizabeth, though they attended church, "it was not the sort of dominant day-to-day living faith that it is for me today" (quoted in Sabar, 2007, p. 1). Then, when his son Wade died in 1996, "my faith came roaring back, and has stayed with me since that time, and helped me deal with the personal challenges we've had" (quoted in Kuo, 2007, pars. 4-5). Referring to his son's death and to his wife's ongoing bouts with breast cancer, Edwards later said, "It was the Lord that got me through that" (quoted in Pickler, 2007, para. 8). Following Wade's death, Edwards joined his wife at United Methodist prayer meetings and Bible study groups. He came to realize "how much I was dependent on my faith, on God, and that I was not in control" (Sabar, 2007).

Though Edwards received no formal theological training, his personal faith journey set the stage for the development of his social-political gospel. His involvement in church life during his early years and in the period following his son's death solidified his concept of social responsibility for caring for the disadvantaged, and motivated him to pursue service on a personal level and to enter into politics in order to serve others on a broader scale ("Q&A: John Edwards," 2006), a commitment solidified through his experiences with Elizabeth's cancer.

THE SOCIAL-POLITICAL GOSPEL OF JOHN EDWARDS

The roots of Edwards's social gospel can be readily seen in his 2004 campaign rhetoric. However, the tenor of this rhetoric was expanded for his 2008 bid, encompassing a virtual quest for social justice, equality of opportunity, racial equality, and universal access to both health care and education. In the following section, we will outline the language from his 2004 campaign, and demonstrate how his message was refined and expanded for 2008.

The 2004 Campaign

In his 2004 presidential bid, Edwards made few references to his personal faith, claiming it was "a private matter" (quoted in Sabar, 2007, p. 1). Rare was the direct expression of religiosity such as this:

> My faith has been enormous to me in my personal life and of course my personal life has a big impact on my political life. I have had an interesting faith journey over the course of my life. I was born and raised in the Southern Baptist church,

I was baptized in the Southern Baptist Church and then later in life joined the Methodist church and like a lot of people, when I was in my college years, and I went to law school and became a lawyer and was raising my young family I moved away somewhat from my faith. And then I lost a son in 1996 and my faith came roaring back and it played an enormous role in my ability to get through that period. It stayed with me and has been enormously important. (Edwards, 2004a, para. 3)

While Edwards touched on his orthodox roots and occasionally shared personal testimony like that above, more common in his public communication were comments about the responsibility of all citizens to care for the needs of individuals, the country, and the world, particularly the responsibility to care for the poor. He tended to frame his antipoverty rhetoric as a moral cause rather than a religious or financial cause: "This is not about economic issues. This is about right and wrong" (quoted in Dionne, 2004, par 6). Linking his presidential bid to his own biography, Edwards noted:

In terms of my political life I believe there are a lot of the things that are part of my faith belief that are also part of my political belief. My responsibilities to others, to help others. . . . To provide help to the homeless in the Raleigh-Durham area in North Carolina is an example of that. So I think it's just part of my entire life. (Edwards, 2004a, para. 4)

Antipoverty messages were at the core of Edwards's campaigns in both 2004 and 2008. He stated openly that "I know this is my life's work" (quoted in Darman, 2007, para. 13). He claimed that Americans can "eliminate poverty within a generation" (quoted in Darman, 2007, para. 12), and proposed as an initial step the appointment of a cabinet-level antipoverty post (Sabar, 2007). He repeatedly emphasized that his dedication to this issue went far beyond mere politics. He told a group of Christian college students that "This is not an issue that I just talk about when I come to you. This is an issue that I talk about all over America in front of all kinds of audiences because it's part of who I am. . . . As long as I am alive and breathing, I will be out there fighting with everything I have to help the poor in this country" (quoted in Burke, 2007, p. 12).

Part of Edwards's social gospel included his commitment to equality of opportunity for all races. In the 2004 campaign, drawing on his own experiences with racism growing up in the South, Edwards stated:

From the time I was very young, I saw the ugly face of segregation and discrimination. I saw young African-American kids sent upstairs in movie theaters. I saw "white only" signs on restaurant doors and luncheon counters. I feel such an enormous responsibility when it comes to issues of race and equality and civil rights. I have heard some discussions and debates about where, and in front of what audiences we should talk about race, equality, and civil rights. Well, I have an answer to that question. Everywhere. (2004b, p. 617)

The 2008 Campaign

In 2008, Edwards expanded his antipoverty theme and opened up about his own faith experiences. While he asserted that his religion was "a private matter" in 2004, Edwards gave it much more airtime in 2008, speaking frankly and frequently about his faith as time went on (Sabar, 2007). Though Republicans had nearly cornered the family values market for the preceding 25 years, Edwards was able to break the Democrats' "determination either to avoid uttering God's name or to stammer while doing so" (Prothero, 2008, para. 2). To that end, Edwards was forthright in talking about his faith during his 2008 political race—yet he vehemently denied that his increase in talk about religion was motivated by his political aspirations. When asked whether he thought that candidates were talking too much about faith, for example, he responded:

> Faith is not a political strategy, and should not be a political strategy. If it is being used as a tool to garner votes, to convince people that they should support one political party or the other, I think that is a huge mistake. I believe with every fiber of my being that God is not a Democrat or a Republican and does not support either party. (quoted in Kuo, 2007, para. 34)

Addressing a theme that would be familiar territory for conservatives, Edwards spoke about sin: "I sin every single day. We are sinners and we all fall short" (quoted in Pickler, 2007, para. 3), though when pressed for an example in an interview he said, "I'd have a very hard time telling you one thing, one specific sin. If I've had a day in my 54 years that I haven't sinned multiple times I'd be amazed. We all fall short, which is why we have to ask for forgiveness from the Lord" (quoted in Boston, 2007, p. 8).

Appealing to religious, conservative voters—staples of the George W. Bush era—was important for all candidates in 2008. Though beset with conflict and claims of religious discrimination, so-called "faith-based initiatives" were nevertheless a "defining policy" of the Bush administration (Steinfels, 2009, para. 2), and clearly one that Edwards, too, supported. Speaking of the importance of the work of faith-based groups, Edwards said:

> Faith-based groups should be central to what we're trying to do—for a whole variety of reasons, including that they can reach large segments of the American

people, they can talk about our mission and why it's so important and why—at least in the case of a Christian like myself—it is Christ-driven. (Edwards, 2008b, p. 22)

Edwards freely invoked Jesus in his campaign rhetoric, an unusual move for almost any presidential candidate, Republican or Democratic. Noting his own philanthropic and humanitarian efforts, including providing learning technology centers for low-income students, funding college scholarships, and building homes for low-income families, Edwards postulated that "I think Jesus would be happy with some of the things we've done" (quoted in Kuo, 2007, para. 23). Edwards also referred frequently to Christian scripture, claiming that Christians need look no further than the Bible for motivation to reach out and lift up others from poverty:

It's the foundation of my belief that we have a responsibility to the least among us and those who are struggling to get a chance. It's not just a personal responsibility, but a collective responsibility that all of us have. It's a huge motivation that if you look for references in the Bible for helping the poor and disenfranchised and those who are struggling, then you have an awful lot of the Bible. It's foundation for me. (Edwards, 2008b, p. 14)

Edwards was even able, on occasion, to bring the subject of his faith into more typically secular conversations. At one rally, when asked about abortion, he said that "Because nobody made me God about [this], I don't believe it's right for government to tell women what to do" (quoted in Sabar, 2007, para. 10). In such situations, Edwards proved to be a master at proclaiming his faith even on subjects that would make more conservative Christians cringe.

Perhaps the most poignant statement made by Edwards, however, and one that focused all of the details of the responsibilities he emphasized, is this one: "I think that Jesus would be disappointed in our ignoring the plight of those around us who are suffering and our focus on our own selfish short-term needs. I think he would be appalled, actually" (quoted in Kuo, 2007, para. 2). This statement revealed not only his personal Christian faith but what that faith meant to him: the belief that Christianity demands social activism.

As noted earlier, Edwards's statements revealed a personal, private faith characteristic of some evangelical/fundamentalist variations, a faith characterized by a strong social flavor. To Edwards, separating religious faith from political activity seemed impossible. Rhetorically, Edwards connected the merely personal aspects of his faith to his campaign call for an American society in need of healing, a blending of the personal and the social that was unique on the campaign trail in the first decade of the 21st century. Edwards seemed to have been motivated by the New Testament verse James 2:26: "Faith without works is dead." His emphasis went beyond personal faith to embrace "more dramatic, more transformational change" (Keen, 2007, para. 29).

Early in the 2008 presidential election cycle, former Bush speechwriter Michael Gerson (2006) spoke about the importance that religion would play in the upcoming election, focusing specifically on the place of evangelicals. He predicted that Republicans would face difficulty in attracting these evangelicals through dogmatic emphasis on such issues as prayer in schools or the Ten Commandments, and that Democrats would need to be more genuine in their declarations of religious faith. Like Rauschenbach and Fosdick, these evangelical activists (including Rick Warren, who led an anti-AIDS, antipoverty crusade in Africa, and Gary Haugen, who worked to stamp out rape and sex slavery in the Third World) emphasized the importance of greater engagement with the world through service to others. This engagement focused on issues including justice and equality of opportunity, poverty, health care, race, labor relations, and education. These were the very same themes that Edwards hammered home throughout his "campaign to transform America" (Bender, 2007, para. 2), freely mixing calls to action and policy proposals with statements of personal faith.

Edwards was driven by a vision of a "just society" (Edwards, 2006), and he consistently framed his antipoverty, anticorruption stand as a moral responsibility. Standing with California custodians who sought wage increases, Edwards declared that "This march for economic and social justice for the men and women who work at this university is a part of a bigger march in America for fairness and equality" (quoted in Bender, 2007, para. 5). As had been the case in 2004, in the 2008 campaign Edwards's message was focused on "social justice" (Gerstein, 2006, par 2), an emphasis not seen since Lyndon Johnson's War on Poverty in the 1960s (Connelly, 2007; Keen, 2007) or Jimmy Carter's 1976 pledges to reform welfare, restructure the tax code, and stimulate a difficult economy (Steuart & Lietman, 1980). His vision was not limited to helping people survive. He believed that all should have the opportunity to partake in the American Dream, and his idea of a just society was "an America that rewards work to build wealth so that everybody has a chance to succeed" (Edwards, 2006, p. 435). To Edwards, this meant also attacking corporate corruption, calling for major revisions of the tax code, speaking out against corruption in government, and calling for the closure of the U.S. military base at Guantanamo Bay (Canellos & Issenberg, 2007; Connelly, 2007; Edwards, 2006).

Edwards also called for "abolishing the tax code of special privileges for wealth" (2006, p. 436), emphasizing that "The bottom line is that your tax rate should be based on your income each year, not how many lawyers and accountants you can afford to hire each year" (p. 437). Edwards's vision of helping the weak and lending a voice to the disenfranchised stretched far beyond American borders. As part of his plan to "stabilize weak and failing states and provide humanitarian assistance to the victims of disasters across the world," he proposed the creation of the "Marshall Corps . . . [which would] consist of 10,000 civilian experts who could be deployed abroad to serve in reconstruction, stabilization, and humanitarian missions. They will be on the frontline in the United States' reengagement with the world" (Edwards, 2007a).

Edwards's efforts to provide access to the American Dream to all segments of society extended to the provision of universal health care. Speaking on the issue of universal access to health care, Edwards made some of his strongest statements, referring to the need to "make affordable, high-quality health care a part of the social compact," and further stating that the high number of Americans without insurance constituted "a moral disgrace" (2008, para. 6.) Edwards's views on health care were deeply affected by his wife's breast cancer diagnosis and later recurrence (Hauser, 2007). As part of his plan to build one America, Edwards proposed tax incentives for companies to provide reasonable health care premiums, more choices for health care, and a system of health care markets. He also proposed better chronic and preventive care and improved chronic care management (Edwards, 2007b).

Edwards's 2008 campaign also featured an intensified focus on racial equality and civil rights. For Edwards, "The fight for civil rights and equal rights and economic and social justice is still going on across our country" ("Edwards Statement," 2008, para. 4). Commemorating the 42nd anniversary of the march in Selma, Alabama, Edwards noted that the work of achieving equality for all was not yet complete:

> You need not come from the South or grow up in the civil rights era to know that there are still deep inequalities in this country. The commemoration of Selma is an important reminder that the struggle for civil rights and equal rights and economic and social justice still goes on. It's going on right here, right now, and that's why we're here today. (quoted in Bender, 2007, para. 19)

Indeed, civil rights and equal rights were a fundamental part of Edwards's social gospel. In a January 2008 statement in honor of Martin Luther King, Jr.'s, birthday, Edwards called for a commitment to "reigniting the revolution of values that Dr. King dreamed about, to speaking out against unfairness and injustice, to making sure the voice of every American is heard and to building One America" ("Edwards Statement," 2008, para. 5).

Edwards's commitment to diversity extended beyond race issues to include religious diversity as well. Indeed, he walked a fine line between courting the new evangelicals described elsewhere in this chapter, and retaining the support of faithful card-carrying Democrats, at least a third of whom claim to attend church rarely, if ever (Boston, 2007). Emphasizing his ability to serve all the citizens of the United States, religious and irreligious alike, he said, "I think I also understand the distinction between my job as president of the United States [and] my responsibility to be respectful of and to embrace all faith beliefs in this country because we have many faith beliefs in America" ("Candidates on Religion," 2007, para. 4).

Edwards's social gospel extended also to the issue of access to education. Edwards called for at least $500 to be provided to every American child at birth. Until the child's eighteenth birthday, contributions could be made to this government savings account, until it would grow (by Edwards's estimate) to approximately $40,000. At 18, if the student studied hard and stayed in school, she or he could claim the money to be used for college, a house, or retirement (Edwards, 2006). At the higher education level, Edwards proposed that the federal government should pay tuition for students unable to afford college themselves (Beale, 2007). He also called for closing banks that act as intermediaries for student loans (Conniff, 2008).

Edwards's vision of educational opportunities was not limited to the United States. Calling on Americans to "do things beyond our selfish motives" (quoted in Connelly, 2007, para. 18), he proposed spending as much as $3.5 billion a year to provide educational opportunities for millions of elementary-age schoolchildren worldwide, partly as a means of garnering pro-American sentiment around the world (Beale, 2007; Edwards, 2007).

As a whole, then, the campaign rhetoric employed by Edwards in 2008 pointed to an agenda of greater engagement both domestically and inter-nationally, a key virtue espoused by new evangelicals. Yet what Edwards did was link this *new* evangelical theme to classic American values. In fact, Edwards stated that "We must reengage with our history of courage, liberty, and generosity. We must reengage with our tradition of moral leadership. . . . And our government must reengage with the American people to restore our nation's reputation as a moral beacon to the world" (2007, para. 2).

THE DOWNFALL OF JOHN EDWARDS

Edwards was dogged by claims that his luxurious lifestyle was not consistent with the populist, antipoverty message of his social gospel. On the campaign trail, he was continually faced with questions about his $400 haircuts, his 28,000-square-foot mansion, and his work with a questionable hedge fund (Campo-Flores et al., 2007). He deflected these charges by changing the focus to his humble upbringing: "I came from nothing and worked hard and was lucky enough to be successful, and I'm proud of what I did with my life" (quoted in Keen, 2007, para. 17). Edwards openly admitted that "I have a blessed life now, at least in material things. It's not the place I come from. I remember vividly the place I come from" (quoted in Connelly, 2007, para. 2). He countered criticism about his mansion by saying that:

> It doesn't matter what the outside of your house looks like. I know this because I've lived in every kind of house you can live in in this country, including the two-room house that I was brought home to when I was born. What matters is what's inside and what it is you teach your kids and your family about your responsibility to help those around you. (quoted in Keen, 2007, para. 15)

However, despite Edwards's rationalizations for his lavish lifestyle, many voters still dwelled on the inconsistencies. "He's the haircut guy, isn't he?" responded one voter when asked about his feelings about Edwards (Connelly, 2007, para. 25).

In many ways, Edwards's campaign rhetoric echoed that of Robert Kennedy's in 1968. Kennedy stood for erasing poverty, referring to "the other America" where Native Americans, blacks, and other citizens struggled to find food, shelter, and health care (MacAfee, 2004, pp. 40-41). However, in many ways, the comparisons between Edwards and Kennedy fell short. As Darman (2007) concluded, whereas Kennedy had been frequently unkempt and impulsive, and delighted in straying from preset campaign schedules, Edwards was too perfect and too scripted. Still, Edwards did not discourage comparisons of his own antipoverty message with that of Kennedy, telling one audience, "I want you to join us to end the work Bobby Kennedy started" (Darman, 2007, para. 1). He was reportedly sobered when Senator Edward Kennedy endorsed Barack Obama (Bosman & Zernike, 2008, para. 15).

The final nail in the coffin of Edwards's credibility—and, ultimately, his political aspirations—was hammered in August 2008 when he announced that he had been having an extramarital affair with former campaign videographer Rielle Hunter. The revelation was made after ten months of denials by Edwards, his wife Elizabeth, and Hunter herself. As one editorial put it, Edwards "initially did what every politician does when caught in a bed that wasn't his. He lied about it until he couldn't any more" ("Edwards Proves Not So Holy," 2008, para. 4). The announcement, conspicuously timed to coincide with the opening of the Beijing Olympics ("For Edwards, Only Full Truth," 2008), further undermined Edwards's campaign rhetoric regarding wholesomeness, faith, and working-class family values. His excuse that the affair occurred when his wife's cancer was in remission did nothing to mitigate the scandal (King, 2008).

The process by which the affair was revealed publicly was itself a study in politics within the U.S. media hierarchy. The earliest reports of the affair were published by the *National Enquirer* in August 2007, followed by reports in December that Hunter was pregnant. Most major news outlets, both print and broadcast, refused to take up the story, deeming it a matter (as Edwards himself put it) of "tabloid trash" ("For Edwards, Only Full Truth," 2008, para. 5). When the *Enquirer* published photos of Edwards visiting Hunter and her baby at a hotel in July 2008, however, the affair became a feature story in the mainstream media (Perez-Pena & Carter, 2008). The claim of paternity by a campaign staffer, with a subsequent retraction, further muddied the waters (Lewis, 2009). In his tell-all book, the staffer claimed that Edwards told Hunter he would marry her after Elizabeth succumbed to breast cancer (Moore, 2009).

Also curious was the support given to Edwards by his wife in spite of her knowledge early on about her husband's indiscretions. According to Elizabeth Edwards, John told her of the affair shortly after publicly announcing in 2006 that he would run for president a second time. In an interview with Oprah Winfrey, Elizabeth said that "I wanted him to drop out of the race, protect our family from this woman, from his act. It would only raise questions, he said, he had just gotten in the race; the most pointed questions would come if he dropped out days after he had gotten in the race" (quoted in Seelye, 2009, para. 8). Edwards refused to drop out, however, and Elizabeth continued playing the roles of wife, mother, and campaign advocate as she worked to cover up early reports of the affair ("Tail between His Legs," 2008). Ultimately, however, weak performances in the early primaries (including a third-place showing in his own home state of South Carolina) forced Edwards to drop out of the race in January 2008, stating that he would "step aside so that history can . . . blaze its path" (quoted in Bosman & Zernike, 2008, para. 7).

Once a hopeful for the highest office in the land, Edwards proclaimed early in the race that "What America needs most in its next president is honesty and openness and decency" (Keen, 2007, para. 32). The former candidate who wore his religion on his sleeve later set his sights on a cabinet position in the Obama presidency. However, as details of his marital infidelity (and, perhaps more important, of his vigorous cover-up) unfolded, Edwards was not even invited to participate in the Democratic National Convention in Denver ("Edwards Proves Not So Holy," 2008). As evidence of a further slide into opprobrium, at the August 2009 funeral of Senator Edward Kennedy, Elizabeth greeted other attendees cheerfully, standing apart from her husband. When the Edwardses visited a restaurant in Chapel Hill, there was no fanfare and "diners averted their eyes and stared at their plates" (Lewis, 2009, p. 1).

The news of Edwards's indiscretions only grew worse with the passage of time. In early 2010, in advance of the release of a tell-all book by former aide Andrew Young, Edwards issued a statement claiming paternity of Rielle Hunter's child, Frances Quinn Hunter (Bosman, 2010). This announcement was followed closely by the news that John and Elizabeth had separated, in spite of Elizabeth's grim cancer prognosis (Zeleny, 2010). John Edwards, who once stood on moral high ground and passionately and publicly professed his belief in Jesus, now occupied tabloid real estate as gossip hacks discussed whether or not he would marry his mistress. Although vehemently denied, these claims rang reminiscent of previous tabloid claims, which ultimately turned out to be true.

CONCLUSION

Through his public declarations, Edwards constructed a unique Christian faith statement that contained social and political tenets, reaching beyond personal belief and promoting a social gospel—a call to action on behalf of the disadvantaged. Edwards connected with members of his own party by promoting solutions to social issues that consistently appeal to Democrats, such as poverty, healthcare, and education. But in a bold strategic move, in the 2008 presidential campaign he also reached out to evangelicals and conservatives, groups typically committed to the Republican Party, by offering a religious, faith-based rationale for his programs. In doing so, he attempted to appeal to both Democrats and Republicans who were committed to social justice and to easing the plight of the poor and the disadvantaged. By leading the charge and injecting substantial faith talk into his campaign rhetoric, Edwards was at the forefront of the effort to neutralize the Republican chokehold on faith and values (Prothero, 2008). He demonstrated that Democrats could be people of faith, and vice versa—and that being a person of faith could have concrete, pragmatic social applications.

While Edwards's faith statements were consistent with his political platform and inspiring for many, they were ultimately insufficient to attract voters. The preceding decades of political American life had soured many to politics in general as well as to the political use of religious expression. In other words, by the time the 2008 presidential race was underway, faith appeared to be of limited value in attracting voters. In a real sense, the Democrats had faith—as evidenced by the near worshipful tone of many Obama supporters and their embrace of his "Hope," "Change You Can Believe In," and "Yes, We Can" messages—and Edwards in particular had a very clearly articulated faith; again, though, it may have been too much, too late. Contemporary religious-political expression had become mere rhetoric to which few were listening and by which few were influenced.

REFERENCES

A new "social gospel" in politics [Editorial]. (2004, January 13). *Chattanooga Times Free Press,* p. B6.

Advocates for the poor are all around us [Editorial]. (2008, September 2). *Albany Times-Union,* p. A8.

Battle, J. A. (1999, February). A brief history of the social gospel. *WRS Journal, 6,* 5–11.

Bauer, G. (2008, January 4). Democrats and religion: Will secularists fight to remain dominant? *The Washington Times,* p. A21.

Beale, S. (2007, November 9). Edwards: Health care, college for everyone. *Manchester (N.H.) Union Leader,* p. A6.

Bender, K. (2007, March 5). Edwards supports Cal custodians: Democratic presidential candidate moves forum to YWCA to back those seeking "living wage." *Contra Costa (CA) Times,* p. F4.

Bosman, J. (2010, January 22). Edwards admits he fathered girl with mistress. *New York Times,* p. A12.

Bosman, J., & Zernike, K. (2008, January 31). Abruptly, Edwards ends his White House bid. *New York Times,* p. A22.

Boston, R. (2007, September). Inquisition 2008. *Church & State,* pp. 8–11.

Burke, D. (2007, June 26). Democratic rivals at ease with faith talk. *Christian Century,* p, 12.

Campo-Flores, A., Bailey, H., Alter, J., Clift, E., & Ramirez, J. (2007, December 24). The road warrior. *Newsweek,* pp. 28–34.

Candidates on religion: The Democrats (2007, July 16). *Denver Post,* p. A11.

Canellos, P. S., & Issenberg, S. (2007, December 30). Subtle and obvious differences on the trail: Democrats vary on style; GOP on issues. *Boston Globe,* p. A17.

Coleman, R. J. (1972). *Issues of theological conflict: Evangelicals and liberals.* Grand Rapids, MI: Eerdmans.

Collins, G. (2008, August 9). Ken Doll in lust. *New York Times,* p. A19.

Connelly, J. (2007, April 30). Edwards remains true to his roots. *Seattle Post-Intelligencer,* p. B1.

Conniff, R. (2008, March). Split decision. *The Progressive,* pp. 7–9.

Darman, J. (2007, July 30). The down and out tour. *Newsweek,* pp. 34–35.

Dionne, E. J. (2004, January 14). Democrats' new "moral majority." *Bergen County (N.J.) Record,* p. L15.

Domke, D. (2007, December 3). How are the main contenders handling the faith issue? *USA Today,* p. 13A.

Edwards, J. (2004a, July). John Edwards on faith. Retrieved from http://www.beliefnet.com/News/Politics/2004/07/John-Edwards-On-Faith.aspx

Edwards, J. (2004b, August 1). Let's make America stronger. *Vital Speeches of the Day,* pp. 615–619.

Edwards, J. (2006). A tax system that embraces fairness and equality. *Social Research, 73,* 431–442.

Edwards, J. (2007a, September). Reengaging with the world. *Foreign Affairs, 86,* 19–36.

Edwards, J. (2007b, November 26). One for all. *Modern Healthcare,* p. 15.

Edwards, J. (2008a, January 2). My plan to stop corporate abuses. *Wall Street Journal,* p. A11.

Edwards, J. (2008b, January 15). Edwards statement in honor of Rev. Dr. Martin Luther King, Jr.'s birthday. *States News Service.* Retrieved from www.statesnewsservice.com

Edwards, J. (2008c, September). The right thing to do. *Sojourners Magazine, 37*(9), 14–22.

Edwards proves not so holy after all [Editorial]. (2008, August 13). *Fitchburg (Mass.) Sentinel & Enterprise.* Retrieved from www.sentinelandenterprise.com

Edwards vows tough stance on lobbying (2007, December 30). *Boston Globe,* p. A16.

For Edwards, only full truth can pave path to redemption. (2008, August 11). *USA Today,* p. 10A.

Fosdick, H. E. (1917). *The meaning of faith.* New York: The Abingdon Press.

Gerson, M. (2006, November 13). A new social gospel. *Newsweek,* pp. 40–43.

Gerstein, J. (2006, December 18). Edwards 2008 bid to push plight of poor. *New York Sun,* p. 1.

Gibbs, N., & Duffy, M. (2007, July 12). How the Democrats got religion. *Time.* Retrieved from http://www.time.com/time/politics/article/0,8599,1642649,00 .html

Gundry, S. N., & Johnson, A. R. (Eds.). (1976). *Tensions in contemporary theology.* Chicago: Moody Press.

Hauser, C. (2007, November 2). In pledge to voters, Edwards reflects on his wife's fight with cancer. *New York Times,* p. A18.

Healy, P., & Luo, M. (2007, June 5). Edwards, Clinton and Obama describe journeys of faith. *New York Times,* p. A20.

Hicks, D. (2007, August 24). Faith in political life. *Albany Times-Union,* p. A10.

Keen, J. (2007, March 14). Can Edwards win with an "us vs. them" pitch?: Populist message poses a challenge second time around. *USA Today,* p. 1A.

Kennedy, H. (2007, March 4). How Edwards sees faith. *(New York) Daily News,* p. 28.

King, F. (2008, September 15). Adultery through green eyeshades. *National Review,* p. 58.

Klinghoffer, D. (2007, October 19). When Democrats become instruments of God: The disputation. *The Forward,* p. A11.

Kuo, D. (2007, March 5). John Edwards: "My faith came roaring back." *Huffington Post.* Retrieved from http://www.huffingtonpost.com/david-kuo/john-edwards-my -faith-cam_b_42696.html

Lewis, N. A. (2009, September 20). For John Edwards, the drama builds toward a denouement. *New York Times,* p. 1.

MacAfee, N. (Ed.). (2004). *The gospel according to RFK: Why it matters now.* Boulder, CO: Westview Press.

Machen, J. G. (1923). *Christianity and liberalism.* New York: Macmillan.

Moore, T. (2009, September 20). Edwards' child, book proposal. *(New York) Daily News,* p. 4.

Nagourney, A. (2004, November 7). Baffled in loss, Democrats seek road forward. *New York Times,* p. 1.

Nixon, J. W. (1942, October). The status and prospects of the social gospel. *Journal of Religion, 22,* 346–358.

Perez-Pena, R., & Carter, B. (2008, August 9). Reticence of mainstream media becomes a story itself. *New York Times,* p. A14.

Pew Forum on Religion and Public Life. (2008.) *U.S. religious landscape survey.* Washington, DC: Pew Research Center.

Pickler, N. (2007, June 5). Edwards says he prays, sins every day. *Associated Press Online.*

Price, R. M. (1979, November 28). A fundamentalist social gospel? *The Christian Century, 96,* 1183–1186.

Prothero, S. (2008, November 3). An election that is, and isn't, about God. *USA Today,* p. 15A.

Q&A: John Edwards (2006, June 21). *Time.* Retrieved from http://www.time.com/time/nation/article/0,8599,1206606,00.html

Quebedeaux, R. (1974). *The young evangelicals: A story of the emergence of a new generation of evangelicals.* New York: Harper and Row.

Rauschenbusch, W. (1907). *Christianity and the social crisis.* New York: MacMillan.

Ross, J. R. (2004, February 4). Edwards starts ads in Wisconsin, Dean begins run toward primary. *The Associated Press State & Local Wire.*

Rossinow, D. (2005). The radicalization of the social gospel: Harry F. Ward and the search for a new social order, 1898–1936. *Religion and American Culture, 15,* 63–106.

Sabar, A. (2007, September 20). John Edwards: Working-class values and a closely held faith. *Christian Science Monitor,* p. 1.

Seelye, K. Q. (2009, May 6). Edwards's wife speaks of his affair. *New York Times,* p. A20.

Steinfels, P. (2009, August 1). Despite a decade of controversy, the "faith-based initiative" endures. *New York Times,* p. A11.

Steuart, J., & Lietman, S. (1980, September 7). Carter's unkept promises—A time bomb? *New York Times,* p. D19.

Tail between his legs: John Edwards. (2008, August 16). *The Economist,* p. 34.

Zeleny, J. (2010, January 28). John Edwards and wife have separated, friends say. *New York Times,* p. A17.

Zernike, K. (2007, December 31). After the pain of a son's death, a shared mission in politics. *New York Times,* p. A1.

Chapter 6

Al Gore's Rational Faith and Unreasonable Religion

Christina M. Knopf

Early in his run for the U.S. presidency, Albert Gore, Jr., told a meeting of religion reporters that, regarding church-state relations, "National leaders have been trapped in a dead-end debate [between] hollow secularism or right-wing religion." He bemoaned the "allergy to faith that is such a curious factor in much of modern society," saying that though modern science is very powerful it has eradicated appreciation for "many of the most important meanings that are found only in the whole." He complained about the arrogant intellectualism that displayed "contempt for belief in God" and "alternative views based on faith" (Steinfels, 1999, p. A11). But just days before the election, Gore was described as a man whose own faith was still in flux—a man conflicted about his beliefs and especially about how to discuss them (Henneberger, 2000).

This conflict continued to be manifested in the various roles Gore played after his 2000 defeat: those of teacher, advocate, and activist. The same man who in 1992 wrote a chapter titled "Environmentalism of the Spirit," which offered the story of Noah and the Ark as evidence of the need for ecological responsibility, authored a book in 2007 titled *The Assault on Reason,* which called for a rejuvenation of rational debate within the public sphere—a concept that often excludes matters of faith and religion from its blueprint (Habermas, 2001)—but which also supported faith as a guide through life. In his speeches on the environment, on terrorism, and on the Iraq war, Gore both reaffirmed his belief in the Bible (Gore, 2005b) and argued that facts and not ideologies would lead to "a society in which citizens of all faiths enjoy equal standing" (2003a).

This chapter is about those mixed messages. It is about the conflicting sacred and secular ideas that appear in the rhetoric of Al Gore—illustrated, for example, in the reverent way he discusses secular democracy—and how he deals with such contradictions, as with a fine distinction between religion and faith. The chapter begins with a brief biographical look at Al Gore's religious practices and teachings, especially in relation to his understanding and valuing of science, and then reviews the primary arguments surrounding God-centered belief systems in the public sphere and their relationship to liberalism. The chapter then discusses the articulation of key secular and sacred precepts found throughout a collection of Al Gore's post-2000 speeches in order to better understand how ideas of God appear in not only big-"D" Democratic rhetoric but also in small-"l" liberal discourse. Al Gore is an especially interesting speaker to study on this issue because of his own religious roots and his drive to speak out against the Bush presidency and its apparent religious motivations.

AL GORE'S QUEST FOR TRUTH: HIS RELIGION AND FAITH

Biographer Bill Turque wrote, "Al Gore is at home with ideas but deeply wary of people, religious but possessed of an equally abiding faith in the blessings of science and technology . . ." (2000, p. x). Gore told Harvard seniors in a 1994 commencement speech that his belief in serving God was "beyond all arguing and beyond any doubt," but even his friends have questioned how someone so devoted to science could totally surrender to belief (Turque, 2000, pp. 94–95). His brand of Christianity has been labeled "ethical and intellectual but not especially doctrinal" (Steinfels, 1999, p. A11). Since childhood, Gore has remained affiliated with the Southern Baptist denomination, but has chosen to emphasize only those elements of Baptist doctrine that are in step with his other beliefs; the result is Baptist-inflected knowledge of the scriptures infused with understandings of mysticism and New Age spiritualism. Many of Gore's speeches hint at his Southern Baptist background, with its flavors of suffering, redemption, and even (for Gore) uncharacteristic energy, especially when speaking in black churches. On the other hand, his support for women's reproductive rights and for gay rights earned him an "F" from the Southern Baptists' Christian Life Commission during his 1992 vice presidential candidacy. Similarly, the Southern Baptist Convention offered little to no support for Gore's pet project of mobilizing the larger spiritual community around environmental action (Turque, 2000).

Before Gore entered politics, he immersed himself in a news career and in the study of theology (Turque, 2000). While briefly enrolled at Vanderbilt Divinity School, he took a special interest in a series of lectures by Walter Harrelson that established a relationship between theology and politics by focusing on Old Testament prophets and the corruption of ancient Israel's ruling class; to Gore, this demonstrated the needs of the people. Gore also took a course called "Theology and the Natural Sciences" which led him to see environmentalism as a theological obligation—a prime example of his mixing of the sacred and the secular. His book *Earth in the Balance* (1992) was infused with religious and philosophical messages of ecology and spirituality, despite his penchant for facts (Henneberger, 2000; Maraniss & Nakashima, 2000). Gore's environmental rhetoric has been called "apocalyptic" (Turque, 2000, p. 220), "fundamentalist" (Thomas, 2008, p. A17), and "prophetic" (Fiore & Simon, 2007, p. A3). He has referred to his fight against global warming as a "sacred agenda" and he has brought together the scientific and religious communities by launching a coalition of spiritual leaders to speak on environmental issues (Turque, 2000, p. 220).

Gore's teachers at Vanderbilt saw him as a searcher—a person seeking answers to ethical questions—and someone whose perspective was shaped by guilt and a constant sense of sin, all of which pushed Gore to see the world in sharp contrasts (Maraniss & Nakashima, 2000; Turque, 2000). His friends see a man with too much of a technical bent to have an irrevocable faith, but one who is attracted to the belief that personal failings are forgiven (Turque, 2000). Gore himself has said of his year in divinity school that he was looking for the meaning of life, for people's relationship to God and to each other. He admits that he did not find all the answers, but that he "found better questions, and . . . a process for living out better answers" (Steinfels, 1999, p. A11). He told reporters, "I think the purpose of life is to glorify God. I turn to my faith as the bedrock of my approach to any important question in my life," and he denied any separation between the religious and rational parts of his brain (Steinfels, 1999, p. A11). He further asserted that, "Everything in the Bible makes sense to me. I interpret it my own way, and that's what my tradition teaches me to do" (Henneberger, 2000, p. A20).

THE LIBERALISM-RELIGION DEBATE AND THE CONSTRUCT OF THE PUBLIC SPHERE

Anthony Arblaster (1984) defined liberalism—a set of political beliefs and practices—as prioritizing and upholding freedom, tolerance, privacy, reason, and law; within the American context, equality is typically added to this list (Crowley, 2006, p. 5). Nicholas Wolterstorff has argued that liberal democracy is an ideal type and that "no society is anything than *more or less* a liberal democracy" (1997, p. 70). In practice, liberalism has become part of a public philosophy that views government as a balancing of private interests

(Sullivan, 1986). Since the late 17th century, when liberal democracies began to emerge, the assumption has been that responsible citizens will restrict the ways in which they discuss and decide political and civic issues. Empirically based reason, or secular rationale, is the preferred method of argumentation in a liberal democracy, where appeals to tradition, authority, and desire have no place. This rational argumentation takes place in what is often referred to as "the public sphere"—collectives of private people discussing public issues in an open forum, separate from authority and institutions, where the quality of an argument, and not its source, is the primary value (Habermas, 2001). The public sphere is, therefore, regarded as secular space where the quality of public debate is dependent on the general decline of God-centered belief systems (Meyer & Moors, 2006).

In modern history this conceptualization frequently puts liberalism in opposition to religion—that is, to belief systems relating to God and the spirit—but in truth the two concepts were originally conceived as compatible. Members of the Royal Society and the Latitudinarian Churchmen, Cambridge neo-Platonic philosophers, and Whig ideologues, including John Locke, argued all elements of religion, such as belief and faith in God, were compatible with reason because reason held the potential to reveal the existence of Providence—if one acknowledged that the individual's capacity for reason came from nature, not from the divine (Zaret, 1992). In his *Essay on Human Understanding,* Locke (1823/1963) described reason as having to do with knowledge and opinion. Reason, he wrote, determines the certainty and probability of an idea and therefore helps a person to regulate his or her agreement to ideas. Thus, reason made it possible for humans to know of the existence of God; without the faculty of reason, a person would be unable to share with others knowledge of, or from, God. According to Locke, the key of responsible citizenship was consensus regarding natural law through a social contract.

Currently, however, liberalism is often contrasted with conservatism, and conservatism is typically equated with evangelicalism. This produces a rhetoric of "us" versus "them" (Bolce & De Maio, 2002; Crowley, 2006), effectively polarizing reason and belief in the divine. Within the United States, the we/they dichotomy between liberalism and God-centered belief systems is often framed within the context of "the separation of church and state" (Habermas, 2006, p. 3); opinions vary about whether the separation indicates government's tolerance of all belief systems, the lack of an established or mandatory belief system, or the government's complete neutrality regarding theological beliefs (Audi, 1997; Thieman, 1996). At the heart of the issue, again, is the notion of a social contract that relies on natural reason. "The parties themselves must reach an agreement on the always contested delimitations between a positive liberty to practice a religion of one's own and the negative liberty to remain spared from the religious practices of the others" (Habermas, 2006, p. 4). Some politically active and religiously observant persons, such as Steven Carter (1993), feel that the separation has morphed into the treatment of religion as a hobby. Richard John Neuhaus (1984), among others, feels that the separation has pushed American liberal democracy to treat God-centered belief systems with hostility, or at least as irrelevant.

Liberalism automatically presumes that all citizens of a liberal democracy will be willing and able to debate issues using a secular rationale that is deemed appropriate for all persons. It overlooks the disagreement that informs the political sphere, assuming that humans are capable of separating personal experience from reason and that everyone will use reason in a similar fashion (Crowley, 2006). Nancy Fraser has ably demonstrated how such a structure of acceptable debate has historically excluded a number of peoples from the public sphere, in some cases because the structure does not recognize their language as familiar or deems their contributions too disruptive (Fraser, 1990/1991). Much of the problem, as Wolterstorff (1997) sees it, is that through Locke's social contract some beliefs are entitled but others are not. He argues that distinctions made by Locke between reason and faith, as well as John Rawls's claims that only some doctrines are justifiable (Rawls, 1987, 1993), asks citizens to carry out the impossible task of stepping outside of their traditions, and unfairly puts them in the position of potentially having to hide their sacred understandings of the world. The burden is on them to learn and adapt to the secular worldview (Habermas, 2006). Paul J. Weithman (2002) argues that religious or spiritual communities have too much to offer American democracy on moral issues and political socialization to be excluded from debate and treated with only tolerant neutrality. Moreover, for many religious or spiritual persons, there are often no divisions among knowledge, belief, truth, and faith—God is truth and faith is a way of knowing God—making the task of secular argumentation incomprehensible.

Secularists, however, may also feel trapped by common workings of a liberal democracy in practice. Oftentimes translation of sacred-to-secular falls on the shoulders of secularists and politicians:

As long as secular citizens are convinced that religious traditions and religious communities are to a certain extent archaic relics of pre-modern societies that continue to exist in the present [they] can obviously no longer be expected to take religious contributions to contentious political issues seriously and even to help to assess them for substance that can possibly be expressed in a secular language and justified by secular arguments. (Habermas, 2006, p. 15)

The paradox is that as a result of such tensions, liberals find religious fundamentalism to be intolerant because its tenets do not appear rational; meanwhile, fundamentalists feel that liberals are intolerant for devaluing their way of life (Crowley, 2006; McClay, 2001). America has been called the 50/50 nation, largely as a result of pervasive religiosity seen to divide the electorate into camps of red and blue, fundamentalist and secular (Fiorina, Abrams, & Pope, 2006; Guth, Kellstedt, Green, & Smidt, 2001). For Habermas (2006), the right-left/sacred-secular split indicates that a vast number of Americans have not yet been willing or able to meet the demands of liberalism and the public use of reason.

Inherent in this 50/50 polarization of the United States is the notion of a culture war between the orthodox and the progressive members of American society (Hunter, 1991). From the 1970s to the beginning of the 21st century, secularists became increasingly attracted to the progressive policies of the Democratic Party (Bolce & De Maio, 2002), and public discourse largely viewed religion as a right-wing force (Dionne, 2008), dividing the parties along religious lines. The underlying assumption has been that liberals cannot possibly be religious and conservatives cannot possibly be secular (Carter, 1993; Dionne, 2008; Fiorina, Abrams & Pope, 2006; Sullivan, 2008; Wallis, 2005). This supposition is, however, beginning to change. A number of prominent journalists, thinkers, and theologians have been increasingly calling for a less partisan, and more respectful, inclusion of religious thought into public and political life. E. J. Dionne, Jr., for example, in his book *Souled Out,* "intended to make the case that liberals dare not relegate people of faith to some outer darkness of supposed ignorance—even if liberals have every right to oppose ideologues on the right who invoke faith for narrow electoral purposes" (2008, p. 7). Democratic evangelical preacher Jim Wallis (2005) has argued that the political Left needs to reclaim religion from being the sole property of the political Right because God is neither a Republican nor a Democrat, a sentiment echoed in journalist Amy Sullivan's (2008) book *The Party Faithful.*

Sharon Crowley has argued that rhetoric is the key to overcoming this problem and bridging the divide. She wrote:

> Rhetorical argumentation, I believe, is superior to the theory of argument inherent in liberalism because rhetoric does not depend solely on appeals to reason and evidence for its persuasive efficacy. Since antiquity rhetorical theorists have understood the centrality of desires and values to the maintenance of beliefs. Hence rhetorical invention is better positioned than liberal means of argument to intervene successfully in disagreements where the primary motivation of adherents is moral or passionate commitment. (2006, p. 4)

A similar case is made by Bill O'Neill (2004) from a philosophical, legal, and theological standpoint, as he, too, speaks of the power of rhetoric in the construction and maintenance of a moral community and the usefulness of narratives in the process of public discourse. All of this brings us to the case of Al Gore, Jr.—another figure who, by all indication, finds some concord or connection between religion and reason, and between the spiritual and the secular, in the modern public sphere of liberal democracy.

METHODOLOGY: CLUSTER CRITICISM

Kenneth Burke has demonstrated how writers and speakers use associational clusters—implicit equations of "what kinds of acts and images and personalities and situations go with . . . notions of heroism, villainy, consolation, despair, etc." (1973, p. 20). Through examining these clusters and charting what goes with what, the critic can identify the speaker's situation or motive and, in so doing, can reach some generalizations about what the meaning is for both the speaker and for the audience. Because spiritual matters, such as his religious identification with the Southern Baptists, his religious schooling, and his expressions of personal faith, have featured so prominently in the life of Al Gore, because he worked so diligently after his exit from politics to promote the ideal of a liberal democracy, and because these forces are often understood as being in opposition, examining the associational clusters for this dichotomy can help us to understand not only how Gore grapples with such differences, but also how he and his audience perceive religion and liberalism in practice.

Twenty-two speeches, delivered by Gore between 2001 and 2008, the years following his exit from public office, were collected and analyzed for this project. The selection of texts for analysis was a convenience sample; speeches were chosen based on availability and were collected from a variety of Web-based sources, making for a somewhat arbitrary selection of speeches. They fell into three purpose-driven categories, with some overlap: political speeches delivered at partisan-sponsored events; environmental speeches about global warming and climate change; and speeches criticizing the Bush administration's practices and policies. (See the Appendix for a complete list of addresses included in the study.)

Based on the common understandings of God-centered belief systems and liberalism described above and on readings of a variety of Al Gore texts, a set of high intensity, and moderate to high frequency, key words for each concept emerged. High frequency words were identified with the help of the "Advanced Text Analyser," available online at www.UsingEnglish.com. Gore's speeches were entered into the program both individually and collectively, and the texts were mapped into graphic word clouds based on their rates of recurrence. For the sacred element, ideas connected to spiritual matters, the key words identified are *belief(s)*, *believe, faith(s), faithfully, God(s)*, and *religion*. The secular counterparts, ideas connected to notions of liberalism, were *reason(s)(ed)*, *fact(s), information, law(s)*, and *democracy* (and *democratic*). Associational clusters for these were identified based on the subjects, modifiers, and god or devil terms surrounding the secular and sacred key words.

FINDINGS

Gore is considered a skillful rhetor, one who is "smooth and fluent," uses well constructed sentences and is assertive, yet who is also calm and controlled (Bilmes, 2001, pp. 153–154). Some argue that his career as a reporter taught him how to ask both sensitive and blunt questions as a politician (Parmelee, 2002). At the same time, of course, Gore is also well known for being a stiff wonk, using little figurative or metaphorical language (Cienki, 2004). Nonetheless, his film *An Inconvenient Truth* (2006) has been described as monomythic—using narratives of personal trial and transformation (Rosteck & Frentz, 2009)—and this element of personal narrative is apparent throughout many of Gore's other communications (Gore & Gore, 2002; Parmelee, 2002). Gore's ability to simplify facts in a way that appeals to an audience has won him acclaim, not to mention an Oscar and the Nobel Peace Prize for public science communication (Greco, 2007; Rosteck & Frentz, 2009). His straightforward, minimally embellished, and yet passionate and personal style was evident throughout the speeches considered here. We will first look at the secular associational clusters for key terms related to liberalism in Gore's activist speeches, and then at the sacred associational clusters for key terms related to spiritual matters.

Secular Clusters

Secular associational clusters are those ideas that are connected to notions of liberalism in Gore's speeches. They are identified by Gore's uses of the words *law(s), democracy* (and *democratic*), *reason(s)(ed)*, and *fact(s)* or *information*. These clusters illustrate Gore's understanding of liberalism in practice.

Associations with Law

As Gore expresses it, laws provide the framework and the support for society, specifically for democracy. Gore, echoing the words of John Adams, repeatedly makes the distinction that "ours is a government of laws and not of men.

What is at stake today is that defining principle of our nation, and thus the very nature of America" (2003b). Law, more precisely "the rule of law," is central to the *Constitution* and the *Declaration of Independence*. *Respect* for and *enforcement* of the law are necessary to the proper functions of the *government*, specifically the *president* and *Executive Branch*, the *Congress* and *Senate*, and the *Supreme Court* and the judiciary. Gore links law with *regulations, treaties, policies*, and *traditions*. He attributes *liberty, rights, security, survival, strength, power*, and *moral authority* to the *rule of law*. "Vigilant adherence to the rule of law strengthens our democracy and strengthens America. It ensures that those who govern us operate with our constitutional structure . . ." (2006a). In this way, Gore intricately connects law to both reason and democracy.

Associations with Democracy

Democracy for Al Gore is not an ideal but a living entity, with a particular *nature* and an *immune system* that it is at *risk* and in *danger* to various *threats*. According to Gore, democracy's *health* and *vitality* are *dependent* on common *people* engaged in *debate, conversation, expression, dialogue*, and *communication*:

> I came here today because I believe that American democracy is in grave danger. It is no longer possible to ignore the strangeness of our public discourse. I know that I am not the only one who feels that something has gone basically and badly wrong in the way America's fabled "marketplace of ideas" now functions. (2005c)

Occasionally, democracy appears more mechanical than organic, made of *fabric* and with specific *operations, workings*, and *processes*, set along a particular *course*, which may be *changed*. Gore's democracy is both *representative* and *deliberative*, and is often distinctly *American*. It encompasses *skills* and *dreams* and *destiny*, encouraging *cooperation* and providing *opportunity*. It has *enemies*, especially *fear*. Highlighting Gore's appreciation for and intermingling of both secular and sacred systems, Gore also speaks of democracy as being a sort of religion, which has *power* and in which a person can have *belief*, closely associating democracy with *tradition, values, strength*, and *good*ness.

Associations with Reason

Though Gore speaks eloquently on the Rule of Reason, arguing that "the very idea of self-government depends upon honest and open debate as the preferred method for pursuing the truth—and a shared respect for the Rule of Reason as the best way to establish the truth" (2003a), reason does not figure prominently into his addresses. The word *reason* is mainly employed to indicate a justification—good or bad—for actions. He uses phrases like "for these and other reasons," "one of the reasons," or "reason why," and he repeatedly conveys reasons for *concern* and *worry.* Gore does, however, make occasional Enlightenment use of the term, connecting it to *deliberation, debate,* and *discourse.*

Associations with Information/Fact

The closely related key terms of information and facts play a much larger role in Gore's speeches, as they are central to his conception of a healthy democracy. He associates these terms with *news, data, figures, intelligence, evidence,* and *reports,* recognizing that these can be *complex* or *difficult* but should nonetheless be *objective, reliable,* and *accurate* because they are *important* parts of *knowing* and *understanding.* Gore is especially interested in the *source, collection, flow, availability* and *accessibility* of information and therefore often mentions the media, including the *printed word, television,* and the *Internet,* in relation to information:

> [M]ore than 40 years have passed since the majority of Americans received their news and information from the printed word. Newspapers are hemorrhaging readers and, for the most part, resisting the temptation to inflate their circulation numbers. Reading itself is in sharp decline, not only in our country but in most of the world. The Republic of Letters has been invaded and occupied by television. Radio, the Internet, movies, telephones, and other media all now vie for our attention—but it is television that still completely dominates the flow of information in modern America. (2005c)

Because Gore links information to *debate, accountability, decisions, power,* and *control,* it is no surprise he concerns himself greatly with the problems of *phony, false,* or *wrong* information, and the *twisting, distorting,* and *manipulating* of facts and places *myth* and *ideology* in opposition:

> Americans in both parties should insist on the re-establishment of respect for the Rule of Reason. We must, for example, stop tolerating the rejection and distortion of science. We must insist on an end to the cynical use of pseudo studies known to be false for the purpose of intentionally clouding the public's ability to discern the truth. (2005c)

True to the principles of sound argumentation, the word "fact" often appears in Gore's speeches as an indication that he is providing a warrant for a claim, as in, "The quickest, cheapest and best way to start using all this renewable energy is in the production of electricity. In fact, we can start right now using solar power, wind power and geothermal power to make electricity for our homes and businesses" (2008a). Like laws, information and facts are central to democracy in Gore's worldview.

In these ways, Gore largely reinforces the common distinctions between liberalism and religion. In his emphasis on law and information, there appears to be little room for more sacred matters. Indeed, democracy, law, information, and reason are all clustered with the words *truth* or *true,* whereas none of the key terms of religion are associated with the truth. This occurrence is especially notable because the Bible claims that "the Lord is near and all His commandments are truth" (Psalm 119:151 King James Version), and Gore has said "everything in the Bible makes sense to me" (Henneberger, 2000, p. A20)—which brings us to the use of sacred terms in his speeches.

Sacred Clusters

Sacred associational clusters are those ideas that are connected to notions of liberalism in Gore's speeches. They are identified by Gore's uses of the words *God(s)*, *belief(s)* and *believe, religion,* and *faith(s)* or *faithfully.* These clusters illustrate Gore's understanding of how spiritual matters fit into public discourse and/or political issues.

Associations with God

Gore's few references to God are primarily in the deistic sense of a God who exists, and who listens to *prayers,* but who does not intervene. Such references appear in the association Gore makes between God and *Earth*—viewing Earth as a *gift* from God, as one of His *blessings,* for which people are responsible: "Let them say we were wise in our time because we worked to protect the Earth God gave us for all of time" (2002b). God is differentiated from man, and Gore claims that man cannot know God's will:

> It is no accident that this assault on the integrity of our constitutional design has been fueled by a small group claiming special knowledge of God's will in American politics. They even claim that those of us who disagree with their point of view are waging war against "people of faith." How dare they? (2005a)

Democracy is more of a God-figure in Gore's speeches than God is; he speaks of democracy as having more form and presence in life than he does of God, and it is democracy, rather than God, in which he is more likely to profess conviction.

Associations with Belief

Belief is the most complex of either the sacred or the secular terms examined in Gore's speeches. Most of the time, beliefs in Gore's rhetoric have nothing to do with religion, but are nonetheless harmful to a liberal democracy. *Belief*, the noun, appears rarely, and is noticeably disparaged through its use in a George Orwell quote that Gore uses repeatedly, "sooner or later a false belief bumps up against solid reality, usually on a battlefield." Positive beliefs, though not false, are nonetheless outrageous, as in, "The revolutionary departure on which the idea of America was based was the audacious belief that people can govern themselves" (2006a). And most beliefs, at least those of others, are often misguided, such as the "broadly-held belief system of grass-roots extremist organizations that have made the destruction of judicial independence the centerpiece of their political agenda" (2005a). Gore, however, does not doubt that belief, even religious belief, is *genuine* and *important.* But, like Locke and Rawls, Gore privileges some beliefs above others:

> It is ideology—and not [President Bush's] religious faith—that is the source of his inflexibility. Most of the problems he has caused for this country stem not from his belief in God, but from his belief in the infallibility of the right-wing Republican ideology that exalts the interests of the wealthy and of large corporations over the interests of the American people. (2004b)

For Gore (in contrast to Locke and Rawls), entitled beliefs have less to do with their secular justifications and more to do with whether or not Gore agrees with them. In fact, Gore takes pains to differentiate between religious beliefs and other belief systems (namely political) that he finds troublesome, repeatedly assuring his audiences that problems caused by the Bush administration were political and not religious in nature.

Though he is not hostile to religious beliefs *per se,* Gore contrasts entitled beliefs and those that are not entitled through his use of *believe,* the verb. Similar to the way Gore uses *in fact* to predicate warrants, he often uses *I believe* to predicate the conclusion in whatever argument he is making, as in this sentence: "I'm speaking today in an effort to recommend a specific course of action for our country, which I sincerely believe would be better for our country than the policy that is now being pursued by President Bush" (2002c). When he speaks about what others believe, however, it is usually in an effort to demonstrate that they are wrong, as he does here: "I thought maybe it was an aberration when three-quarters of Americans said they believed that Saddam Hussein was responsible for attacking us on September 11, 2001" (2005c). Whereas Gore's beliefs are treated as admirable, the beliefs of others are rarely shown as worthy or sympathetic.

Associations with Religion

Gore suggests some distaste for religion in many of his speeches. In multiple instances, when he mentions religion, it is often surrounded by references to *right-wing, zealots, extremists,* or *bigots.* He refers to "a growing part of the media characterized by paranoia presented as entertainment—the part that allows drug-addled hypocrites, compulsive gamblers, and assorted religious bigots to masquerade as moral guides for the nation" (2004a). Gore also speaks of "narrow ideology" supported by "right-wing religious extremists and exceptionally greedy economic special interests" both seeking power (2005a). In other instances, religion is more an issue of *difference* and demography than a matter of the spirit, as he places it in laundry lists with *race, ethnicity, disability, gender, sexual orientation,* and *culture.* "Climate refugees have migrated into areas already inhabited by people with different cultures, religions, and traditions, increasing the potential for conflict" (2007b).

Associations with Faith

Gore's own Baptist understandings are frequently removed from the confines of *religion* and are instead placed within the area of *faith.* When Gore speaks of his religious orientation he usually calls it his "faith tradition." He couples his faith tradition with the idea of *teaching* and explains to his audience how his faith is relevant to the issue at hand, affording him insight. Whereas religion provides *doctrine,* faith provides *perspective* and *standards.* It is faith, and not religion, that Gore associates with the *Bible,* with *Jesus,* and with *values.* "The Bible in which I believe, in my own faith tradition, says, 'Where there is no vision, the people perish'" (2005b). He even makes a point of distinguishing religious zealots from *people* and *communities* of faith:

> Most people of faith I know in both parties have been getting a belly-full of this extremist push to cloak their political agenda in religiosity and mix up their version of religion with their version of right-wing politics and force it on everyone else. They should learn that religious faith is a precious freedom and not a tool to divide and conquer. I think it is truly important to expose the fundamental flaw in the arguments of these zealots. (2005a)

Religious zealots are detrimental to Gore's conception of democracy, whereas people of faith he includes with leaders of "government, science, business, labor, agriculture, [and] grass-roots activists" (2006b) as important participants in public dialogue. Gore even reminds his audience that people of faith exist in both parties—indicating that not all Democrats are atheists and not all Republicans are fundamentalists. He makes this same acknowledgment in *The Assault on Reason,* recognizing "people of faith in both parties" and

setting them apart from the "extreme religious conservatives and fundamentalists" who want to undo the progressive social change of the last century
(2007a, pp. 67–68).

DISCUSSION: RECONCILING REASON AND RELIGION

The differentiation Gore makes between faith and religion is the key to
Gore's reconciliation of sacred ideas with secular argumentation. For many,
faith and religion are synonymous; for example, journalist and author Amy
Sullivan writes about Catholics and evangelicals, people within two distinct
religious denominations, as being part of the "community of the faithful"
(2008, p. vii). Indeed, faith is a necessary component of those, and other,
practices—faith in God, in Christ, in the Eucharist, or in miracles. What
Gore implicitly acknowledges in his rhetoric, however, is that though Judeo-
Christian religion cannot exist without faith, faith may exist without religion.
This reflects a fairly contemporary understanding of the sacred, as numbers
of unaffiliated faith in the United States are on the rise with people explaining
their decisions to leave organized religions as a result of thinking religious
organizations are too judgmental and rigid, and not because they think that
modern science has disproved religion (Pew Forum, 2009).

Gore views religion as something fixed, as it is clustered with unalterable
characteristics like race and ethnicity and with unfavorable descriptors as in
"narrow version of religious doctrine" (2005a). In the pages of *The Assault
on Reason,* as well, he cites a "historic temptation of religious zealots to
subordinate the rule of law to their ideological fervor" (2007a, p. 70). This
association may be a residual effect of his upbringing, as Gore's mother and
father did not favor organized religion, in part because of the intolerance they
witnessed in it (Henneberger, 2000). His frustration with organized religion is
certainly not new or a result of the actions during the Bush administration. In
his 1992 book *Earth in the Balance,* Gore complained of organized religion
being too narrowly focused to include environmentalism on their agendas.

Faith, on the other hand, does not carry this dogmatic connotation for
Gore and is, therefore, compatible with reason. Faith, in the religious sense,
is prominently clustered with tradition and teachings, as in the example of,
"The faith tradition I share with Ashcroft includes this teaching from Jesus:
'whatsoever you do unto the least of these, you do unto me'" (2003b). For
Gore, then, faith, though not dogmatic religion, offers information that may
be used in deliberations for the advancement of a healthy democracy. This is
especially apparent when he links the teachings of his own faith tradition to
those of another:

What is "evil" anyway? I do not pretend to have the answer to such a question but my faith tradition teaches me that all of us have the potential inside of us for both good and evil. Indeed, the first example of murderous violence in the Bible is the story of the two sons of Adam and Eve. With slight differences, it is the same story told in Chapter five, verses 27 through 31 of "Sura" in the Koran, where Muslims read that both Cain and Abel "offered an offering, but it was accepted from one of them and was not accepted from the other." Feeling disrespected by God, Cain said to his brother, "I will most certainly slay you . . . then his mind facilitated to him the slaying of his brother, so he slew him; then he became one of the losers." (2002a)

George Weigel argued that a society without religious faith is unsustainable because it lacks a commitment to posterity (2005). In his book *The Assault on Reason,* Gore reflects on issues like abolition, where religious belief, more than reason, often motivated change. He writes, "for most people, a balance between reason and faith is a better guide than either alone" (2007a, p. 47). For Gore, faith is not only compatible to democracy, but is in fact one of its vital components.

Indeed, it may be that Gore's sense of compatibility between the teachings of faith and deliberative liberal democracy may have come from his faith tradition:

The Senate's tradition of unlimited debate has been a secret weapon in our nation's arsenal of democracy as well. It has frequently served to push the Senate—and the nation as a whole—toward a compromise between conflicting points of view, to breathe life into the ancient advice of the prophet Isaiah: "Come let us reason together," to illuminate arguments for which the crowded, busy House of Representatives has no time or patience, to afford any Senator an opportunity to stand in the finest American tradition in support of a principle that he or she believes to be important enough to bring to the attention of the nation. (2005a)

Not only does he include people of faith as important participants in debate, but also he uses an excerpt from his Bible to argue for debate and collective reasoning.

Gore puts a new spin on Lockean and Rawlsian philosophy. He presents and supports a rational approach to spiritual matters, while acknowledging a multiplicity of worldviews. In true liberal tradition, Gore espouses "a society in which citizens of all faiths enjoy equal standing" in "a nation that places the highest values on facts, not ideology, as the basis for all its great debates and decisions" (2003a). But, whereas Locke thought reason could support religion, Gore finds religion to be the antithesis of reason. Also, whereas Locke wrote of faith as flawed, defining it as "nothing but a firm assent of the mind" (1963, Book 4, ch. 17, § 24) used by people when their reason fails them, Gore sees its ability to fill in the gaps of reason to be the great strength of faith.

Nonetheless, some of the tensions between faith and reason, religion and liberalism, sacred and secular, remain. Gore's call for a society that both tolerates peoples of all faiths and lauds facts over ideology may be a functional oxymoron. Ideologies, like religions, are systems of concepts that orient people to life. Even Gore is unable to entirely rectify belief in his faith tradition with his distrust of ideology. He repeatedly claims "unbridled passions of ideology" (2005a) are undesirable in America, that they are too narrow for complex reality (2008b), and that they are naturally in opposition to one another (2007a). Ideology, however, is visionary (Pettigrew, 1979; Thompson, 1990), and it is vision that Gore emphatically calls for following the devastation of Hurricane Katrina, thrice repeating Proverbs 29:18, "Where there is no vision, the people perish" (King James Version). A similar conundrum can be seen in how one might differentiate between a "person of faith" and a "religious zealot," as Gore does not always achieve the liberal goal of translating his arguments of faith into purely universal language. For example, Gore's own use of Biblical allusions may not make sense to all members of his audience, even to those who profess belief in the same Bible, given that he once told reporters that he interprets the Bible in his "own way" (Henneberger, 2000, p. A20).

CONCLUSION

Al Gore often turns to the Bible when faced with life's harder questions (Henneberger, 2000), and he openly admits to praying for ways to fulfill his purpose in life (Gore, 2007b). But his penchant for facts and his commitment to faith have long been at odds with each other. He has been compared to Abraham Lincoln—tortured by questions of God and of life and shaped by Calvinist teachings (Maraniss & Nakashima, 2000). As a Democrat of faith and a liberal activist with religious convictions, Al Gore is certainly a person of interest; wary of religion and its destructive potential but confident that it has something— namely, faith—to contribute to American public discourse, he has attempted to find a reasonable balance, knowing full well that, "Fear displaces reason, reason challenges faith, faith overcomes fear" (Gore, 2007a, p. 45). By separating faith from religion Gore is able to rhetorically, if not practically, find some resolution to the tension between these opposing philosophies. Of course, Al Gore is also a politician and his rhetoric can be viewed as an attempt not only to find personal concord but also to appeal to an audience—to acknowledge the faithful among them while embracing the secularist persons, not to mention reputation, of his party. In either instance, his rhetorical hair-splitting of terminologies is an attempt to bring spirituality and the spiritual back to the Democratic Party and to bring the Party back to the type of religious perspectives that helped it usher in grand ideas, such as civil rights, in decades past.

APPENDIX: SPEECHES ANALYZED

I. January 3, 2001: *Remarks to the Congressional Black Caucus.*

II. September 29, 2001: *Keynote Address, Iowa State Democratic Party's 2001 Jefferson-Jackson Day Dinner.*

III. February 2, 2002: *Keynote Address, Tennessee Democratic Party's 2002 Campaign Kick-off.*

IV. February 12, 2002: *A Commentary on the War against Terror: Our Larger Tasks,* at the Council on Foreign Relations.

V. April 22, 2002: *Earth Day Speech,* at Vanderbilt University.

VI. September 23, 2002: *Iraq and the War on Terrorism,* in San Francisco for the Commonwealth Club of California.

VII. August 7, 2003: *Iraq War Aftermath,* at New York University for MoveOn. Org.

VIII. November 9, 2003: *Freedom and Security,* at Constitution Hall, Washington, DC, for MoveOn.Org and the American Constitution Society.

IX. January 15, 2004: *Global Warming and the Environment,* in New York at Beacon Theater for MoveOn.Org.

X. February 5, 2004: *Fear: It's* [sic] *Political Uses and Abuses,* at New School University for a Conference on Politics.

XI. May 26, 2004: *Foreign Policy: Rumsfeld Should Resign,* for MoveOn.Org.

XII. June 24, 2004: *Our Founders and the Unbalance of Power,* for the American Constitution Society for Law and Policy.

XIII. July 26, 2004: *Let's Make Sure this Time Every Vote Is Counted,* in Boston for the Democratic National Convention.

XIV. October 18, 2004: *Iraq,* at Georgetown University, for MoveOn.Org.

XV. April 27, 2005: *An American Heresy: Breaking the Rules to Destroy Our Courts,* for MoveOn.Org.

XVI. September 9, 2005: *On Katrina, Global Warming,* in San Francisco for the National Sierra Club Convention.

XVII. October 5, 2005: *The Threat to American Democracy,* remarks to the Media Center.

XVIII. January 16, 2006: *Restoring the Rule of Law,* in Washington, DC, for the American Constitution Society.

XIX. September 18, 2006: *Global Warming: What Should We Do,* at New York University.

XX. December 10, 2007: *Nobel Lecture.*

XXI. July 17, 2008: *Renewable Energy,* in Washington, DC.

XXII. August 28, 2008: *Speech at Invesco Field,* for the Democratic National Convention.

REFERENCES

Arblaster, A. (1984). *The rise and decline of Western liberalism.* Oxford: Basil & Blackwell.

Audi, R. (1997). Liberal democracy and the place of religion in politics. In R. Audi & N. Wolterstorff (Eds.), *Religion in the public square: The place of religious conviction in political debate* (pp. 1-66). Lanham, MD: Rowman & Littlefield.

Bilmes, J. (2001). Tactics and styles in the 1992 Vice Presidential debate: Question placement. *Research on Language and Social Interaction, 34,* 151-181.

Bolce, L., & De Maio, G. (2002). Our secularist Democratic Party. *Public Interest, 149,* 3–20.

Burke, K. (1973). *The philosophy of literary form,* 3rd ed. Berkeley: University of California Press.

Carter, S. L. (1993). *The culture of disbelief: How American law and politics trivialize religious devotion.* New York: Anchor Books.

Cienki, A. (2004). Bush's and Gore's language and gestures in the 2000 U.S. presidential debates: A test case for two models of metaphors. *Journal of Language and Politics, 3,* 409–440.

Crowley, S. (2006). *Toward a civil discourse: Rhetoric and fundamentalism.* Pittsburgh: University of Pittsburgh Press.

Dionne, E. J., Jr. (2008). *Souled out: Reclaiming faith & politics after the religious right.* Princeton, NJ: Princeton University Press.

Fiore, F., & Simon, R. (2007, March 22). Congress warms to Gore's return: He's greeted like a movie star and treated like prophet. *South Florida Sun-Sentinel,* p. A3.

Fiorina, M. P., Abrams, S. J., & Pope, J. C. (2006). *Culture war? The myth of a polarized America.* New York: Pearson Longman.

Fraser, N. (1990/1991). Rethinking the public sphere: A contribution to the critique of actual existing democracy. *Social Text, 25,* 56–80.

Gore, A. (1992). *Earth in the balance.* Boston: Houghton Mifflin.

Gore, A. (2002a, February 12). *A commentary on the war against terror: Our larger tasks.* Retrieved from http://www.cfr.org/publication/4343/commentary_on_the_war_against_terror.html

Gore, A. (2002b, April 22). *Earth Day speech.* Retrieved from http://www.danaroc.com/guests_algore_042108.html

Gore, A. (2002c, September 23). *Iraq and the war on terrorism.* Retrieved from http://www.commonwealthclub.org/archive/02/02-09gore-speech.html

Gore, A. (2003a, August 7). *Iraq War aftermath.* Retrieved from http://www.moveon .org/gore-speech.html

Gore, A. (2003b, November 9). *Freedom and security.* Retrieved from http:// www.acslaw.org/files/2003%20programs_Gore_speech%20transcript.pdf

Gore, A. (2004a, February 5). *Fear: It's* [sic] *political uses and abuses.* Retrieved from http://www.rappdems.org/gore_politicalabuses.htm

Gore, A. (2004b, October 18). *Iraq.* Retrieved from http://pol.moveon.org/gore5/

Gore, A. (2005a, April 27). *An American heresy: Breaking the rules to destroy our courts.* Retrieved from http://pol.moveon.org/algore/rally.html

Gore, A. (2005b, September 9). *On Katrina, global warming.* Retrieved from http:// www.sierraclub.org/pressroom/speeches/2005-09-09algore.asp

Gore, A. (2005c, October 5). *The threat to American democracy.* Retrieved from http://www.buzzflash.com/alerts/05/10/ale05154.html

Gore, A. (2006a, January 16). *Restoring the rule of law.* Retrieved from http:// www.acslaw.org/node/2096

Gore, A. (2006b, September 18). *Global warming: What should we do?* Retrieved from http://thinkprogress.org/gore-nyu/

Gore, A. (2007a). *The assault on reason.* London: Penguin Books.

Gore, A. (2007b, December 10). *Nobel lecture.* Retrieved from http://nobelprize.org/ nobel_prizes/peace/laureates/2007/gore-lecture_en.html

Gore, A. (2008a, July 17). *Renewable energy.* Retrieved from http:// climateprogress .org/2008/07/17/gore-speech/

Gore, A. (2008b, August 28). *Al Gore's speech at Invesco Field.* Retrieved from http://www.cnn.com/2008/POLITICS/08/28/gore.transcript/index.html

Gore, A., & Gore, T. (2002). *Joined at the heart: The transformation of the American family.* New York: Henry Holt.

Greco, P. (2007, December). A Nobel prize to public science communication. *Journal of Science Communication, 6,* 1.

Guth, J. L., Kellstedt, L. A., Green, J. C., & Smidt, C. E. (2001, October). America fifty/fifty. *First Things: A Journal of Religion and Public Life, 116,* 19–26.

Habermas, J. (2001). *The structural transformation of the public sphere: An inquiry into a category of bourgeois society.* (T. Burger & F. Lawrence, Trans.). Cambridge, MA: MIT Press. (Original work published 1962)

Habermas, J. (2006). Religion in the public sphere. *European Journal of Philosophy, 14,* 1–25.

Henneberger, M. (2000, October 22). The 2000 campaign: Spiritual seeker; Gore has explored a range of beliefs from old time to new age. *New York Times,* p. A20.

Hunter, J. D. (1991). *Culture wars: The struggle to define America.* New York: Basic Books.

Locke, J. (1963). *Works.* Germany: Scientia Verlag Aalen. (Original work edited 1823)

Maraniss, D., & Nakashima, E. (2000). *The prince of Tennessee: Al Gore meets his fate.* New York: Touchstone Books.

McClay, W. M. (2001). Two concepts of secularism. In H. Heclo and W. M. McClay (Eds.), *Religion returns to the public square* (pp. 31–61). Washington, DC: Woodrow Wilson Center Press.

Meyer, B., & Moors, A. (Eds.). (2006). *Religion, media, and the public sphere.* Bloomington: Indiana University Press.

Neuhaus, R .J. (1984). *The naked public square: Religion and democracy in America* (2nd ed.). Grand Rapids, MI: William B. Eerdmans.

O'Neill, B. (2004). Modernity and its religious discontents: Religion and public reason. *Jesuit Philosophical Association Proceedings, 1–21.*

Parmelee, J. (2002). Presidential primary videocassettes: How candidates in the 2000 presidential primary elections framed their early campaigns. *Political Communication, 19,* 317–331.

Pettigrew, A. M. (1979). On studying organizational cultures. *Administrative Science Quarterly, 24,* 570–581.

Pew Forum on Religion & Public Life. (2009, April 27). *Faith in flux: Changes in religious affiliation in the U.S. executive summary.* Retrieved from http://pewforum.org/newassets/images/reports/flux/summary.pdf

Rawls, J. (1987). The idea of an overlapping consensus. *Oxford Journal of Legal Studies, 7,* 1–25.

Rawls, J. (1993). *Political liberalism.* New York: Columbia University Press. (Original work published 1921)

Rosteck, T., & Frentz, T. S. (2009). Myth and multiple readings in environmental rhetoric: The case of *An Inconvenient Truth. Quarterly Journal of Speech, 95,* 1–19.

Steinfels, P. (1999, May 29). In a wide-ranging talk, Al Gore reveals the evangelical and intellectual roots of his faith. *The New York Times,* p. A11.

Sullivan, A. (2008). *The party faithful: How and why Democrats are closing the God gap.* New York: Scribner.

Sullivan, W. M. (1986). *Reconstructing public philosophy.* Berkeley: University of California Press.

Thieman, R. F. (1996). *Religion in public life.* Washington, DC: Georgetown University Press.

Thomas, C. (2008, January 2). Al Gore a prophet; global warming a religion. *South Florida Sun-Sentinel,* p. A17.

Thompson, J. B. (1990). *Ideology and modern culture.* Stanford, CA: Stanford University Press.

Turque, B. (2000). *Inventing Al Gore.* Boston: Mariner Books.

Wallis, J. (2005). *God's politics: Why the right gets it wrong and the left doesn't get it.* New York: HarperSanFrancisco.

Weigel, G. (2005). *The cube and the cathedral: Europe, America, and politics without God.* New York: Basic Books.

Weithman, P. J. (2002). *Religion and the obligations of citizenship.* Cambridge, UK: Cambridge University Press.

Wolterstorff, N. (1997). The role of religion in decision and discussions of political issues. In R. Audi & N. Wolterstorff (Eds.), *Religion in the public square: The place of religious conviction in political debate* (pp. 67–120). Lanham, MD: Rowman & Littlefield.

Zaret, D. (1992). Religion, science, and printing in the public spheres of England. In C. Calhoun (Ed.), *Habermas and the public sphere* (pp. 212–235). Cambridge, MA: MIT Press.

Part III

The Religious Rhetoric of Barack Obama

Chapter 7

The Audacity of Faith

An Inclusive Political Rhetoric

James T. Petre and Lenore Langsdorf

The tradition of pragmatism—the most influential stream in American thought—is in need of an explicit political mode of cultural criticism that refines and revises Emerson's concerns with power, provocation, and personality in light of Dewey's stress on historical consciousness and Du Bois's focus on the plight of the wretched of the earth. . . . Prophetic pragmatism, with its roots in the American heritage and its hopes for the wretched of the earth, constitutes the best chance of promoting an Emersonian culture of creative democracy by means of critical intelligence and social action.

—Cornel West, *The American Evasion of Philosophy* (1989, p. 212)

We don't know if Barack Obama has studied John Dewey's work, which was foundational for classical pragmatism, or Cornel West's contemporary work on prophetic pragmatism. We do know that Obama was a student at Harvard and a faculty member at the University of Chicago—and that pragmatism's academic history was based at Harvard, West taught at Harvard, and Dewey taught at the University of Chicago. And we know that, whether because of explicit classroom instruction, or what was in the intellectual air at these institutions, or coincidence, the four markers of what Cornel West (1993) calls "prophetic pragmatism" are present in Barack Obama's 2004 Democratic National Convention Keynote Address. These elements are discernment, connection, tracking hypocrisy, and hope.

We argue that the presence of these markers in Obama's rhetoric invites audiences to envision progressive alternatives to the faith-based politics of the George W. Bush administration. To use a phrase from John Dewey's work, Obama's use of prophetic pragmatism points toward a new understanding of "a common faith" that is rooted in a more inclusive interpretation of religion. More specifically, it evokes a means through which progressives may root public policy arguments in particular religious traditions as an alternative to conservative constructions of faith-based politics. For example, in the 2000 and 2004 elections, Bush used a great deal of religious imagery, and Democratic politicians were positioned as "liberal secularists" by his campaign. Even though Democratic politicians used a great deal of religious imagery themselves, as Weiss (this volume) points out regarding John Kerry's campaign, throughout the 2004 campaign and its aftermath, Democrats were seen to have a problem with attracting religious voters (see Gibbs & Duffy, 2007; Kuhn, 2007; Murphy, 2004). For example, Nancy Gibbs and Michael Duffy (2007) outline how major Democratic political figures such as Barack Obama, Hillary Clinton, and John Edwards seem to be more comfortable talking about how religion informs their politics than were Kerry and his primary opponent Howard Dean (pp. 4–5). We argue that the presence of West's elements of prophetic pragmatism in Obama's Keynote Address at the 2004 Democratic National Convention offers a progressive interpretation of what an alternative faith-based politics could look like.

In what follows we sketch those elements as West describes them and as we see them manifested in Obama's speech. We follow West in linking prophetic pragmatism to Ralph Waldo Emerson's conception of "creative democracy," and argue that this conception provides a basis for the inclusive political rhetoric that we find enacted in many of Obama's speeches, and particularly in his 2004 Keynote Address. Obama's use of personal examples, along with his repeated declaration that "I am my brother's keeper, I am my sister's keeper" (a Biblical phrase) evokes an empathetic, forward-looking, experimentalist strand of pragmatism that flows through the writings of Emerson, Dewey, and West.[1] This pragmatism is rooted in an idea that we can look toward our shared intelligences and experiences to envision a better tomorrow—a *faith* in what West (1989) describes as "a culture of Emersonian creative democracy" (p. 213). Moreover, this strand of prophetic pragmatism in American philosophy illustrates the development of an "American theodicy" that flows through the writings of Emerson, Dewey, and West himself, and is present in Obama's political rhetoric.

West (1989) describes Emerson as "a cultural critic who devised and deployed a vast array of rhetorical strategies in order to exert intellectual and moral leadership over a significant element of the educated classes of his day" (p. 10). West goes on to say "[t]he rhetorical strategies, principally aimed at explaining America to itself, weave novel notions of power, provocation, and personality into a potent and emerging American ideology of voluntaristic invulnerability and utopian possibility" (p. 10). After outlining prophetic pragmatism, West elaborates further: "To speak then of an Emersonian culture of creative democracy is to speak of a society and culture where politically adjudicated forms of knowledge are produced in which human participation is encouraged and for which human personalities are enhanced" (p. 213). The presence of all four prophetic elements speaks to both a "voluntaristic invulnerability" and "utopian possibility." It is inherently democratic and experimentalist: we are constantly in a process of new understandings and experiences, based on the contributions of human participation, development, and ingenuity. Prophetic pragmatism draws upon the pragmatic tradition that West outlines.

ANALYSIS

We explore prophetic pragmatism in Obama's political rhetoric by explicating moments of his 2004 Democratic National Convention Keynote Address in which West's four prophetic elements are present. The first prophetic element is *discernment*. West (1993, p. 3) refers to discernment as "the capacity to provide a broad and deep analytical grasp of the present in light of the past." He calls for a "nuanced historical sense . . . an ability to keep track, to remain attuned to the ambiguous legacies and hybrid cultures in history" (p. 3). This "nuanced historical sense" is his preferred way to analyze the multiculturalism and Eurocentrism that characterizes contemporary politics (p. 4).

Obama's (2004) speech begins with his discernment of possibility in America's history and future. "I stand here," he says, "knowing that my story is part of the larger American story, that I owe a debt to all those who came before me, and that, in no other country on Earth, is my story even possible" (para. 10). He goes on to provide a historical interpretation of the American narrative as a positive one about hard work, sacrifice, and upward mobility, then connects this story to the Declaration of Independence and the 2004 election: "This year, in this election, we are called to reaffirm our values and our commitments, to hold them against a hard reality and see how we're measuring up to the legacy of our forebears and the promise of future generations" (para. 14). This passage evokes Emersonian creative democracy in its reflection on our history, where we are, and where we are going. Democracy is dynamic, always in flux, and dependent on citizens' actions. Obama's praise of the American story is also an invitation to citizens to "reaffirm our values and commitments," and he characterizes this reaffirmation as a necessary part not only of democracy in America, but also of this particular electoral process. These statements are similar to many religious and faith-based ceremonies that begin by declaring their belief in and affirmation of the faith as well as the community of believers. Judith Trent and Robert Friedenberg (2008) also identify this reaffirming and legitimizing of the American system as the first function of political nominating conventions: "The convention rituals are, in short, a kind of emotional/spiritual/patriotic catharsis in which we can, if necessary, lament current shortcomings within the party or the country while remaining proud of and faithful to our legacy" (p. 59).

The second prophetic element is *connection.* West (1993) describes connection as "a value of empathy" that informs "the capacity to get in contact with the anxieties and frustrations of others . . ." (p. 5). He recalls William James's 1903 essay on the "U.S. invasion, occupation, and annexation of the Philippines" in order to contrast this element of connection with the political rhetoric of that time, which "cast them [the citizens of the Philippines] as . . . often stereotypical pictures and portraits" (p. 5) and thus denied their humanity. A creative democracy, West holds, is one that "always attempt[s] to remain in contact with the humanity of others" (p. 5) and speaks in terms of individuals, rather than an abstract humanity. Obama's speech exemplifies this belief:

> And fellow Americans, Democrats, Republicans, Independents, I say to you tonight: We have more work to do—more work to do for the workers I met in Galesburg, Illinois, who are losing their union jobs at the Maytag plant that's moving to Mexico, and now are having to compete with their own children for jobs that pay seven bucks an hour; more to do for the father I met who was losing his job and choking back the tears, wondering how he would pay 4500 dollars a month for the drugs his son needs without the health benefits that he counted on; more to do for the young woman in East St. Louis, and the thousands more like her, who has the grades, has the drive, has the will, but doesn't have the money to go to college. (para. 15)

Thus, along with affirming the greatness of our nation (para. 11), Obama dramatizes the claim that there is work that must be done by recounting the needs of individuals. These are people who are falling through the cracks; those for whom the system is not working. The specificity of their stories complements, on the individual level, West's abstract analysis: "The condition of truth to emerge must be in tune with those who are undergoing social misery—socially induced forms of suffering" and that we must be honest about who is being left out and the suffering that is occurring (West, 1993, pp. 4, 6). One way to address this suffering is to hear these stories and devise meliorating policies, with the understanding that no policy will ever be perfect, and so melioration is an ongoing task.

Obama emphasizes that connection is not antithetical to the American story: "Alongside our famous individualism, there's another ingredient in the American saga, a belief that we're all connected as one people. If there is a child on the south side of Chicago who can't read, that matters to me, even if it's not my child" (para. 31). This reminder of our belief in connection, despite "our famous individualism," invites audiences to see individualism and interconnectedness as "ingredients in the American saga," rather than as mutually exclusive concepts. Again, Obama speaks of the interconnectedness of individuals in making this point:

> If there is a senior citizen somewhere who can't pay for their prescription drugs, and having to choose between medicine and the rent, that makes my life poorer, even if it's not my grandparent. If there's an Arab American family being rounded up without the benefit of an attorney or due process, that threatens my civil liberties . . . it is that fundamental belief: I am my brother's keeper; I am my sister's keeper—that makes this country work. (para. 32–33)

Obama goes on to give more examples of people who are falling through the cracks of our system in order to invite audiences to see themselves as sharing a common faith in the possibilities of what could be accomplished through our shared empathy. He refers to the Hebrew Bible ("I am my brother's keeper," a slight variation on Genesis 4:9), but broadens out the scriptural allusion to make a nondenominational yet still religious argument about the power of faith and connection. According to Obama, even if our individual lives are free from crisis, we should turn our attention toward those experiencing crisis, and do the work that's needed if the system is to work for them, also.[2] In other words, ensuring that no one falls through the cracks makes us all stronger—it is what "makes this country work." Such a claim is important to take note of because it uses religious scripture to challenge the repeated arguments Christian Republicans such as Bush have made against welfare-state liberalism and social programs to help the poor.

Tracking hypocrisy is West's third marker of prophetic pragmatism. This requires "accenting boldly, and defiantly, the gap between principles and practice, between promise and performance, between rhetoric and reality" (1993, p. 5). West is a philosopher, not a rhetorician, and rhetoricians might object to the negative connotation of using the term *rhetoric* in contrast to *reality* here. That connotation carries a reminder of the centuries of separation between philosophy, which claimed to operate on *principles* grounded in transcendent truth about reality, and rhetoric, denigrated as a *practice* that pandered to audiences' limited apprehension of truth. However, we suggest that the negative connotation is erased when we recognize the gap as one between words and actions: Rhetorical words rely on principles held by an audience in giving us *promises* for the future; actions transform those words into *performances,* deeds that change reality. West reminds us that "keeping track of human hypocrisy, in a self-critical, not a self-righteous mode . . . one must point out human hypocrisy while remaining open to having others point out that of your own" (p. 5). Reflexivity, then, is vital to bridging the gap between our rhetorical words and the actions we perform; to moving audiences toward identifying with principles that promise to transform the all-too-evident failures in the past and present reality of the American story.

Obama focuses his tracking of hypocrisy on objections to the gaps between principles and practices—words and actions—in the current administration's policies:

> When we send our young men and women into harm's way, we have a solemn obligation not to fudge the numbers or shade the truth about why they're going, to care for their families while they're gone, to tend to the soldiers upon their return, and to never ever go to war without enough troops to win the war, secure the peace, and earn the respect of the world. (para. 29)

Referring to this responsibility as a *solemn obligation* reminds us that sending soldiers off to fight has moral and even spiritual consequences. In order for our faith in the American story to continue, it is imperative to recognize our past shortcomings about how the war was handled, (i.e., confess our sins) so that we can be open to future possibilities.

Immediately following this passage, Obama acknowledges that the United States does have *real* enemies in the world (para. 30), and illustrates the present gap between principles and practice by addressing deeds of the Bush administration which the United States should *never* do: actions that forsake what the United States has stood for in the past and should stand for now. The gap that Obama identifies "between principles and practice, between promise and performance, between rhetoric and reality" is a gap between the principles, promises, and rhetoric of the Constitution, and the practices, performance, and reality of the policies of the Bush administration. This gap is the *sin* of the Bush administration, and Obama tracks this hypocrisy as a crucial step in moving America forward.

West identifies *hope* as the fourth element of a prophetic pragmatism: "to talk about human hope," he says, "is to engage in an audacious attempt to galvanize and energize, to inspire and to invigorate a world-weary people" and "keep alive the notion that history is incomplete, that the world is unfinished, that the future is open-ended and that what we think and what we do can make a difference" (1993, p. 6).

Obama's hope is rooted in that American story we quoted at the beginning of this chapter: "I believe that we have a righteous wind at our backs and that as we stand on the crossroads of history, we can make the right choices and meet the challenges that face us" (para. 42). Words such as *righteous wind* again evoke religious imagery, and work to respond to the proliferation of religious rhetoric by the Republicans in the 2004 election (e.g., Republicans referring to the GOP as "God's Own Party," etc.). Obama's *hope* reflects his "audacious attempt to galvanize and energize" his audience in his concluding paragraph:

> America! Tonight, if you feel the same energy that I do, if you feel the same urgency that I do, if you feel the same passion that I do, if you feel the same hopefulness that I do—if we do what we must do, then I have no doubt that all across the country, from Florida to Oregon, from Washington to Maine, the people will rise up in November, and John Kerry will be sworn in as President, and John Edwards will be sworn in as Vice President, and this country will reclaim its promise, and out of this long political darkness a brighter day will come. (para. 43)

As the conclusion of a keynote speech at a convention that will nominate a presidential candidate, this linking of hope for a brighter day to the election of particular candidates for a particular election is both appropriate and explicitly prophetic, as *brighter day* evokes religious themes for adherents of many different faiths; this may be the day of the resurrection, going to heaven, being *saved*, etc. Images of the populace *rising up* with *energy, urgency, passion,* and *hopefulness* also contain religious connotations of a community of worshippers filled with optimism for the future. Yet, this immediate goal creates a dilemma for Obama. Given the conventions of this sort of speech, he must both inspire his audience and deliver a persuasive endorsement of his party's candidates. If his own speech is too inspirational, it could overshadow Kerry's, and possibly, thereby, point up the criticism made of Kerry at the time; namely, that he lacked the very sense of *urgency*—much less, *energy, passion,* and *hopefulness*—that was needed to bring an end to "this long political darkness." In 2008, Obama would face no such dilemma with his optimistic campaign slogan: "Yes we can"—another phrase that underscores the importance of interconnection and inclusion.

IMPLICATIONS

In his 2004 Keynote Address, Obama evokes prophetic pragmatism through the presence of West's four prophetic elements. In particular, Obama's use of personal examples, which emphasize connection and empathy, implies an orientation toward "the plight of the wretched of the earth" (West, 1989, p. 212). Furthermore, Obama's pragmatic orientation carries the potential of "promoting an Emersonian culture of creative democracy by means of critical intelligence and social action" (West, 1989, p. 212). An orientation toward critical intelligence and social action was similarly evident throughout the 2008 presidential campaign, and continued through the early days of the Obama administration as new ideas were put forward to attempt to solve the economic crisis and improve U.S. relations around the world.

An optimistic inclination toward melioration of social ills in Obama's rhetoric, rooted in empathy for others, shares a common thread with Emerson, Dewey, and West. This shared faith in the efficacy of constituting and reconstituting a "culture of creative democracy" is quite evident among these thinkers. In this light, we can understand Obama's political rhetoric as evoking a prophetic pragmatism that shares Dewey's concern with "the experiences of everyday people" (West, 1989, p. 213). For example, Dewey (1962) argues:

> The ideal ends to which we attach our faith are not shadowy and wavering. They assume concrete form in our understanding of our relations to one another and the values contained in these relations. We who now live are parts of a humanity that extends into the remote past, a humanity that has interacted with nature. The things in civilization we most prize are not of ourselves. They exist by grace of the doings and sufferings of the continuous human community in which we are a link. Ours is the responsibility of conversing, transmitting, rectifying and expanding the heritage of values we have received that those who come after us may receive it more solid and secure, more widely accessible and more generously shared than we have received it. Here are all the elements for a religious faith that shall not be confined to sect, class, or race. Such a faith has always been implicitly the common faith of mankind. It remains to make it explicit and militant. (p. 87)

We argue that this faith outlined by Dewey is linked to West's prophetic pragmatism—evoking an Emersonian culture of creative democracy that lives on in the political rhetoric (and policy proposals) of Barack Obama and his administration. Like Dewey and West, Obama offers a faith-informed argument that is not "confined to sect, class, or race" and builds coalitions based on shared experiences rather than opposition to outsiders. While the full implications of such a view remain to be seen, the rhetorical landscape of faith and religion can no longer be seen as dominated by Republicans.

Obama (2008) reminds audiences that U.S. citizens are part of a proud tradition of people who have used innovation to spur progress, economic growth, and greater social justice. He invites audiences to see that different problems the nation faces are connected (i.e., fixing health care creates more jobs, funding education makes U.S. Americans more competitive in a global economy) and that U.S. citizens themselves are connected as a people. He holds the United States accountable for its past mistakes, while celebrating its successes (e.g., Obama's [2009a] admission of U.S. involvement in a 1953 Iranian coup during his speech in Cairo, in which he also praised U.S. support of human rights around the globe). Finally, he evokes a sense of hope and optimism, urging audiences to see the nation's best days as set in the future and not the past—in a "new era of responsibility" (2009b). His use of religious phrases to describe U.S. citizens' interdependence continued throughout the 2008 campaign. As president, he has expanded the scope of such phrases to include all of the people of the world.

This orientation, and the policy proposals flowing from it, has been met with much criticism from the political opposition. For example, conservatives have been particularly critical of Obama's use of the word *empathy* in relation to Sonia Sotomayor's nomination to the Supreme Court, as well as in economic policy and foreign policy writ large. However, empathy is what indicates an orientation toward prophetic pragmatism in Obama's rhetoric that is in line with a tradition of "Emersonian creative democracy" as outlined by West. Perhaps what draws criticism is that privileging empathy—and repeatedly using Biblical phrases to underscore the connections that U.S. Americans and people throughout the world share—challenges a socially conservative approach to religion. In other words, rather than criticizing Republican policies through a secular-liberal approach, Obama is offering a liberal approach to a faith-informed politics. Instead of a faith-based politics focused on a pro-life stance on abortion, free market fundamentalism, and opposition to same-sex marriage as its major planks, Obama offers a faith-informed politics rooted in empathy and inclusion. Although criticized by conservatives for many of his other decisions, this particular aspect of Obama's approach to politics does not appear to have had a significantly detrimental effect on his popularity to date. According to RealClearPolitics (2009), six months into his presidency, Obama enjoyed an average approval rating consistently above 55 percent, although that rating dipped below 50 percent in the final months of 2009.

The inclusiveness displayed by Obama is a stark contrast to the frequent divisiveness of the Bush administration. For example, Ellen Goodman recalls Bush's 2001 Inauguration and the fact that "[t]he minister at the inauguration had invoked Jesus Christ the savior, and millions of Americans from Sikhs to Unitarians had to choose between saying 'amen' and feeling excluded" (2006). While Obama's quotes also derive from Judeo-Christian teachings, his use of phrases such as "I am my brother's keeper" focuses on drawing connections between those who are religious and nonreligious, rather than drawing divisions between these groups. Obama's rhetorical efforts in the 2004 Keynote Address and throughout his own presidential campaign, along with the approaches of other Democratic politicians described in these pages, indicates a pendulum shift toward Democrats' increasing comfort in discussing how their faith informs their approach to politics. While some may argue that faith should be left out of politics, it is also important to consider the benefits flowing from a more progressive and inclusive alternative to Republican manifestations of faith-based politics. Such inclusion is especially important since, as Goodman (2006) points out, the United States is "the most religiously diverse country in the world."

CONCLUSION

The presence of West's four prophetic elements was evident throughout Obama's successful 2008 presidential campaign, and in speeches and town hall meetings he now delivers and conducts as president. In contrast to the role he played in the 2004 Democratic National Convention Keynote Address, he is now free to promote his own ideas of hope, rather than seeking to inspire hope for a different candidate. It is important to note that although West critiqued Obama early on in his presidential run, he later endorsed Obama's campaign and "signed on as an unpaid advisor" (Wolffe & Briscoe, 2007, p. 1). Although we cannot discern whether Obama has read West's work, it is clear West's four prophetic elements are manifest in Obama's rhetoric. Reporting on West's decision to endorse Obama, Richard Wolffe and Daren Briscoe state that Obama called West to "clarify some things" that he had said in a speech challenging the candidate to answer a stark set of questions:

> I want to know how deep is your love for the people, what kind of courage have you manifested in the stances that you have and what are you willing to *sacrifice* for. That's the fundamental question. I don't care what color you are. You see, you can't take black people for granted just 'cause you're black. (quoted in Wolffe & Briscoe, 2007, p. 1)

That call, Wolffe and Brisco report, instigated further conversations. We wish we could have been listening in, for we suspect that West's endorsement came as the result of what must have been some very persuasive conversations. It remains to be seen whether or not West will play any continued advisory role (unpaid or otherwise) in the Obama administration, and more broadly, how the political ramifications of prophetic pragmatism will take shape in the coming years. It is clear, however, that Obama's use of prophetic pragmatism offers audiences a progressive and inclusive interpretation of a faith-informed politics.

NOTES

1. West (1989) thoroughly outlines a lineage between these philosophers.

2. Obama would go on to evoke these same themes in his successful 2008 presidential campaign. As president, he emphasizes interconnection and the importance of owning up to past mistakes in several foreign policy speeches, such as his speech in Cairo (Obama, 2009b).

REFERENCES

Dewey, J. (1962). *A common faith*. New Haven, CT: Yale University Press.

Gibbs, N., & Duffy, M. (2007, July 12). How the Democrats got religion. *Time*. Retrieved from http://www.time.com/time/politics/article/0,8599,1642649,00 .html

Goodman, E. (2006, October 20). Faith-based politics is reason to worry. *Boston Globe*. Retrieved from http://www.boston.com/news/globe/editorial_opinion/oped/ articles/2006/10/20/faith_based_politics_is_reason_to_worry/

Kuhn, D. P. (2007, June 10). Democrats take religion out of the closet. *Politico*. Retrieved from http://www.politico.com/news/stories/0607/4416.html

Murphy, J. (2004, November 4). Should Democrats get religion? *CBS News*. Retrieved from http://www.cbsnews.com/stories/2004/11/04/politics/main653667 .shtml

Obama, B. (2004). The audacity of hope. Retrieved from http://www.americanrhetoric .com/speeches/convention2004/barackobama2004dnc.htm

Obama, B. (2008, August 28). Barack Obama's acceptance speech. *New York Times*. Retrieved from http://www.nytimes.com/2008/08/28/us/politics/28text-obama .html

Obama, B. (2009a, June 4). Full text: President Barack Obama's speech to the Muslim world. *Time*. Retrieved from http://www.time.com/time/printout/0,8816,1902738,00 .html

Obama, B. (2009b, January 20). Barack Obama's Inaugural Address. Retrieved from http://www.whitehouse.gov/blog/inaugural-address/

RealClearPolitics [President Obama Job Approval]. (2009). *RealClearPolitics.com*. Retrieved from http://www.realclearpolitics.com/epolls/other/president_obama _job_approval-1044.html

Trent, J. S., & Friedenberg, R. V. (2008). *Political campaign communication: Principles and practices* (6th ed.). Lanham, MD: Rowman & Littlefield.

West, C. (1989). *The American evasion of philosophy.* Madison: University of Wisconsin Press.

West, C. (1993). *Beyond eurocentrism and multiculturalism: Prophetic thought in postmodern times.* Monroe, ME: Common Courage Press.

Wolffe, R., & Briscoe, D. (2007, July 16). Across the divide: How Barack Obama is shaking up old assumptions about what it means to be black and white in America. *Newsweek.* Retrieved from http://www.newsweek.com/id/33156

Chapter 8

Dancing on the Wall

An Analysis of Barack Obama's "Call to Renewal" Keynote Address

Biff Rocha and Jeffrey L. Morrow

When did the Democrats lose the "religious values voter"? For all its commitment today to a secularist worldview (the notion that religion should be pushed out of the public realm), the Democratic Party through much of American history has been the party comprising religiously motivated individuals, particularly Christians, who sought to make society more just, charitable, and equitable. New Deal Liberals advocated a moral vision of a just society and pursued that vision by harnessing the power and resources of the government to shape the American civil landscape. During the civil rights and women's movements of the 1960s, Democrats enshrined moral arguments as civil laws, criminalizing racial segregation and requiring gender equality. But the 1973 Supreme Court *Roe v. Wade* decision dramatically changed the way Democrats integrated their religious faith into society. "Shifting the focus of contemporary liberal politics, the argument for abortion rights forced the Democratic Party to recast liberalism, emphasizing personal autonomy and a libertarian view of moral issues. This approach was virtually guaranteed to turn off religiously motivated voters" (Winters, 2008, p. 114). Persons of faith became *personae non gratae,* regardless of their liberal credentials on other issues (Wolfe, 2004).[1]

Indeed, the new Democratic strategy expunging religion set in motion a 30-year exodus: moderate voters who valued the role of faith in their lives fled to the Republican Party. As Notre Dame professor R. Scott Appleby observes, "in short, the Democratic Party's long string of counterproductive responses to the enduring influence of the religious right has had the cumulative effect of driving away any type of base with the word 'faith' attached to it" (2008, para. 5). As a result the Republicans became the party of the religious right while the Democrats became identified as the party of the secular left. The 1970s and

1980s saw the formation of new politically minded religious groups such as the Moral Majority and the Christian Coalition. The "God gap" continued to widen through the presidencies of Ronald Reagan and George H. W. Bush. In the early 1990s, Pew researchers identified a clear correlation between regular religious attendance at worship and voting behavior (Steinfels, 2006). Democrats became suddenly aware that they needed a way to reach religious voters. At approximately the same time, a relatively new teacher of constitutional law at the University of Chicago captured sufficient constituent attention to secure three terms in the Illinois Senate. Barack Obama infused his campaigns with religious appeals, created a faith steering committee, and held forums across the state with the title "What's faith got to do with it?" (Domke, 2007). Obama stepped forward, offering hope to the Democratic Party as a candidate who could speak the language of faith to the common American citizen.

In 1995, Jim Wallis, editor of the Christian magazine *Sojourners* and author of the best-selling book *God's Politics: Why the Right Gets it Wrong and the Left Doesn't Get it* (2005),[2] founded the liberal group Call to Renewal, uniting progressive churches and other faith-based organizations in an effort to exercise their political power. When, nearly a decade later, Wallis, his magazine, and his organization decided to sponsor a Call to Renewal Conference, the young Senator from Illinois appeared to be the obvious choice to serve as the keynote speaker, as he would be addressing an emerging movement of politically active progressive Christians.

REACTION TO OBAMA'S "CALL TO RENEWAL"

Barack Obama gave his Call to Renewal keynote address in Washington, D.C., on Wednesday, June 28, 2006. In retrospect, the address may be fairly identified as a successful disaster. The *New York Times* praised the speech as "remarkable for its honesty [and] its sensibleness" (McMullen, 2006, para. 5) while political columnist E. J. Dionne, Jr., declared in the *Washington Post* that the speech was the "most important pronouncement by a Democrat on faith and politics since John F. Kennedy's Houston speech in 1960" (2006a, para. 6), and *The New Yorker* described the speech as simply "remarkable" (Boyer, 2008, para. 29). Writing in the *Washington Post,* Michael Gerson, a self-identified evangelical and former speechwriter for President George W. Bush, contrasted Obama with the "series of Democratic presidential candidates who seemed to suffer from a theological disability," noting how "one of Obama's genuine contributions had been a renewed, liberal appreciation of the role of religious motivation in politics" (2008, para. 7). In a column published a week after the speech, Dionne identified Obama's keynote address as a road map for Democrats struggling to speak to people of faith (2006b, para. 12). This sentiment was echoed by other commentators, including a *Washington Post* reporter who observed that Obama's words "could easily be adopted as well as guidelines for all governments" (Hoagland, 2006, para. 12). Conservatives, too, applauded Obama's foray into faith talk. Douglas Kmiec, a Republican professor of constitutional law, noted that the speech was "significantly different" and "significantly better" than other Democrats' attempts to use religious language because Obama recognized that "religion necessarily is a source of morality, and morality is necessarily the place we draw laws from" (quoted in Boyer, 2008, para. 34).

Although well received by his intended audiences, and praised by commentators, Obama's speech to his fellow Democrats used techniques more commonly employed when addressing a hostile audience; at the same time, he unintentionally insulted certain people of faith. Furthermore, while attempting to use the language of faith in his speech, Obama revealed a lack of theological and historical understanding, and proposed solutions that sounded appealing in their presentation, but that when applied to particular instances proved to be unsustainable.

It is clear from the Call to Renewal speech that Obama is a gifted and experienced public speaker. While there is much to be praised in his keynote address, our chapter will also focus on some of the more unusual aspects of the speech such as his use of hostile audience techniques and his inclusion of Christian testimony. We will begin by analyzing the text of the speech, establishing its rhetorical situation and highlighting some of its more distinctive components. We will then narrow our focus to look in some depth at Obama's problematic treatment of a significant scriptural passage, the *Aqedah* in Genesis 22, and consider how his understanding of religion shapes his approach to faith and politics. From there we will dive into some faulty assumptions commonly held by the American public (as evidenced by Obama's comments) that hinder the current debate on the role of religion in public. Our method, therefore, will involve both a textual approach to the speech, and a brief review of some historical situations for which the modern characterization of religion as dangerous is based.

OVERVIEW OF SPEECH

Barack Obama was invited by the Call to Renewal group to deliver the keynote address at their 2006 convention. Obama chose to discuss the role of religion in politics. In his speech, Obama affirms the place of private individuals motivated by their religious concerns to engage with politicians to initiate change. Yet Obama also recognizes that not everyone acknowledges the rights of the religiously motivated to act on their faith publicly. The dominant theme in Obama's speech is the idea of two Americas: one religious, the other secular. He first discusses the disadvantage to Democrats of avoiding religion, then proposes that progressives tolerate and even attempt to dialogue with the religiously minded America. While some may see Obama's speech as merely a campaign maneuver, it is clearly, also, an extension of his personal experience of life as a dance between faith and politics, a tension that he had addressed in his books *Dreams From My Father* (1997) and *The Audacity of Hope* (2006), each of which devoted a chapter to his reflections on faith and politics.

The warm and folksy Call to Renewal keynote address follows a simple path. Opening with the affirmation that the religiously minded have much to offer this nation through their thoughtful prescriptions and policy suggestions, Obama identifies as a significant rhetorical obstacle the mutual suspicion that exists between religious America and secular America. "The political divide in this country has fallen sharply along religious lines. Indeed, the single biggest 'gap' . . . [is] between those who attend church regularly and those who don't" (para. 15). Admitting that some liberals dismiss religion in the public square as inherently irrational and offensive, Obama warns his party[3] of the consequences of ignoring religion in America, as over 90 percent of U.S. citizens believe in God and over 70 percent affiliate themselves with a Christian denomination or other religious organization. As Obama points out, the lives of most Americans are replete with religious meaning and experiences.

Obama speaks to both Americas as he presents himself as an example of a person who finds comfort in the spiritual dimension of reality. He confronts the secular fundamentalists in his audience with a startling claim: "secularists are wrong when they ask believers to leave their religion at the door before entering the public square" (para. 47). Obama then asks how "we progressives" (para. 48) can build a bridge between religious and secular people of good will. Throughout his speech he offers suggestions for us ("religious and secular people") (para. 52) to move forward: "Conservative leaders" (para. 53) must understand the critical role of the separation of church and state (para. 54); we (the nation) must respect religious pluralism (para. 55); the religiously motivated must learn to translate their concerns into secular language (para. 57); and both sides must adopt a sense of proportion on the subject (para. 62). To illustrate this good will Obama concludes his speech with a personal anecdote about a pro-life doctor calling into question an entry posted on Obama's campaign Web site concerning abortion. The audience repeatedly interrupted the senator with cheers and applause. Afterward the speech's full text was posted online, and a video was made available for viewing on YouTube. Months, even years, after the address was given, audiences continued to extol Obama's historic attempt to address the connection between religion and politics in the United States.[4]

Given Obama's message that people of faith have much to contribute to our national discussion regarding the future betterment of America, the Call to Renewal coalition of politically minded progressive Christians was an ideal audience. The words of the address suggested that the divide between religious and secular America is so deep that acknowledging and facing the issue of suspicion was a significant goal in and of itself. Yet Obama wished to do more than merely draw America's attention to the intellectual wall separating the religious from the secular constituencies. In his Call to Renewal address, Obama offered solutions for society's ills.

ANALYSIS

A Tale of Two Worldviews: Secular and Religious America

Obama opens his speech with the recognition that the Call to Renewal group had written a document entitled "Covenant for a New America." He praises their efforts, then declares his own purpose: talking "about the connection between religion and politics" (para. 2). He introduces his "two Americas" theme in the third paragraph where he divides the nation into "religious America and secular America" (para. 3). These audiences become further defined in paragraph 15, where Obama observes that the political divide in America falls sharply along religious lines: that is, between those who attend church regularly and those who do not. Religious America is composed of conservatives and Christians (para. 16). On the other side of the gap stand Democrats and liberals, the groups implicitly constructed as the constituents of secular America. Near the end of his speech Obama nods his head toward Jews and Muslims (para. 50), who could be added to the people-of-faith America, while expanding secular America to include "secular people of good will" (para. 52) and nonbelievers (para. 55). For a speech given to readers of *Sojourners* it seems odd that the repeated chorus is the positioning of people of faith against Democrats, or the framing of Christians as contrary to liberal progressives. Obama casts his Democratic supporters as the major participants in secular America, people who typically do not attend church and are uncomfortable with public expressions of religion.

Although Obama addresses his message to Americans of both the secular Democratic and religious Republican persuasions, the actual audience members in attendance at his talk were overwhelmingly progressive in their orientation. Obama specifically acknowledges that both he and these progressives are Democrats: "Democrats, for the most part, have taken the bait. At best, we may try to avoid the conversation about religious values altogether" (para. 17). Repeatedly throughout his speech Obama identifies himself with this group through the use of the inclusive pronouns *we* and *us:* "As progressives," Obama encourages his listeners, "we cannot abandon the field of religious discourse" (para. 34). Later he states, "If we progressives shed some of these biases, we might recognize some overlapping values that both religious and secular people share" (para. 48).

To persuade what he sees as a group of progressive secular Democrats to shed their biases against religion and against their fellow religious Americans, throughout his keynote address Obama employs a wide variety of common strategies for dealing with a hostile audience. Among these are highlighting one's experience on the given topic in order to establish credibility; admitting past mistakes in order to increase one's believability; and using humor and compliments to increase one's likeability (Tracy, 1990). In order to limit his exposure, Obama uses techniques such as keeping the speech short, narrowing the speech's goals, and focusing on the single most important issue (Dutton, 1986; Tracy, 1990). He also uses effective tension-reducing techniques such as storytelling, repetition, and speaking with a rhythmic cadence (Dutton, 1986).

In the first paragraph he begins by complimenting the attendees: "I'd like to congratulate you on all the thoughtful presentations you've given so far" (para. 1). He affirms past actions of his audience and where they stand in agreement: "I'd like to congratulate you . . . for putting fire under the feet of the political leadership here in Washington" (para. 1). He clarifies potential misunderstandings; for example, when he explains the significance of religion to Americans: "Americans are a religious people. Ninety percent of us believe in God, seventy percent affiliate themselves with an organized religion. Thirty-eight percent call themselves committed Christians and substantially more people in America believe in angels than they do in evolution" (para. 19). Obama then clarifies his point: "This religious tendency is not simply the result of successful marketing by skilled preachers or the draw of popular mega-churches" (para. 20).

Another technique used to gain the audience's empathy is admitting to past mistakes; as Tracy (1990) notes, confessing personal faults may be advantageous, especially when such a past flaw and its present correction complements or reinforces the main message. Obama skillfully recounts his 2004 senatorial campaign debate against Republican candidate Alan Keyes (para. 4–13). When pushed by Keyes on the biblical consistency of his public testimony as a Christian and on his abortion advocacy, Obama explains that he reflexively responded "with what has come to be the typically liberal response in such debates. Namely, I said that we live in a pluralistic society. That I can't impose my own religious views on another. That I was running to be the U.S. Senator of Illinois and not the minister of Illinois" (para. 12).

After Obama states that religion motivates a great number of Americans, he advises progressives to permit religious language in public policy debates. Near the end of his speech Obama explains that his earlier response to Keyes was an error because it did not recognize that laws, by their very nature, institutionalize a morality for the society. By prohibiting or permitting certain behaviors, beliefs, or activities, laws "impose" specific values and practices. Obama elaborates, "To say that men and women should not inject their 'personal morality' into public policy debates is a practical absurdity. Our law is by definition a codification of morality, much of it grounded in the Judeo-Christian tradition" (para. 47). Admitting his own flawed response to Keyes allows Obama to display his humanity and his ability to grow. It also complements his larger point of the necessity for progressives to learn the language of faith; further, it serves as a model for his liberal supporters to emulate when working with the cooperation of religious Americans toward the renewal of America.

In his speech, Obama paints a vision for future collaboration with his audience: "We have the ability to reach out to the evangelical community and engage millions of religious Americans in the larger project of American renewal" (para. 48). Obama's speech has two messages: one for religious Republicans and the other for his secular Democrats. Religious Republicans must learn a second language and culture: that of the dominant society, which is secular America. Obama states, "The religiously motivated [should] translate their concerns into universal, rather than religion-specific, values" (para. 57). The message for the Democrats is quite simple: "we cannot abandon the field of religious discourse" (para. 34). While this is his main call for action for progressives, Obama clarifies his proposal for action: "I am not suggesting that every progressive suddenly latch on to religious terminology . . . As Jim [Wallis] has mentioned, some politicians come and clap off rhythm to the choir.[5] We don't need that" (para. 45). He clarifies: "But what I am suggesting is this. Secularists are wrong when they ask believers to leave their religion at the door before entering into the public square. Frederick Douglass, Abraham Lincoln, William Jennings Bryan, Dorothy Day, Martin Luther King—indeed a majority of great reformers in American history . . . used religious language to argue for their cause" (para. 47). Requesting people to tolerate and perhaps even use religious language is a modest but necessary first step in Obama's vision for renewing America. Employing a typical strategy of engagement with a hostile audience (Dutton, 1986) Obama's call to action is quite limited, perhaps even more than one would expect from a liberal Senator addressing a sympathetic liberal crowd.

Obama's Christian Testimony

Another technique for persuading a hostile audience is to convince them that you possess sufficient experience or knowledge on the topic you are addressing (Tracy, 1990). Throughout his speech, Obama vacillates between religious and secular self-presentations. His political (and thus secular) credentials are assumed since he has previously held and is again running for a political office. To establish his religious credentials Obama offers a testimony, a public profession of faith that recounts how an individual came to accept Jesus Christ as one's savior and lord and therefore identifies one as a follower of Jesus (Kennedy, 1996; King, 2009). Obama's own brief testimony to his faith in Jesus Christ comes in paragraphs 22–33, where he provides background about his life before his decision to follow Jesus:

> I was not raised in a particularly religious household, as undoubtedly many in the audience were. My father, who returned to Kenya when I was just two, was born Muslim but as an adult became an atheist. My mother, whose parents were non-practicing Baptists and Methodists, was probably one of the most spiritual and kindest people I've ever known, but grew up with a healthy skepticism of organized religion herself. As a consequence, so did I. (para. 23)

While his testimony is fairly standard in some ways, at the same time it obfuscates what Obama means by religion, as he contrasts the religious with the spiritual, and, in doing so, highlights his skepticism about organized religion. He recounts how working with an African American Christian church in Chicago helped him to see "that without a vessel for my beliefs, without a commitment to a particular community of faith, at some level I would always remain apart, and alone" (para. 26).

As historical Protestant Christianity has always maintained, God sent Jesus to die in our place as a substitute, as the divine redeemer paying the penalty for human sin. This substitutionary atonement is alluded to in scaled-down form when Obama states, "You need to come to church in the first place precisely because you are first of this world, not apart from it. You need to embrace Christ precisely because you have sins to wash away" (para. 31). Elaborating on his own acceptance of Jesus as savior and lord, he explains, "kneeling beneath that cross on the South Side, I felt that I heard God's spirit beckoning me. I submitted myself to His will, and dedicated myself to discovering His truth" (para. 32). For this particular audience, many of whose members may be unfamiliar with how one's faith can be integrated into an overall approach to life, Obama feels it necessary to explain the result of becoming a follower of Jesus Christ: "That's a path that has been shared by millions upon millions of Americans—evangelicals, Catholics, Protestants, Jews and Muslims alike; some since birth, others at certain turning points in their lives. It is not something they set apart from the rest of their beliefs and values. In fact, it is often what drives their beliefs and their values" (para. 32).

The telling of one's faith journey (i.e., the story of how God has changed one's life) is a common practice among Christians, both Protestant and Catholic. Although the testimony Obama gives falls within the standard genre of this Christian public expression by presenting an account of his life before and after placing his faith in Jesus, throughout his speech several statements indicate the newness of his Christian faith. His comments frequently reveal a lack of depth behind the experience; indeed, a *Washington Post* journalist was among the kinder evaluators when she observed Obama lacked "spiritual nuance" (Saslow, 2009, para. 19).

Obama does explicitly and implicitly identify himself as a Christian by use of phrases such as "my religion" and "my God" (para. 8). He notes that when political opponent Alan Keyes pointed out that Obama advocated policies and positions contradictory to positions taught by God in the Bible,[6] Obama confesses that the "accusation that I was not a true Christian nagged at me" (para. 13). Yet Obama does not directly refute the charge that his policies and actions are often contradictory to the teaching of Scripture, or to specific Christian communities' interpretations of Scripture. It is enough for him that he had an experience, and then could "affirm my Christian faith" (para. 32). Within his testimony Obama indicates that part of the appeal of joining a church was its ability to affect politics and "spur social change" (para. 28). His pragmatic approach to faith here can make demands upon society without necessarily requiring much change in his own person, attitudes, or behavior. Such an approach is frequently associated with an immature understanding of the Christian life (Sproul, 1998). Since, according to his own testimony, he is a new believer, such a limited grasp of Christianity is totally appropriate and understandable.

In paragraph 33, Obama displays a lack of familiarity with basic differences between various religions by claiming that in the same way that he accepted Christ by walking down the aisle in church, so too, "that's a path that has been shared by millions upon millions of Americans— evangelicals, Catholics, Protestants, Jews, and Muslims alike." One might point out that Muslims and Jews neither teach nor accept the divinity of Jesus Christ. Furthermore, Catholics do not "walk down the aisle" to accept Christ, and evangelicals are typically considered a subgroup of Protestants.

Similarly throughout his speech Obama's words display his unfamiliarity with rudimentary principles of reading and interpreting the Bible (see para. 56). It is the perception of Obama's genuine good will combined with his self-admitted ignorance that combine to make his floundering attempts to speak the language of faith appealing to such a wide audience. Yet secular America, which does not typically employ the language of faith, does not perceive Obama's gaffes or notice the ways in which Obama is "tone deaf" to the language of faith (Winters, 2008, p. 105). Meanwhile, "Religious America," which Obama apparently identifies with Republicans, or at least conservative Christians, is so pleasantly surprised that a Democratic candidate is even attempting to express himself in their language, that they as conservatives are willing and even eager to overlook his faltering attempts (Editorial, 2006).[7]

Obama's naiveté is frequently quite endearing, such as when he observes that in America there have been debates "for the last 30 years over the role of religion in politics" (para. 14). Born in 1961, Obama was 45 years old when he made this claim, and like many Americans, his awareness of history coincides with his own lifetime. Historians, of course, would trace conflicts between religion and politics in America all the way back to its founding. Many of the first colonists came to this country in search of religious freedom and to escape the political persecution of other governments. So while Obama's comments may indicate awareness only of a few years of tension between religion and politics, he is at least attempting to address the issue as best he can.

FAITH AND POLITICS IN THE SPEECHES OF BARACK OBAMA AND JOHN F. KENNEDY

Pundits and commentators frequently draw laudatory parallels between Barack Obama and John F. Kennedy (Judis, 2008; Lockwood, 2008). Greenberg (2007) states, in fact, that "the most important aspect of Kennedy's campaign mirrored in Obama's may be the way that JFK handled his Catholicism."

As the 1960 Democratic presidential candidate, Kennedy gave a speech to the Greater Houston Ministerial Association addressing the question of whether a Catholic citizen could be considered for the nation's highest office. Kennedy faced the problem of a normative anti-Catholicism in the dominant Protestant culture. Public opinion frequently assumed the popular myths of the Crusades, Inquisition, Galileo, and Wars of Religion to be true. The dominant Protestant culture was convinced that a Catholic was unfit to serve as president because his religious beliefs were unreasonable and would lead to violence or a papal usurpation of governmental power. Kennedy's speech was meant to mollify his Baptist audience, who feared that Catholic priests were scheming for political control through a Catholic president. In his speech, Kennedy repeatedly denied any role for faith in the public arena; indeed, at least seven times in his five-minute address, Kennedy disavowed any impact of his Catholic faith on his political decisions, a move that was necessary, Greenberg observes, because his religion was a political hindrance: "Kennedy seemed only to be pleading that his loyalty to country preceded his loyalty to any religious dictates" (2007, para. 3).

Likewise, Obama admits in his 2006 Call to Renewal address that the standard approach of Democrats to religion is "that regardless of our personal beliefs, constitutional principles tie our hands" (para. 17). Loyalty to politics or the state is given priority over religious principles or particular denominations or churches. Because anti-Catholicism was normative in 1960s American culture, social commentator Lockwood (2008) reminds us that, "Kennedy was at pains to privatize his faith, to assure his listeners that his Catholic faith would not impact on his public life" (para. 13). Although Obama maintains the advocacy of privatized belief, and requires people of faith to "translate their concerns into universal, rather than religion-specific, values" (para. 57), he does permit religious people to be motivated by their religion and he tolerates their use of religious imagery and terminology in public debates (para. 37).

But comparisons between Obama's "Call to Renewal" and Kennedy's "Address to the Houston Ministerial Association" must also observe points of divergence in the suggested relationship between faith and politics. One such difference is in the two politicians' recognitions of the religious components of many political issues. Kennedy opened his 1960 speech by acknowledging the religious issue of his Catholicism, going on to state that the more serious issues of the election were not religious:

> While the so-called religious issue is necessarily and properly the chief topic here tonight, I want to emphasize from the outset that we have far more critical issues to face in the 1960 election; the spread of Communist influence, until it now festers ninety miles off the coast of Florida, the humiliating treatment of our President and Vice President by those who no longer respect our power, the hungry children I saw in West Virginia, the old people who cannot pay their doctor bills, the families forced to give up their farms. An America with too many slums, with too few schools, and too late to the moon and outer space: these are the real issues which should decide this campaign. And they are not religious issues, for war and hunger and ignorance and despair know no religious barriers. (Kennedy, 1960, para. 2)

Thus Kennedy categorized poverty, communism, hunger, ageism, war, and the space race as explicitly nonreligious. Quite to the contrary, Obama opens his own speech by identifying poverty and the environment (para. 3), then later a range of issues such as AIDS, debt relief (para. 49), gun control (para. 41), and a national commitment to diversity (para. 42), as social problems containing religious components. As Lockwood (2008, para. 12) recalls, Kennedy "spent most of his speech not defending the role of religion in the public arena, but denying that his faith could or would play any role at all." By contrast, Obama promises that his faith *will* play a role in his leadership. Obama also commends the religiously motivated, such as the historically black churches, to be "an active, palpable agent in the world" (para. 28) as long as they translate their concerns into secular values, amenable to reason (para. 57).

UNINTENDED CONSEQUENCES

Although invited by Jim Wallis and the Call to Renewal group to speak at a religious forum held within the walls of a church, Obama unintentionally and frequently insults numerous religious traditions–Christianity, Judaism, and Islam–while attempting to affirm or compliment them. For example, Obama praises his Catholic audience members for their use of contraception and birth control (para. 65), and chides Catholic candidate Alan Keyes in particular for following the teachings of the Pope (para. 11). As will be discussed in much greater detail below, Obama likewise dismisses the *Aqedah,* the famous "binding of Isaac" story in Genesis 22, humorously suggesting that instead of trust in Abraham's God, the state in the form of the Department of Children and Family Services should be savior to little Isaac (para. 61). To the progressive Call to Renewal members in his audience, he divides America into secular and religious and implicitly categorizes his audience as secular and thus as needing to shed antireligion biases (para. 48), failing to attend church regularly (para. 15), desiring to scrub language of all religious content (para. 37), and dismissing religion as intolerant and irrational (para. 17). Evangelicals receive repeated criticism as those who believe in the inerrancy of the Bible, suggesting that a literal reading of the Bible is folly (para. 11). He even maintains that evangelicals will have an especially difficult task working with others in a pluralistic society since policy proposals need to be supported by tolerance and rational thought (para. 57-58).

Still, having noted some of Obama's unintentional rebuffs, we must also consider the overwhelmingly positive response to his keynote address. As mentioned earlier, many people of faith had heard so little discussion of substance from prior Democratic candidates that they were excited and over-joyed that Obama affirmed the role of their faith in the public square. Writing in the conservative evangelical magazine *Christianity Today,* Collin Hansen observed: "Sen. Barack Obama explained with some depth his views on the relationship between faith and public policy. The speech drew widespread praise as a long awaited Democratic affirmation of religion's contribution to American society" (2008, para. 2). Indeed, people on either side of the religious/secular divide applauded Obama's speech because he voiced criticisms of the other side that they feel were often ignored. The hopeful appeal to a future where both religious and secular people join together to renew America elicited strong positive reactions, especially from younger voters (Pew, 2008; Stange, 2007). Another factor in the speech's positive reception is the way in which Obama positioned himself as a thoughtful moderate between the extremes of zealous theocrats and hard-line secular separationists. Furthermore, Obama offered ground rules for collaboration that were sufficiently vague. The religious must understand the critical role of the wall of separation of church and state (para. 54), while the secularists should not view every mention of God as a breach in that wall (para. 66).

But such principles become quite difficult to apply. Take, for example, Obama's recommendation that the religiously motivated translate their concerns from religion-specific to universal values (para. 57). Most religious people feel they are already appealing to universal principles when they argue that one individual does not have the right to take the life of another individual. How could the pro-life position be made more universal? To what could they appeal to other than reason, justice, and compassion? Another factor that may have earned grace for Obama from the religiously minded was the general understanding that Obama cannot be read literally. Unlike former President Bill Clinton, who weighed his word choices with the precision of a medieval Scholastic, Obama often uses language imprecisely[8] and the reader, as the axiom goes, must listen to what he means rather than what he says. Obama's audience is required to interpret his comments loosely and often in the process they hear him in more pleasant tones. Thus for a number of reasons Obama and his keynote address were well received.

LOST IN TRANSLATION: THE (UN)BINDING OF ISAAC

As we have already mentioned in passing, Obama's discussion of the *Aqedah* is one place where he may be found "clapping off rhythm." The *Aqedah,* from the Hebrew word meaning "binding," refers to the account in Chapter 22 of the book of Genesis in which Abraham must choose between following the wisdom of man and following the direction and character of God. However, the *Aqedah* is not simply a section of the Bible that happens to fall within the sacred Jewish Torah (the Old Testament books of Genesis, Exodus, Leviticus, Numbers, and Deuteronomy); rather, it is a passage that has an important place in the belief system of all three of the major monotheistic ("Abrahamic") world religions: Islam, Judaism, and Christianity.

Abraham's offering of his son plays a significant role in Muslim interpretive circles (Caspi & Cohen, 1995; Leemhuis, 2002). The binding of Abraham's son occurs in Surrah 37 of the Qur'an. Indeed, Leemhuis (2002) underscores that for Muslims, "the story of Ibrāhīm [Abraham] willing to sacrifice his son is certainly not just a story. It is part of God's message to the world as contained in the Koran. And from this story lessons are to be learnt for those who understand: lessons about obedience to God's will and His reward for those who obey Him" (p. 125).[9]

In Judaism, there is an incredibly long and elaborate history of diverse interpretations associated with the *Aqedah* (Barth, 1990; Ellis, 1999; Feldman, 1985, 2002; Fitzmyer, 2002; García Martínez, 2002; Hayward, 1981; Levenson, 1993; Rojtman, 1990; van Bekkum, 2002; van den Brink, 2002; Vermes, 1983). Central to these interpretations are the Jewish traditions that associate the binding with the later sacrifice of the Passover lambs. In fact, some Jewish traditions connect the rock in the central sanctuary of the Temple in Jerusalem with the rock on top of which Abraham placed Isaac. Thus a clear link was formed with the lambs offered at the Temple in sacrifice and Isaac's binding. Recent scholarship has emphasized the importance of the *Aqedah* for the rest of the Abrahamic narratives within Genesis as a whole.

Abraham's sacrifice of Isaac became even more important for Christians, as Isaac was read as a type, or foreshadowing, of Jesus in light of the numerous similarities the early church fathers found between the two (Bolliger, 2006; Brock, 1981; Harl, 1986). Jesus and Isaac both carried the wood to the place of sacrifice, both offerings were upon hilltops, and more important, both Isaac and Jesus were textually identified as the only beloved son of their respective fathers.

In his Call to Renewal speech, in order to offer an example of the danger inherent in basing political (secular) policy on religious commitments, Obama refers to the *Aqedah* as follows:

> If God has spoken, then followers are expected to live up to God's edicts, regardless of the consequences. To base one's life on such uncompromising commitments may be sublime, but to base our policy making on such commitments would be a dangerous thing. And if you doubt that, let me give you an example.

We all know the story of Abraham and Isaac. Abraham is ordered by God to offer up his only son, and without argument, he takes Isaac to the mountaintop, binds him to an altar, and raises his knife, prepared to act as God has commanded. Of course, in the end God sends down an angel to intercede at the very last minute, and Abraham passes God's test of devotion.

But it's fair to say that if any of us leaving this church saw Abraham on a roof of a building raising his knife, we would, at the very least, call the police and expect the Department of Children and Family Services to take Isaac away from Abraham. We would do so because we do not hear what Abraham hears, do not see what Abraham sees, true as those experiences may be. So the best we can do is act in accordance with those things that we all see, and that we all hear, be it common laws or basic reason. (para. 58–61)

When Obama interprets Genesis 22 in a way that appears to be dismissive, he can only appear to Muslims, Jews, and Christians who are aware of their respective communities' interpretive traditions to be clapping off rhythm (para. 45). Indeed, some conservative Christian leaders such as Dr. James Dobson questioned whether Obama was "deliberately distorting the traditional understanding of the Bible to fit his own worldview" (quoted in Associated Press, 2008, para. 5). In his treatment of the *Aqedah,* Obama's facile analogy appears to sweep away the import of Genesis 22, with the expectation that the proper attitude toward this text is disbelief, or at least some form of dissent from the text.

What is Obama's purpose in using the Abrahamic narrative if not to highlight the potential dangers of religion in general, and worse yet, the disaster that would result if government policy were based on religion? Obama states, "religion does not allow for compromise. It's the art of the impossible . . . to base our policy making on such commitments would be a dangerous thing. And if you doubt that, let me give you an example" (para. 58). One might bring up the numerous societies where public policy was based on the integration of politics and religion. Yet those who object to religion having a role in public affairs traditionally will cite the Crusades, the Inquisition, the Galileo affair, and the Wars of Religion as historical instances where the influence of religion led to violence. These objectors to religion assume the state or government must be secular (free from religion) so it may restrain the religiously motivated from their irrational and dangerous actions. This appears to be the point of Obama's use of the *Aqedah*—that while from his own private religious perspective it was sublime and good for Abraham to follow God's command, from a secular and public position, Abraham was acting irrationally and dangerously; indeed, so dangerously that a normal person would feel it necessary to call upon a government agency to ensure public safety.

The religiously motivated neither think their faith to be unreasonable, nor do they believe that religion necessarily leads to violence. Many would argue that the much cited examples of religious violence were actually situations in which both religion and politics were involved in struggling for power. If Obama selects the binding of Isaac as a representative passage of the dangers posed by followers of God, then it behooves him to become better informed about how Jews, Muslims, and Christians have traditionally interpreted and understood this central and significant text. Within Jewish traditional interpretations, the *Aqedah* points forward to the Passover, which saves (and then commemorates) the Israelite firstborn sons, and initiates the exodus event, which in the canonical Hebrew Bible becomes the paradigmatic example of how God saves His people. In later prophetic literature, the exodus from Egypt is the prime case of God's saving and merciful love. For the New Testament, this exodus/Passover imagery becomes even more sharply focused in the person and saving works of Jesus, who lies at the center of Christianity. For some New Testament authors (for example, the apostle Paul), the *Aqedah* becomes the foundation on which the gospel of Jesus rests (Hahn, 1995, 2004, 2005a). If Obama cannot speak with credibility on this text, a passage fundamental to three of the world's largest and most ancient religions, how can religious adherents take seriously his explanation of any lesser text, practice, or doctrine?

SHOULD RELIGION BE PUBLIC? DEFINING "RELIGION" AND "SECULAR"

Obama confronts his audience with the issue of the role of religion in the public sphere. We think his powerful affirmation of religion's positive role in the public sphere is one of the greatest strengths of his presentation, and at the same time is also one of its greatest weaknesses. In his claim that religion must play a role in public discussions, Obama has captured an important insight about American (and perhaps human) public life. Indeed, his grasp of this insight appears more sophisticated than Kennedy's, at least insofar as Obama understands that issues Kennedy considered secular (e.g., poverty) have deep religious implications; such global and national problems do not lie outside the religious sphere. But the disputed question is in *how* religion is to enter the public sphere, and this is where Obama's proposals in the Call to Renewal address run into difficulty.

Part of the difficulty here lies in the very concepts of religion and of a public (i.e., secular) sphere, which have changed over time. Like Obama, modern audiences have been raised to believe religion and secular are opposite terms; religion should be private, while the public sphere should be secular, that is to say, free from religion. In the medieval period, religion pertained to specific religious orders or to monastic disciplines (Aquinas, 1964; Cavanaugh, 1995; Morrow, forthcoming, b; Smith, 1962). It was only in the early modern period that religion became redefined to refer to private systems of belief (Asad, 1993; Bodin, 1962; Cavanaugh, 2009; Ficino, 1480; Grotius, 1971; Harrison, 1990; Locke, 1963; Morrow, forthcoming, c; Rousseau, 1997). This transformation went hand-in-hand with the emergence of the secular, which, in the modern sense of the word, is the creation of a public space devoid of the particular, especially of religious particularity.

As Milbank (2006) has pointed out, however,

> Once, there was no "secular." And the secular was not latent, waiting to fill more space with the steam of the "purely human," when the pressure of the sacred was relaxed. Instead there was the single community of Christendom, with its dual aspects of *sacerdotium* and *regnum.* The *saeculum,* in the medieval era, was not a space, a domain, but a time—the interval between fall and *eschaton* where coercive justice, private property and impaired natural reason must make shift to cope with the unredeemed effects of sinful humanity. (p. 9)

Historically, secularity had to do with being in the world among the society. Secular priests were and are distinguished from religious priests by their not belonging to a particular order or community. In the early modern period, the same period when religion was being redefined, secular enters the English language with the primary meaning pertaining to the transformation of church land into state land (Simpson & Weiner, 1989). Such transformations were almost always violent, and the paradigmatic example remains the dissolution of the monasteries (Baskerville, 1937; Duffy, 2005; Gros, 2004; MacCulloch, 2003; Morrow, forthcoming, a; Tumbleson, 1998). Like Obama, many people today take the idea of secular or public space (as a religion-free zone) for granted, just as they take the justification for such space as a given, and indeed, the givenness of such assumptions lies at the heart of the tensions in Obama's address.

The high school textbook version of the "religion is dangerous" story is ubiquitous in the West: the medieval Crusades, the Spanish Inquisition, the Galileo Affair, and the Sixteenth and Seventeenth Century Wars of Religion. Religion, so we are taught, had to be privatized and banished from the public sphere for our own protection. Religion, unchecked, produces frightening violence. More recent events like the 9/11 attacks and other acts we attribute to religious fanaticism seem only to confirm what we have been taught to take for granted. All we need to do to see how problematic our inherited assumptions are regarding the wedding of religion and violence is take a closer historical look at four paradigmatic examples we assume we know so well: the Crusades, the Inquisition, Galileo, and the Wars of Religion. Specifically, recent scholarship has shown that (a) the Crusades had much more to do with the political order than religious imperatives as regional European rulers vied with the papacy for temporal authority (Tschanz, 2007); [10] (b) the Spanish Inquisition was more a tool used by the state to extract land and wealth than a religiously motivated scheme to persecute Jews (Kamen, 1997; Yovel, 2009); (c) the persecution of Galileo had far more to do with the pope's personal problems with Galileo's arrogance and biblical interpretation than it did with his Copernican findings (Finocchiaro, 2005; Lessl, 1999); and (d) the 16th and 17th centuries' so-called wars of religion, which justified the advent of modern nation-states and their monopoly on coercive violence, were not primarily religious at all (Cavanaugh, 2009; Marx, 2003; Morrow, forthcoming, d). Thus when modern politicians make claims such as those in Obama's Call to Renewal speech, which assume and assert that religion inherently leads to violence necessitating the secular state, they are operating on false understandings of the past and the nature of religion.

The commonly held beliefs couched in Obama's reference to the *Aqedah,* that religion inherently leads to violence and that the secular state was created to keep the peace by restraining the religiously motivated, has been shown by modern scholarship to be inaccurate understandings of the historical events, understandings that transfer power from religious organizations and peoples to political nation-states. Obama's understanding of the conflict between church and state leads him to suggest that the minority culture of religiously motivated individuals must learn to express themselves in the language of the dominant secular culture.

As Gillespie's (2008) work has demonstrated, however, we need to be careful not to make too sharp a distinction between the secular and the religious. Secularity, politics, and theological concerns are more closely related, intertwined, and enmeshed with one another than we usually assume. We would suggest that secularization is better understood as the privatization of religious commitments, practices, and concerns, and increases the mutual suspicion that exists between religious America and secular America. What we might call a secularizing trend, however, may be the degree to which individuals and societies implicitly or explicitly reject the natural publicness of their faith commitments.

Finally, we need to briefly address the problem of translation, namely, Obama's idea that religion can and should be public, but only when translated into common public (secular) discourse as if such discourse were neutral, which is itself the great myth taught by secular modernity (Schindler, 1996). Rather, our particularity is essential to who we are as individuals and members of communities (Kallenberg, 2001). Few scholars have highlighted the difficulties of translation as thoroughly as Alasdair MacIntyre (1988, 1990, 2007). Traditions of inquiry and discourse, as well as academic disciplines represented in universities, operate with different and often mutually exclusive norms concerning acceptable sources of authority, forms of argumentation and reason, as well as evidence, not to mention goals and motivations. Any attempts at translating religious language and behavior into some ostensibly universal language and behavior not only fail because no such universal language and behavior exist, but also because such attempts privilege one type of particularity—the secular or privatized religion—over all other forms. We might remind ourselves that the very examples Obama upholds in his speech—Frederick Douglass, Abraham Lincoln, William Jennings Bryan, Dorothy Day, Martin Luther King—did not "translate" their religious language into some universal public language, even when they did attempt to use more commonly shared sources and arguments alongside their religious ones. This issue of public religion remains one of the greatest sources of tension within Obama's Call to Renewal address.

At this point, we must applaud Obama's intentions. The goal of tolerance and the desire for peace that undergird his comments concerning religious translation in the public sphere (which ironically create a severe, perhaps insurmountable, tension with his desire for religion to be public) are laudable. Difficulties arise, however, with both the notion of tolerance engendered in such a discussion, as well as with the very idea of translation assumed. Attempts at tolerance such as those Obama suggests inevitably fall flat on their face. This is the case for at least two reasons. Such tolerance is by nature exclusive; it of necessity excludes those who are unwilling to privatize particular aspects of their traditions. Modern forms of tolerance based upon a principle of pluralism cannot but exclude those who are unwilling to privatize their public religious traditions (D'Costa, 2005; Griffiths, 2001; Hauerwas, 2007).

CONCLUSION

Barack Obama's Call to Renewal keynote address is a fascinating specimen of political and religious rhetoric. While the speech violated numerous technical principles of good communication, it was well received by liberals and conservatives alike. Historical conditions in the United States combined with Obama's *ethos* as a speaker in such a way as to elicit a positive response from what Obama called "Religious America." Obama's call to fellow Democrats to refrain from silencing or excluding religious language was heartily welcomed by people of faith, while secular Americans were reassured that Obama upheld the wall of separation. Still, Obama's understanding of religion as privatized belief shaped his suggestions regarding how to negotiate the waters between church and state. Having subsequently won the election to the presidency, Barack Obama will hopefully continue to elaborate on ways religious America and secular America might respond to his call for renewal and cooperate for the good of the nation.

NOTES

1. Symbolic of this orientation, Democratic Party convention managers silenced pro-life Pennsylvania governor Robert Casey, denying him the opportunity to address the 1992 national convention.

2. *God's Politics* remained on the *New York Times* bestseller list for four months. His book is identified by some social commentators as the political manifesto of the emerging evangelical left, predominantly composed of liberal Christians whose religious motivations find their expression in social justice, feeding the homeless, and poverty issues.

3. While Wallis's Call to Renewal group is officially listed as nonpartisan for tax purposes, the group tends to attract Democrats and is commonly identified as progressive. In a similar vein the National Rifle Association is also categorized as a nonpartisan organization although it is most commonly thought of as a somewhat more Republican/conservative group. Throughout our chapter we follow Obama's practice of using the terms *Democrats, liberals,* and *progressives* interchangeably, and of using *Republicans* and *conservatives* interchangeably.

4. Sarah Posner commented in *The Nation* in 2008 that Obama "further energized young Christian activists with an electrifying speech at the Call to Renewal Conference" (para. 2).

5. Here Obama and Wallis are employing a racial stereotype that suggests people of color have rhythm and are musically inclined while white people, or individuals of European descent, can't dance, clap, or sing. The analogy suggests a white person visiting an African American church might attempt to participate, but if she lacks the necessary skills, she might clap her hands off the beat and therefore appear inauthentic (Anything, 2010; Ivins, 2000; Todd, 2009).

6. Keyes's expectation of consistency is not unusual. The standard course of action of a testimony is that the person claiming to follow Jesus Christ will bring his life into conformity with Jesus's will as revealed in the Bible. As Reeves (2008) explains, "The very existence of the confession testifies that here is truth that demands a response. A confession therefore demands that we have the integrity to respond appropriately to the truth being confessed. In this way the doctrine becomes profoundly life-shaping. For example, to confess with integrity that Jesus is Lord, and that the Spirit works in us to make us Christlike, means rejecting sin and altering every aspect of our lives" (p. 82).

7. Obama's testimony and adoption of religious language did inspire a minority of evangelicals to consider whether the term *evangelical* might be losing its linguistic moorings "because it has been misunderstood, misappropriated, and maligned" (Grossman, 2007, para. 13).

8. Several people have commented on the gaps between what Obama says and what he means or does; see, for example, Long, 2009; Mirengoff, 2009; Rosenthal, 2010; and Russo, 2008.

9. Leemhuis points out, however, that Muslims tend to view Ishmael as the son of the intended sacrifice, not Isaac, since Ishmael was Abraham's firstborn son (in Judaism and Christianity as well as in Islam).

10. We are indebted to Lamin Sanneh for this discussion of the Crusades, for this citation, and for his February 2009 presentation at the University of Dayton, entitled "The Fall of Constantinople and the Fall of the Twin Towers: Religion in a Post 9/11 World."

REFERENCES

Anything, S. (n.d.). Senator Obama: White men can't clap. *AnswerBag.com* Retrieved from http://www.answerbag.com/article/Senator-+Obama:+White+Men+Can't+Clap/9f7b3970-960b-7447-5942-c8d2a3c2a4ee/coupled

Appleby, R. S. (2008, Feb. 10). Left wing and a prayer. *New York Times.* Retrieved from http://www.nytimes.com/2008/02/10/books/review/Appleby-t.html

Aquinas, St. T. (1964). *Summa theologiae.* Cambridge, UK: Blackfriars.

Asad, T. (1993). *Genealogies of religion: Discipline and reasons of power in Christianity and Islam.* Baltimore: Johns Hopkins University Press.

Asad, T. (2003). *Formations of the secular: Christianity, Islam, modernity.* Stanford, CA: Stanford University Press.

Asad, T. (2007). *On suicide bombing.* New York: Columbia University Press.

Associated Press (2008, June 25). Conservative Christian leader blasts Obama speech. *Boston Globe.* Retrieved from http://www.boston.com/news/nation/articles-/2008/06/25/conservative_christian_leader_blasts_obama_speech

Barth, L. M. (1990). Introducing the akedah: A comparison of two midrashic presentations. In P. R. Davies & R. T. White (Eds.), *A tribute to Geza Vermes: Essays on Jewish and Christian literature and history* (pp. 125–138). Sheffield, UK: Journal for the Study of the Old Testament Press.

Baskerville, G. (1937). *English monks and the suppression of the monasteries.* New Haven, CT: Yale University Press.

Bodin, J. (1962). *The six books of a commonweale.* Cambridge, MA: Harvard University Press.

Bolliger, D. (2006). Dramatisches symbol konfessioneller grundhaltungen zwischen glaube und politik. Die opferung Isaaks in frühen reformierten auslegungen von Huldrych Zwingli bis Jean Crespin. In J. A. Steiger & U. Heinen (Eds.), *Isaaks opferung (Gen 22) in den konfessionen und medien der frühen neuzeit* (pp. 259–308). Berlin: Walter de Gruyter.

Boyer, P. J. (2008, Sept 8). Party faithful: Can Democrats get a foothold on the religious vote? *The New Yorker.* Retrieved from http://www.newyorker.com/reporting/2008/09/08/080908fa_fact_boyer

Brewer, J. (1990). *The sinews of power: War, money and the English state, 1688–1783.* Cambridge, MA: Harvard University Press.

Brock, S. P. (1981). Genesis 22 in Syriac tradition. In P. Casetti, O. Keel, & A. Schenker (Eds.), *Mélanges Dominique Barthélemy: Études bibliques offertes à l'occasion de son 60ᵉ anniversaire* (pp. 1–30). Fribourg, Switzerland: Editions Universitaires.

Byrd, L. (2008, Aug. 22). The case against Obama in his own words. *Real Clear Politics.* Retrieved from http://www.realclearpolitics.com/articles/2008/08/the_case_against_obama_in_his.html

Caspi, M. M., & Cohen, S. B. (1995). *The binding (aqedah) and its transformations in Judaism and Islam.* Lewiston, UK: Edwin Mellen Press.

Cavanaugh, W. T. (1995). "A fire strong enough to consume the house": The wars of religion and the rise of the state. *Modern Theology, 11,* 397–420.

Cavanaugh, W. T. (2007). Does religion cause violence? Behind the common question lies a morass of unclear thinking. *Harvard Divinity Bulletin, 35* (2–3). Retrieved from http://www.hds.harvard.edu/news/bulletin_mag/articles/35-23_cavanaugh.html

Cavanaugh, W. T. (2009). *The myth of religious violence: Secular ideology and the roots of modern conflict.* Oxford, UK: Oxford University Press.

Collins, J. B. (1997). State building in early-modern Europe: The case of France. *Modern Asian Studies, 31,* 603–633.

D'Costa, G. (2005). *Theology in the public square: Church, academy, and nation.* Oxford, UK: Blackwell.

Dionne, E. J. (2006a, June 30). Obama's eloquent faith. *Washington Post.* Retrieved from http://www.washingtonpost.com/wp-dyn/content/article/2006/06/29/AR2006062901778.html

Dionne, E. J. (2006b, July 3). Obama's message on faith. *San Francisco Chronicle.* Retrieved from http://www.sfgate.com/cgi-bin/article.cgi?file=/c/a/2006/07/03/EDGOBIPTDV1.DTL

Domke, D. (2007, Dec. 3). How are the main contenders handling the faith issue? *USA Today,* p. 13A.

Duffy, E. (2005). *The stripping of the altars: Traditional religion in England, c. 1400–c. 1580.* New Haven: Yale University Press. (Original work published 1992)

Dunn, R. S. (1970). *The age of religious wars: 1559–1689.* New York: Norton.

Dutton, J. L. (1986). Mellowing the hostile audience. *Training and Development Journal, 40,* 8.

Editorial. (2006, Sept.). God's will in the public square: Democratic senator Barack Obama gets it mostly right. *Christianity Today,* pp. 23–24.

Ellis, R. S. (1999). Human logic, God's logic, and the akedah. *Conservative Judaism, 52,* 28–32.

Ertman, T. (1997). *Birth of the leviathan: Building states and regimes in medieval and early modern Europe.* Cambridge, UK: Cambridge University Press.

Feldman, L. H. (1985). Josephus as a biblical interpreter: The aqedah. *Jewish Quarterly Review, 75,* 212–252.

Feldman, L. H. (2002). Philo's version of the aqedah. *Studia Philonica Annual, 14,* 66–86.

Ficino, M. (1480). *De Christiana religione.* Microform obtained from Ohio State University. Florence, Italy: Nicolaus Laurentii.

Finocchiaro, M. A. (2005). *Retrying Galileo, 1633–1992.* Berkeley: University of California Press.

Fitzmyer, J. A. (2002). The sacrifice of Isaac in Qumran literature. *Biblica, 83,* 211–229.

García Martínez, F. (2002). The sacrifice of Isaac in 4Q225. In E. Noort & E. Tigchelaar (Eds.), *The sacrifice of Isaac: The Aqedah (Genesis 22) and its interpretations* (pp. 44–57). Leiden, Netherlands: Brill.

Gerson, M. (2008, April 16) Better than the bitter. *Washington Post.* Retrieved from http://www.washingtonpost.com/wp-dyn/content/article/2008/04/15/AR2008041502665.html

Gillespie, M. A. (2008). *The theological origins of modernity.* Chicago: University of Chicago Press.

Greenberg, D. (2007, April 20). Playing the tolerance card: How Obama is like JFK. *Slate.* Retrieved from http://www.slate.com/id/2164662

Griffiths, P. J. (2001). *Problems of religious diversity.* Oxford, UK: Blackwell.

Gros, M. B. (2004). *The war on Catholicism: Liberalism and the anti-Catholic imagination in nineteenth-century Germany.* Ann Arbor: University of Michigan Press.

Grossman, C. L. (2007, Jan. 23). Evangelical, can the "E-word" be saved? *USA Today.* Retrieved from http://www.usatoday.com/news/religion/2007-01-22-evangelicals -usat_x.htm

Grotius, H. (1971). *True religion.* New York: Da Capo Press.

Hahn, S. W. (1995). *Kinship by covenant: A biblical theological study of covenant types and texts in the Old and New Testaments* (Unpublished doctoral dissertation). Marquette University, Milwaukee, WI.

Hahn, S. W. (2004). A broken covenant and the curse of death: A study of Hebrews 9:15-22. *Catholic Biblical Quarterly, 66,* 416–436.

Hahn, S. W. (2005a). Covenant, cult, and the curse-of-death: Diaqh/kh in Heb 9:15-22. In G. Gelardini (Ed.), *Hebrews: Contemporary methods—new insights* (pp. 65–88). Leiden, Netherlands: Brill.

Hahn, S. W. (2005b). Covenant, oath, and the *aqedah:* Diaqh/kh in Galatians 3:15-18. *Catholic Biblical Quarterly, 67,* 79–100.

Hansen, C. (2008, June 30). Reading the Bible with Obama. *Christianity Today.* Retrieved from http://www.christianitytoday.com/ct/2008/juneweb-only/127-11.0.html

Harl, M. (1986). La "ligature" d'Isaac (Gen. 22, 9) dans la Septante et chez les Pères grecs. In A. Caquot, M. Hadas-Lebel, & J. Riaud (Eds.), *Hellenica et Judaica: Hommage à Valentin Nikiprowetzky* (pp. 457–472). Leuven, Belgium: Peeters.

Harrison, P. (1990). *"Religion" and the religions in the English enlightenment.* Cambridge, UK: Cambridge University Press.

Hauerwas, S. (2007). *The state of the university: Academic knowledges and the knowledge of God.* Oxford, UK: Blackwell.

Hayward, R. (1981). The present state of research into the targumic account of the sacrifice of Isaac. *Journal of Jewish Studies, 32,* 127–150.

Hoagland, J. (2006, July 2). Melding faith and tolerance. *Washington Post.* Retrieved from http://www.washingtonpost.com/wp-dyn/content/article/2006/06/30/AR2006063001479.html

Ivins, M. (2000, Aug. 3) White people can't clap on beat. *The Free Press.* Retrieved from http://freepress.org/columns/display/1/2000/173

Judis, J. B. (2008). Is Obama Al Smith or John F. Kennedy? *The New Republic.* Retrieved from http://www.tnr.com/story.html?id=66e16e0d-572f-4a38-9ed8-340a4f602341

Kallenberg, B. J. (2001). *Ethics as grammar: Changing the postmodern subject.* Notre Dame, IN: University of Notre Dame Press.

Kamen, H. (1997). *The Spanish inquisition: A historical revision.* New Haven: Yale University Press.

Kennedy, D. J. (1996). *Evangelism explosion.* Carol Stream, IL: Tyndale House Publishers.

Kennedy, J. F. (1960). Address to the Houston Ministerial Association. Retrieved from www.americanrhetoric.com/speeches/jfkhoustonministers.html

King, P. (2009) Augustine on Testimony. *Canadian Journal of Philosophy, 39,* 195–214.

Leemhuis, F. (2002). Ibrāhīm's sacrifice of his son in the early post-koranic tradition. In E. Noort & E. Tigchelaar (Eds.), *The sacrifice of Isaac: The Aqedah (Genesis 22) and its interpretations* (pp. 125–139). Leiden, Netherlands: Brill.

Lessl, T. S. (1999). The Galileo legend as scientific folklore. *Quarterly Journal of Speech, 85,* 146–168.

Levenson, J. D. (1993). *The death and resurrection of the beloved son: The transformation of child sacrifice in Judaism and Christianity.* New Haven: Yale University Press.

Locke, J. (1963). *A letter concerning toleration.* The Hague, Netherlands: Nijhoff.

Lockwood, R. (2008). JFK, Obama, and the role of religion. *Catholic Online* (originally published in *Pittsburgh Catholic*). Retrieved from http://www.catholic.org/diocese/diocese_story.php?id=27388

Long, J. (2009, Sept. 1). Obama's ambiguous campaign persona doesn't suit presidency. *The Hoya.* Retrieved from http://www.thehoya.com/opinion/obamas-ambiguous-campaign-persona-doesnt-suit-presidency

MacCulloch, D. (2003). *The reformation.* New York: Penguin Books.

MacIntyre, A. (1988). *Whose justice? Which rationality?* Notre Dame, IN: University of Notre Dame Press.

MacIntyre, A. (1990). *Three rival versions of moral enquiry: Encyclopaedia, genealogy, and tradition: Being Gifford Lectures delivered in the University of Edinburgh in 1988.* Notre Dame, IN: University of Notre Dame Press.

MacIntyre, A. (2007). *After virtue: A study in moral theory* (3rd ed.). Notre Dame, IN: University of Notre Dame Press. (Original work published 1981)

Marx, A. W. (2003). *Faith in nation: Exclusionary origins of nationalism.* Oxford, UK: Oxford University Press.

McMullen, C. (2006, July 15). Obama's new perspective on religion and politics. *Naples (FL) Daily News.* Retrieved from http://m.naplesnews.com

Milbank, J. (2006). *Theology and social theory: Beyond secular reason.* Oxford, UK: Blackwell. (Original work published 1990)

Mirengoff, P. (2009, Dec 28). Lawyers at war. *Powerline Blog.* Retrieved from http://www.powerlineblog.com/archives/2009/12/025260.php

Morrow, J. L. (2007). *Evangelical Catholics and Catholic biblical scholarship: An examination of Scott Hahn's canonical, liturgical, and covenantal biblical exegesis* (Unpublished doctoral dissertation). University of Dayton, Dayton, OH.

Morrow, J. L. (forthcoming, a). The Bible in captivity: Hobbes, Spinoza and the politics of defining religion. *Pro Ecclesia.*

Morrow, J. L. (forthcoming, b). The early modern political context to Spinoza's Bible criticism. *Scottish Journal of Theology.*

Morrow, J. L. (forthcoming, c). *Leviathan* and the swallowing of Scripture: The politics behind Thomas Hobbes's early modern political biblical criticism. *Christianity & Literature.*

Morrow, J. L. (forthcoming, d). The politics of biblical interpretation: A "criticism of criticism." *New Blackfriars.*

Obama, B. (2006). Call to Renewal keynote address. Retrieved from www.barackobama.com/2006/06/28/call_to_renewal_keynote_address.php

Pew Forum. (2008). Event transcript: Religious voters in 2008 election. *Pew Forum.* Retrieved from http://pewforum.org/events/eventID=184

Posner, S. (2008) Democrats chase evangelical vote. *The Nation.* Retrieved from http://www.thenation.com/doc/20081027/posner

Reeves, M. (2008). Why do we have a declaration of belief? *Evangel, 26,* 80–83.

Rojtman, B. (1990). Le récit comme interprétation (à partir de Gen. 22 et du Midrach Rabba). *Revue de Théologie et de Philosophie, 122,* 157–169.

Rosenthal, J. (2010, Jan. 19). Obama and God. *USNewswire.* Retrieved from http://www.prnewswire.com/news-releases/joel-rosenthal-carnegie-council-obama-and-god-82076437.html

Rousseau, J.-J. (1997). *The social contract and other later political writings* (V. Gourevitch, Ed. and Trans.). Cambridge, UK: Cambridge University Press.

Russo, A. (2008, Dec 2). Obama staff vs reformy crowd. *This Week in Education.* Retrieved from http://scholasticadministrator.typepad.com/thisweekineducation-/2008/12/transition-obam.html

Saslow, E. (2009, Jan. 18) Obama's path to faith was eclectic. *Washington Post.* Retrieved from http://www.washingtonpost.com

Schindler, D. L. (1996). *Heart of the world, center of the church: Communio ecclesiology, liberalism, and liberation.* Grand Rapids, MI: Eerdmans.

Simpson, J. A., & Weiner, E. S. C. (Eds.), (1989). *The Oxford English dictionary Vol. XIV: Rob-Sequyle* (2nd ed.). Oxford, UK: Clarendon Press.

Smith, W. C. (1962). *The meaning and end of religion.* New York: Macmillan.

Sproul, R. C. (1998). *Essential truths of the Christian faith.* Carol Stream, IL: Tyndale House.

Stange, M. Z. (2007, April 7). Obama's believers. *USA Today.* Retrieved from http://blogs.usatoday.com/oped/2008/04/obamas-believer.html

Steinfels, P. (2006, Dec. 9). In politics the "God Gap" overshadows other differences. *New York Times.* Retrieved from http://www.nytimes.com/2006/12/09/us/politics/09beliefs.html

Tilly, C. (Ed.). (1975). *The formation of national states in western Europe.* Princeton, NJ: Princeton University Press.

Todd, R. (2009, March 18). White people, please stop clapping off beat. Seriously. *The Sling Blog.* Retrieved from http://www.sling.com/blog/2331/White-People,-Please-Stop-Clapping-Off-Beat-Seriously

Tracy, L. L. (1990). Taming the hostile audience. *Training and Development Journal, 44,* 32–36.

Tschanz, D. W. (2007). History's hinge: 'Ain jalut. *Saudi Aramco World, 58,* 24–33.

Tumbleson, R. D. (1998). *Catholicism in the English Protestant imagination: Nationalism, religion, and literature 1600–1745.* Cambridge, UK: Cambridge University Press.

van Bekkum, W. J. (2002). The Aqedah and its interpretations in midrash and piyyut. In E. Noort & E. Tigchelaar (Eds.), *The sacrifice of Isaac: The aqedah (Genesis 22) and its interpretations* (pp. 86–95). Leiden, Netherlands: Brill.

Vermes, G. (1983). *Scripture and tradition in Judaism: Haggadic studies.* Leiden, Netherlands: Brill.

Wallis, J. (2005). *God's politics: Why the right gets it wrong and the left doesn't get it.* San Francisco: HarperCollins.

Winters, M. S. (2008). *Left at the altar: How the Democrats lost the Catholics and how the Catholics can save the Democrats.* New York: Perseus Books.

Wolfe, A. (2004, Sept. 19). The God gap: How religion divides the Democrats. *Boston Globe.* Retrieved from http://www.boston.com/news/globe/ideas/articles/2004/09/19/the_god_gap?pg=full

Yovel, Y. (2009). *The other within: The Marranos: Split identity and emerging modernity.* Princeton, NJ: Princeton University Press.

Chapter 9

Change the Context, Build the Coalition

Democrats, Abortion Reduction, and the Politics of Articulation

Samuel Boerboom

In much the same way that John F. Kennedy's notable 1963 Commencement Address at American University called upon U.S. and Soviet citizens to pursue achievable peace, President Barack Obama used the occasion of his 2009 Notre Dame Commencement speech to call Americans to work together to reduce abortion. Whereas Kennedy spoke to new graduates about the importance of "practical" peace, Obama used religious discourse to defend a practical approach to addressing the divisive issue of abortion. Kennedy[1] called for an "attainable" peace between the United States and the Soviet Union, a peace based on a "series of concrete actions and effective agreements which are in the interest of all those concerned" (para. 9)." He urged his audience to reexamine their assumptions about the Soviets in order to see which values they held in common. As Kennedy observed, peace between the two superpowers could only be achieved through the common interest of avoiding war:

> With such a peace, there will still be quarrels and conflicting interests, as there are within families and nations. World peace, like community peace, does not require that each man love his neighbor–it requires only that they live together in mutual tolerance, submitting their disputes to a just and peaceful settlement. (1963, para. 15)

Kennedy reminded the American University audience that the world could unite around the common cause of peace, even in the presence of seemingly irresolvable differences. In much the same way, President Obama asserted to the Notre Dame audience that political stances like abortion reduction are in the common interest of all those who care deeply about the issue. Using language similar to that of Kennedy, Obama[2] asked his audience to "find a

155

way to reconcile our ever-shrinking world with its ever-growing diversity" and abandon crass "zero-sum" mentalities (2009, para. 16). Like Kennedy, Obama warned his audience not to dismiss the opposing viewpoint, asking "How does each of us remain firm in our principles, and fight for what we consider right, without . . . demonizing those with just as strongly held convictions on the other side?" (Obama, 2009, para. 23). In his address Obama identified abortion as the most divisive and important issue demanding a civil dialogue. Echoing the words of the Notre Dame president, Obama called upon his audience to be both a "lighthouse" and a "crossroads," by asserting their religious convictions while remaining humbled by their faith that God's wisdom surpasses their own. Obama's address asserted that the abortion debate needs those driven by conviction but tempered by humility to seek common ground with others.

Both Kennedy and Obama attempted to translate problems historically understood as ideologically bound into conflicts resolvable instead through pragmatic means. Murphy (2004) explains that Kennedy "redefined" the Cold War by "offer[ing] a new way of talking about an old set of problems" (p. 145). Kimble (2009) adds that Kennedy also attempted to redefine the national attitude toward the war. Both presidents acknowledged the role principled pragmatism plays in addressing both real-world crises and the attitudes necessary to meet those crises. Both presidents also engaged in what Jasinski (2001) calls "articulation practices" to redefine and thereby reorient issues and attitudes. Articulation, Jasinski explains, is the use of discourse to "shape and reshape our understanding of reality by establishing connections or severing established connections" (2001, p. 65). Kennedy and Obama both sought to de-emphasize particular ideological dimensions of a crisis in order to reorient its solution through an appeal to common ground. Whereas Kennedy spoke of common ground while asserting a pro-United States ideology, Obama offered common-ground solutions to the abortion debate, recasting it in the language of "progressive" evangelical Christian ideology focused on the collective welfare.

Obama's address at Notre Dame resembles Kennedy's speech in both style and strategy. Just as Kennedy's address simultaneously decried stagnant ideologies and called upon seemingly pragmatist notions of common purpose, so too did Obama critique ideologies of the left and right while proposing that common ground be the new criterion upon which the abortion issue be measured and evaluated. This exemplifies Jasinski's observation that "warranting principles that are successful in one context are articulated to new circumstances" (2001, p. 65). Both presidents' pragmatic common-ground appeals were actually infused with significant ideological markers: for Kennedy, a pro-West ideology rejecting the proscription of individual liberties; for

Obama, a progressive/liberal religious ideology, deeply influenced by progressive evangelicals like Jim Wallis, that rearticulated the abortion issue from one of individual rights to one adjudicated by broad social solutions. Obama engaged in an act of articulation by insisting that the abortion issue be discussed in a different context than it had been previously. The Kennedy and Obama addresses provide discursive examples of how presidents can employ the common ground trope to advance particular ideologies—in Kennedy's case, an ideology of Western-style democracy; in Obama's, a progressive religious ideology concerned with social welfare.

This chapter argues that Obama's Notre Dame address is heavily influenced by Jim Wallis's (2008) notion of conservative radicalism. At Notre Dame, Obama appealed to his audience through progressive evangelical Christian ideology, with its emphasis on social values and serving the common good, to reconnect the abortion issue to such a moral framework. I argue that the concept of articulation best explains the strategy behind Obama's work, because he, like Wallis, sought to unhinge the conservative Christian ideological understanding of abortion, with its focus on individual rights, and reframe the issue as one best addressed by common-ground means to which committed yet oppositional groups can agree. President Obama's articulatory rhetoric drew from Wallis's (2005, 2008) work, which provided fertile resources for invention in his address to Notre Dame. The concept of articulation elucidates the rhetorical work taking place in Obama's approach to reorienting the abortion debate. Articulatory rhetoric makes possible the move from considering abortion in an individualist context of women's versus fetus rights, to one bridging the divide between opposing viewpoints.

In this chapter I contend that through the figurative gesture of common ground, Obama made an articulatory argument using religious argumentation to shift the context of abortion discourse from the sanctity of life to a context of upholding common-ground solutions like abortion reduction. Obama made such a gesture in order to provide Democrats a more effective way to appeal to the pro-life voting public as well as to religious moderates and progressives. Articulation practices and common-ground appeals are intimately linked as the former makes possible the necessity of the latter. Put differently, articulatory rhetoric appeals to the need for a new understanding, a new linkage of ideas that rejects the static understanding of old. The common ground trope works as a figurative gesture to allow a rhetor to establish a new articulation. As a corollary this analysis underscores the larger theme of this collection, that Democratic Party officials and the progressive religious community collectively develop rhetorical strategies.

This chapter proceeds as follows: I first discuss articulation processes of forging and breaking discursive linkages, demonstrating the ways in which

Obama's rhetorical work embodies a particular type of articulatory politics. I then explain the importance of Wallis's strategy of conservative radicalism to President Obama during his address at Notre Dame. I next review key dimensions of Obama's oration. Finally, I discuss Obama's use of Wallis's work, and offer some conclusions about the prospect of Obama's middle-ground discourse for religious voters.

ARTICULATION PRACTICES AND THE
HISTORICAL SHAPING OF UNDERSTANDING

Grossberg (1992) explains that articulation is the "construction of one set of relations out of another; it often involves delinking or disarticulating connections in order to link or rearticulate others" (p. 54). For Grossberg, articulation is a "theory of contexts" that explains how communicative practices have "specific effects, that identities and relations exist" (p. 55). Because contexts are historically contingent, the meaning of a controversy is always variable. That is, articulation "reshape[s] how people understand the relationship" between a controversy and an attitude taken toward it. The Democratic Party's official platform position on abortion evolves based on the historical context. For example, President Bill Clinton made popular the slogan "safe, legal, and rare" (Morley, 2002). This position connected the party to a particular position on abortion. Contexts are composed of a variable, ever-changing set of relations. President Obama's campaign discourse and his resulting election suggest strongly that his bipartisan appeals resonated with the voting populace and that the political context supported the bipartisan connections Obama linked to voting issues (Waldman, 2008). Similarly, contexts enable certain articulations to be made between a religious faith and a political issue. Just as they enable certain links, they constrain others.

Jasinski (2001, p. 65) reminds us that articulation is a manner in which discourse is used to build links between different things, "different events, different social movements, different ideas, different people," and admits to many theoretical possibilities. Nevertheless, articulation is not the same thing as an analogy. As Jasinski notes (2001, p. 66), articulation does not suggest one thing resembles another, rather it attempts to "reshape how people understand the relationship" between two things linked together by discourse. Articulation is a postmodern phenomenon in that it assumes the relationships between things and their received meaning is unstable and therefore subject to change; as Laclau (1977) argues, there is no necessary relationship between a given representation and what it represents. Hanczor (1997) points to the example of religious conservatives and the Republican

Party. No necessary relationship exists between the two; that is, "there is no determined relationship between the ideological force and its potential constituents" (p. 6). The appeal to abortion reduction is an attempt, in part, to resist the "naturalizing tendencies" of the articulation organizing religious voters and the pro-life position on abortion.

The discourse of abortion reduction attempts to disrupt the articulation of ideological rigidity seen in the conflicting positions between mothers' abortion rights and the rights of the unborn. By specifically attempting to break the historical links between pro-life voters and the Republican Party, Democrats hope to expand their constituency. In order to do so, however, Democrats need to make their appeals with the language of faith, because many religious voters have historically voted against the Democrats on the abortion issue (Kirkpatrick, 2007). Political power depends upon "historical forces which have produced the present, and which continue to function as constraints and determinations on discursive articulation" (Hall, 1986, p. 58). These historical forces, or context, come to make possible articulatory practice. As Hall observes, "you have to ask, under what circumstances, *can* a connection be forged or made? The so-called unity of a discourse is really the articulation of different, distinct elements which can be rearticulated in different ways" (1986, p. 53; emphasis in original).

For Hall religion is one of the most important cultural resources[3] people use to make their world knowable, and so it is necessary to look to the politics of contemporary culture to see how it links up and becomes affiliated with particular religious practices. Any analysis of political culture will surely have to account for the "'lines of tendential force' articulating [a] religious formation to political, economic and ideological structures" (Hall, 1986, pp. 53–54). Once a religious formation, such as a position taken on torture or the environment or abortion, becomes established, it gains a "tendential historical connection"—that is, it gains inertia and becomes difficult to disrupt. As Hall explains, "if you want to move religion, to rearticulate it in another way, you are going to come across all the grooves that have articulated it already" (1986, p. 54).

The naturalness with which religion seems to be linked to an ideology over time can be explained, in part, by the politics of "common sense" wherein the dominant articulation, through a process of co-optation, defuses the articulation of political alternatives (Angus, 1992). As Mumby (1992) argues, a politics of common sense demonstrates how communities struggle over the meaning of traditions. In this sense, the common sense understanding many Americans share is that to be religious is to approach and engage political issues like abortion in a nonnegotiable fashion. To put it differently, the pro-life position has in recent history been articulated to the Republican Party.

DeLuca (1999) explains that articulation has two aspects, which he calls "speaking forth elements" and "linking elements" (p. 335). Articulating these two types of elements together involves an attempt to "fix meaning within the field of discursivity" and an attempt to "fix the context," which attempts to "temporarily define[s] the field of discursivity itself" (pp. 335–336). An appeal to common ground works through a change in context, from ideological partisanship to pragmatic grounds of problem solving. Context is important for articulation because it "defines parameters for enactment" (Stormer, 2004, p. 64). An articulation that both functions on the level of meaning and that sets the context in which that particular understanding is enacted is a rhetorically powerful move, for it shifts the grounds for understanding a controversy, thereby potentially modifying the hegemonic understanding of the controversy itself.

Certain rhetorical scholars believe that any study of articulation should avoid the term *ideology* and instead use *discourse*. DeLuca (1999) explains that ideology too often is set opposite Truth. In such a configuration rhetoric serves as an instrument for delivering truth. By preferring "discourse" over "ideology," critics gain an understanding of articulation from a discursive perspective, which "suggests that the meaning of the world is not discovered, but constructed through rhetorical practices" and that "within a discursive frame, rhetoric is no longer an instrument in the service of reality, but, rather, becomes constitutive of the meaning of the world" (DeLuca, 1999, pp. 338, 342). For our purposes we might understand ideology to be the set of values given form through discursive practice by competing political parties.

DeLuca's move to claim articulation for rhetoric is important because it highlights the struggle for meaning taking place through the discourses of religion and politics. Both of these institutions seek to create social change, sometimes in conjunction with one another, other times in the absence of the other. Regardless, they do so in a social universe where meaning is historically contingent and unstable. As DeLuca explains, "in a world without foundations, without a transcendental signified, without given meanings, the concept of articulation is a means to understanding the struggle to fix meaning and define reality *temporarily*" (1999, p. 334, emphasis added). No group advocating social change endeavors to achieve temporary solutions; nevertheless, they labor in a social environment where reality is ever-negotiable and shifting. While personal visions of the good life, of justice and propriety, can be foundational, it is impossible for a social vision of the same to ever be total. That is, there are far too many competing visions of the good and the true for the social to ever wholly reflect all of them simultaneously. As DeLuca explains, competing versions of the truth testify "to the opening of reality as a site of struggle" (1999, p. 334). Not all versions of the truth are equally likely to succeed in the social, thus we might understand the social environment to be a very contested space. Laclau and Mouffe (2001) observe that articulation is "any practice establishing a relation among elements such that their identity is modified" (p. 105). Because there is no necessary relationship between any two given elements, articulation forges the link between the two.

THE CONSERVATIVE RADICAL AND THE COMMITMENT TO COMMON CAUSE

Jim Wallis, leader of the antipoverty, pro-peace group Sojourners, editor in chief of the monthly journal of the same name, and best-selling author of *God's Politics* (2005) and *The Great Awakening* (2008), is one of the most influential progressive Christian leaders in the Obama administration. Wallis was a key consultant on the abortion reduction language change and is a senior advisor for Obama's newly appointed White House Office of Faith-Based and Neighborhood Partnerships. Wallis's work on abortion reduction undoubtedly influenced President Obama's public statements at Notre Dame. Wallis's recent influence on the Democratic Party is well documented. He accepted an invitation from Senate Majority Leader Harry Reid in December 2006 to deliver the Democrats' weekly radio broadcast (Olsen, 2006). After Bush's reelection in 2004, Wallis conducted seminars for Democratic officials, including then Representative Nancy Pelosi, that aimed to develop a "spiritual left" (Wallis, 2005). After publishing his best-selling *God's Politics,* Wallis stated that he advised Democrats to rethink big issues like abortion (Guthrie, 2005). His *God's Politics* chapter calling for a practical approach to abortion reduction reads as if it were directed squarely at Democratic politicians. He noted that emphasizing abortion reduction as a common-ground initiative would "allow many pro-life and progressive Christians the 'permission' they need to vote Democratic. Again, there are millions of votes at stake here" (2005, p. 299).

Obama's common-ground stance in his Notre Dame address on abortion reflects earlier changes to language in the Democratic Party platform—changes primarily brought forth by religious progressives like Wallis. Before accepting the party's nomination, Obama called upon religious progressives to help draft new language on the issue of abortion. At the 2008 convention the Democratic Party amended its platform position to include, for the first time, language calling for a reduction in the need for abortion, establishing abortion reduction within the context of a woman's right to choose. This move was significant for some pro-life Democrats because it "include[d] not just contraception, but also economic and other supports for women who are already pregnant" (Polter, 2009, p. 12). For both pro-life and pro-choice Democrats, the language shift represented an attempt to make the Democratic Party amenable to the interests of both. According to notable progressive evangelical Tony Campolo, the language gave religious Americans—evangelicals and Catholics in particular—"the sense that they could participate in the Democratic Party without the compromise of their convictions" (quoted in Warner, 2008, para. 4). Waldman points out that Obama's inclusion of pro-life progressives in the language-change process signaled that these folks were "in the conversation," which "changed the terms of the debate" (2008, para. 22).

The Democrats' platform language reflects Wallis's notion of "conservative radicalism," which is "rooted in strong tradition but radical in seeking social justice" (2008, p. 7). Wallis observes that the current political options for persons of faith are limited by an "ideological rigidness [that] blocks social cooperation and political solutions" (2008, p. 99). Conservative radicalism is a type of politics that is conservative in its dedication to "traditional" theological principles of personal behavior and responsibility yet simultaneously committed to social responsibility. Wallis's project, as he explains it, attempts to move beyond the polarizing political categories of membership, calling for a politics more in tune with the moral sensibilities of many religious Americans. He notes "if we are to preserve the values (a conservative goal) of equality and justice, for example, they require a radical application to the needs of a broken world (a liberal goal)" (2008, p. 101). Under this line of reasoning, deeply held theological beliefs mean little unless they are acted upon in ways that address present problems. As Wallis notes,

> Ultimately, we are known and judged by what we say yes to and what we say no to. We say yes to the conservative values that root us, and then say a radical no when those values require it. A conservative radical doesn't fall neatly into any of our modern political categories and options but could help transform them all. And that might lead us to some real solutions, and perhaps even bring a measure of peace to a political culture that is still at war. (2008, p. 101)

For Wallis, the political system is broken; only a new type of politics can attempt to forge the common ground necessary to break impasses over pivotal issues like abortion.

Wallis asserts that more and more evangelicals and other Christians are coming to terms with the seemingly paradoxical combination of conservative, fundamental faith on one hand and liberal politics on the other. E. J. Dionne, interviewed by Wallis (2008) in his chapter on the conservative radical, observes that the broader moral agenda called forth by many religious

Americans is a "renegotiation" of religion's role in public life. For Dionne, many pro-life religious voters increasingly possess an attitude of "flexidoxy." Flexidoxy resembles Wallis's formulation of conservative radicalism. The term reflects a mixture of flexibility in spiritual practice in one sense, and a desire for orthodoxy of spiritual principles and faith in another.

In his own book, *Souled Out: Reclaiming Faith and Politics after the Religious Right* (2008), Dionne advocates for a less ideological religion free to pose a challenge to all ideologies, promoting "radical monotheism" predicated on a fundamental belief in God that promotes a "sensible skepticism" about all other earthly matters. A commitment to common ground suggests a skeptical assumption about one-sided solutions to moral problems. Dionne, citing Reinhold Niebuhr, emphasizes that radical monotheism, or flexidoxy, "dethrones all absolutes short of the principle of being itself" (2008, p. 18). Religion is therefore both conservative and progressive—conservative in that religion is nourished by tradition, progressive in its attempt to challenge and adapt traditions to contemporary exigencies. Dionne emphasizes that religion is also both public and private, arguing that it is the "drama of the interaction between these two spheres that makes public religion so contested" (2008, p. 196).

Dionne defends the public tradition of religion. But public religion, he argues, is best disciplined by democratic rhetorical norms. Those interested in religion's role in public discourse must call for

> a more demanding standard whereby religious people live up to their obligations to religious pluralism and religious liberty by making public arguments that are accessible to those who do not share their assumptions or their deepest commitments. And we need to understand that religion offers its greatest gift to public life not when it promotes certainty, but when it encourages reflection, self-criticism, and doubt. (2008, p. 184)

Dionne's and Wallis's advocacy of a particular kind of public religion is noteworthy in its attempt to defend a collective public/religious stance on political matters. These political positions frequently adopt a pragmatic, results-oriented tone, as in the case for abortion reduction. Indeed, in his 2005 book, *God's Politics,* Wallis begins his chapter on abortion by recounting his experience giving a lecture to Notre Dame students. Surely this example was not lost on the Obama White House as it prepared to defend its common-ground abortion-reduction stance to an audience of young, predominantly pro-life Catholics, many of whom, it is safe to assume, were amenable to voting Democratic.[4] Wallis uses his own conversations with young Catholics at Notre Dame to support his assertion that liberals err in failing to "comprehend how deep and fundamental the conviction on 'the sacredness of human life' is for millions of Christians, especially Catholics and evangelicals, in forming their view on abortion" (2005, p. 297). This liberal "miscalculation" costs Democrats votes, even though young religious voters are often deeply passionate about social justice and policies championed to that effect by Democrats. Wallis explains that many Christians find it difficult to vote for Democrats "given the party's highly ideological and very rigid stance on this critical moral issue" but for this "major and, in some cases, insurmountable obstacle, these voters would be casting Democratic ballots" (2005, p. 298).

In Wallis's view, the Republicans have been able to secure the majority of religious voters by taking a clear stand opposing abortion. The GOP's general party platform, though, insufficiently addresses social problems. For Wallis (2008), Democrats offer the best hope for the conservative radical, for they need only adjust their commitments on abortion in order to better accommodate those religious voters concerned with both personal morality and social justice. As a brand, Wallis (2008) observes, Democrats are strong on social justice but wanting on matters of personal morality so important to Catholics and evangelical voters:

> As I told the Notre Dame students, the Democrats are being quite rigid on the issue of abortion . . . [the party] could take a more respectful and even dialogic approach [which would entail Democrats affirming that] they are still the pro-choice party but then also say what most Americans instinctively believe: that the abortion rate in America is much too high for a good and healthy society that respects both women and children. (Wallis, 2008, p. 299)

For Wallis (2008), party-line discourse about abortion results in ideological rigidity and "merely symbolic" commitment to the issue. To break the stalemate caused by debates, Wallis urges Democrats to pragmatically seek a common-ground gesture in abortion reduction. Using the Catholic students at Notre Dame as an example, Wallis suggests that most Americans want a "consistent ethic of life," as reflected in Catholic social teaching. Democrats win on the social issues, save for abortion. Wallis observes, "Given the bitter partisan division on the issue of abortion, it may be that the Democrats are the only ones who could initiate a common project to make abortion truly 'rare' in America" (2008, p. 300).

The emphasis on dialogue and common interest allows Wallis to make a significant move. First, he asserts that abortion is a serious moral issue, but then denies that its solution is found in any party ideology, that is, in either defending choice or "criminalizing" abortion. Second, by noting that dialogue is a far more productive strategy than diametrically opposed argumentation, Wallis seemingly shifts the burden from ideological consistency to pragmatic problem solving; seeking the common ground means adhering to democratic norms of disagreement and compromise. The move from ideological to pragmatic is also a shift in values, from certainty to a commitment to dialogue. The appeal to common ground is a figurative resource that helps shift the context in which abortion is discussed. In a purely ideological context, party positions reaffirm nonnegotiable principles. In a pragmatic context, however, Democrats hope to articulate through abortion reduction a discourse acceptable to religious moderates and liberals concerned with a consistent ethic of life. In Wallis's example, the Notre Dame students' concerns serve as a synecdoche for moderate and liberal pro-life voters. It is largely through this example that Wallis makes his case for abortion reduction, and it is from this example that Obama modeled his common-ground appeals during his commencement address at Notre Dame.

PRESIDENT OBAMA AT NOTRE DAME

Obama's address at Notre Dame called into question the articulation between two elements: religious faith and its relation to the practice of abortion. There is no necessary relationship between the two. Since this is the case, Obama proposed that a new linkage could be formed between the party and a commitment to abortion reduction, rejecting the former Democratic Party platform language committed solely to a woman's right to choose. Such a move proposed that the abortion issue voiced in the well-worn ideological commitment to choice-only offers little in the way of helping expand the Democratic coalition or of making progress on the fraught issue of abortion.

As an analogy, Obama called upon Notre Dame traditions when he spoke of the metaphorical significance of both a lighthouse and a crossroads. Obama explained that Notre Dame is both "a lighthouse that stands apart, shining with the wisdom of the Catholic tradition, while the crossroads is where differences of culture and religion and conviction and co-exist with friendship, civility, hospitality, and especially love" (2009, para. 31). When Obama referenced serving as both a "lighthouse" and a "crossroads" to his Notre Dame audience, he was drawing from Wallis's paradoxical notion of conservative radicalism—being grounded in faith, yet recognizing contemporary exigencies and the resulting need to seek common ground with others where possible. Obama used the lighthouse and crossroads metaphors to frame the audience's response to the controversy preceding his visit to Notre Dame. To this effect he observed that he was inspired by the "maturity and responsibility with which this class has approached the debate surrounding today's ceremony" (para. 31).

Obama's Notre Dame speech attempted to forge a new understanding for religious voters on abortion by breaking the existing unity linking Christian faith to the pro-life position. He did it by appealing to and repeatedly stressing the trope of common ground. Obama labored to create a new unity, tying religious voters to an abortion reduction platform that still kept abortion legal. Such a carefully crafted move, framed in the language of faith and common-ground appeals, attempted to rearticulate religious belief not to inflexible ideological positions, but to a position of common cause with others on pivotal issues facing the social as a whole. Obama noted:

> Because when we do that—when we open up our hearts and our minds to those who may not think precisely like we do or believe precisely what we believe—that's when we discover at least the possibility of common ground. That's when we begin to say, "maybe we won't agree on abortion, but we can still agree that this heart-wrenching decision for any woman is not made casually, it has both moral and spiritual dimensions." (Obama, 2009, para. 28)

While Obama's address mentioned other issues of pressing importance—poverty and materialism, in particular—none was more prominent than abortion. Obama did not mention abortion-reduction policy language specifically, but he frequently referred to abortion as an issue that called for common purpose. As a parallel, Obama cited other examples of common-ground strategies to illustrate the necessity of working through conflicts in innovative ways. In particular, Obama used the following analogy to emphasize the importance of common ground on issues similar to abortion: "Those who speak out against stem cell research may be rooted in an admirable conviction about the sacredness of life, but so are the parents of a child with juvenile diabetes who are convinced that their son's or daughter's hardships can be relieved" (para. 22).

Obama used this analogy to illustrate the importance of changing the rigid nature of the debates over abortion. Such a move proposed changing the context and form in which controversial moral matters—abortion in particular—are discussed. By so doing, Obama suggested that abortion should not be discussed through agonistic debate (context) but through common-ground appeals around the notion of abortion reduction (form).

By changing the context of the abortion issue to one of dialogue concerned with common ground, Obama tried to disarticulate abortion from the contentious debates that have traditionally linked religious voters to a pro-life position. By shifting the focus of the abortion debate to reduction, Obama hoped to rearticulate a religious position to abortion reduction that still preserved reproductive rights—essentially, a new religious position on abortion, committed to common ground, and synonymous with Democrats. Stressing the importance of common ground on issues mired in moral uncertainty, Obama observed, "And of course, nowhere do these [vexing] questions come up more powerfully than on the issue of abortion" (para. 24).

Through the context of the abortion common ground, Obama stressed to the Notre Dame audience the importance of a commitment to openness on the traditionally divisive issue. Obama talked about the commitment to debate as a "way of life" necessary to provide leadership in the 21st century. Toward the end of his address he returned to the metaphors of the lighthouse and the crossroads. Obama stated:

> And in this world of competing claims about what is right and true, have confidence in the values with which you've been raised and educated. Be unafraid to speak your mind when those values are at stake. Hold firm to your faith and allow it to guide you on your journey. In other words, stand as a lighthouse. But remember, too, that you can be a crossroads. Remember, too, that the ultimate irony of faith is that it necessarily admits doubt. (para. 40–41)

Obama's stress on the "irony of faith" called into question the hegemonic—particularly, the conservative religious—arguments defining the abortion issue. That is, while religious conservatives traditionally root their opposition to abortion in the language of faith, Obama's emphasis on the lighthouse and crossroads made apparent his attempt to link faith and values with a position on abortion that invited moral and spiritual deliberation. In other words, his rhetoric attempted to make possible a "liberal" position on abortion grounded in faith. Such a position—supporting abortion reduction—appeals to both abortion foes and defenders while still preserving abortion as a legal right.

OBAMA AND THE COMMON GROUND

Religious political appeals are made in an ideological style, linked to a particular party. To this effect Democrats have been trying since the 2004 election to shrink the "God gap" and voice their political values through religious appeals (Gibbs & Duffy, 2007; Kirkpatrick 2007; Rosin, 2007). One such gesture is evident in Obama's oratory: breaking the articulation between "conservative" religious belief and "conservative" ideological identification, which, on the issue of abortion, has historically favored the Republican Party. In spite of this trend, Obama's Notre Dame address suggested that pro-lifers can vote for Democrats and that a focus on the common good effectively articulates the pro-life position with Democratic policies.

In his 2009 Notre Dame address President Obama upheld the values of humility through religious language by observing that common ground is difficult to achieve because of "original sin" and "our selfishness, our pride" (2009, para. 20). Reflecting upon faith and doubt, Obama further remarked, "And within our vast democracy, this doubt should remind us even as we cling to our faith to persuade through reason, through an appeal whenever we can to universal rather than parochial principles" (para. 41). Obama's remarks pressed the importance of religious citizens engaging pragmatist means on political issues. The president called for citizens to really "discipline" their public certainty on political issues with democratic, and ultimately religious, principles of humility, and respect for plurality and difference.

Obama's call for humility was well received by certain Catholics for whom a civil dialogue on divisive matters, such as abortion, is more important than ever. Two such Catholic activists posted a comment on Wallis's blog to the effect that dialogue allows religious Americans to respond "pragmatically to social and political realities [and promotes] humility, compassion, and critical introspection" (Gehring & Campbell, 2009, para. 6). The authors noted that ideological opposition to common-ground abortion-reduction efforts amounts to making "perfect the enemy of the good" (para. 1). In other words, the blog posters indicated that hard-line positions asserting ideal, yet divisive, solutions ignore the good achievable through a commitment to common goals and mutual concerns.

The common ground spoken about by Obama relies upon a shift in context that effectively blurs the dependable ideological divide limiting Democratic inroads to moderate and liberal pro-life voters. The articulation of abortion to a common goals pragmatic context, and not one favoring agonistic debate that places values in diametric opposition, shifts the discursive norms in favor of the Democrats. Wallis's example of the conservative radical and Obama's allusion to the Notre Dame values of the "lighthouse" and the "crossroads" speak to the virtue of blending conviction with humility and civil disagreement. These arguments assume that democracy disciplines religious appeals by demanding they demonstrate material and broad social consequence, and also speaks to what Iris Marion Young (2000) calls an inclusive political rhetoric, wherein the criterion of inclusion establishes the political legitimacy of outcomes to collective problems. As Young observes, the appeal to inclusion transforms "an initial self-regarding stance to a more objective appeal to justice" that is ultimately answerable to those who may differ (2000, p. 52).

A pragmatic context for discussing abortion works only if voters accept the shift to democratic norms of discourse. Put differently, many voters, both pro-life and pro-choice, prefer to emphasize the moral force of their convictions, whether it is protecting the unborn or defending a woman's right to her own body. This is clearly an ideological choice, reflecting unbending principled commitment. Wallis and Obama, instead, endorse favoring the public dimension of the abortion debate by appealing to humility, common cause, and the acknowledgment that abortion is fraught with variables appealing to people of well-meaning, yet differing, moral stances.

Obama's articulatory gesture at Notre Dame attempted to change the context in which abortion discourse circulates. The president's rhetoric did not, and did not seek to, change underlying commitments to particular moral stances on abortion. That is, Obama's articulation was not an attempt to say that religious Americans should assume a particular stance vis-à-vis abortion, but was rather an attempt at changing the manner in which abortion is discussed. His Notre Dame rhetoric did not attempt to transcend the abortion debate, but instead shaped a commitment to problem solving in a contested arena of meaning. It reoriented the debate on abortion by de-emphasizing certain ideological commitments in favor of an alternative strategy of engagement. Following Wallis, Obama attempted to link the struggles of both the life and choice factions of the abortion controversy, in an attempt to transform each side's particular struggle into a "broad-based challenge to hegemonic understanding" (DeLuca, 1999, p. 346).

While reframing the abortion controversy through common-ground appeals may prove to be successful for President Obama's administration, it remains to be seen if abortion reduction will gain bipartisan support in the near term. As Polter (2009) observes, "for both sides, framing the abortion debate as a noble battle has been a tried-and-true way of motivating the base and raising funds" (p. 12). It is worth noting that the Democratic Party's official platform on choice emphatically begins: "The Democratic Party strongly and unequivocally supports *Roe v. Wade* and a woman's right to choose a safe and legal abortion, regardless of ability to pay, and we oppose any and all efforts to weaken or undermine that right" (www.democrats.org). Steve Waldman (2008), editor in chief of beliefnet.com, described the difference between the 2004 platform position defending choice and the 2008 position opening the door to reduction as a dramatic gesture cementing the party's commitment to choice.

In spite of the emphatic protection of choice, Obama and the Democrats were able to satisfy faith leaders participating in the platform language change. Even former evangelical conservatives like Dr. Joel Hunter, former president of the Christian Coalition, reported that Obama's willingness to meet with faith leaders on abortion reduction was significant. Hunter defended the Democrats' pragmatic approach by indicating that "if we insist on keeping this an ideological war we're literally not saving the babies they [pregnant mothers] could save," noting that with the move to abortion reduction, Democrats could "steal the thunder from those who are seen as traditionally pro-life" (quoted in Waldman, 2008, para. 26). Waldman indicates that even though Obama impresses with his common-ground rhetoric, his consistent voting record favoring choice will make it difficult for him to advocate for a third way. As Waldman observes,

> The public is accustomed to viewing the abortion debates being about legal rights . . . Obama's approach—to be pro-choice but reduce the number of abortions by making it easier to choose birth instead of abortion—is new, and likely to be viewed with suspicion by both sides. (2008, para. 33)

CONCLUSION

While the notion of the conservative radical might appeal to certain moderate and liberal religious voters, its effect among party loyalists remains to be seen. The blending of styles—the traditional with the inclusive—may in fact limit Obama's attempt to redefine a nation's attitude toward addressing abortion. As Kimble (2009) warns, an androgynous rhetoric that mixes the agonistic "masculine" style with the nurturant "feminine" style probably limited the rhetorical effect of John F. Kennedy's American University address; its polysemy yields a "mixed message" that, instead of fixing meaning, may actually disperse it across varied interpretations. Kimble observes in his analysis of JFK that the president's androgynous style successfully transcended the "typical rhetoric" of the Cold War. Yet Kennedy's Soviet interlocutors likely had a difficult time reconciling the masculinist, hard-line portion of Kennedy's mixed message with its simultaneous plea for peace. As Kimble explains, "the intensity of the Cold War in 1963 . . . might simply have been too hot" (2009, p. 165). One wonders if Obama's attempt to present a similar paradoxical message will really bridge ideological divisions over abortion. What is more likely is that Obama's common-ground appeal will articulate a Democratic Party identity to certain religious voters for whom abortion is an abiding concern.

Obama attempted to shape the understanding of abortion reduction by establishing a common-ground gesture toward moderate and liberal pro-life voters. His articulatory rhetoric worked to build the Democratic coalition while still remaining steadfast in its commitment toward reproductive rights. His use of articulation created the possibilities for a "governing apparatus to judge reality" (Greene, 1998, p. 22).

Rhetoric used in this way is a "technology of deliberation" that reflects the attempt for a governing body—in this case the Democratic Party—to articulate discourses (the conservative radical, flexidoxy, liberalism) to a particular practice (abortion reduction). Such a move is an attempt to establish a hege-monic articulation, one that becomes difficult to sever. Wallis's and Obama's appeals to pragmatism are, of course, fraught with ideological implications. The pragmatic gesture of seeking common ground attempts to expand liberal ideology by establishing the proper context for deliberation about abortion. The abortion-reduction position will succeed for those who already accept the democratic norms of deliberation called for by Obama in his emphasis on the "crossroads." For those whose faith is fundamentalist, and for those party loyalists who worry about ceding ground on the issue of rights, there is and can be no middle way. The articulatory move made by Obama in his address at Notre Dame will succeed or fail based on his ability to maintain a fragile coalition of abortion rights supporters and moderate and liberal religious voters willing to be a part of a coalition committed, at least symbolically, to reducing the need for abortions.

NOTES

1. The full text of Kennedy's address is available at americanrhetoric.com. I cite quotations from the speech by referring the reader to the appropriate paragraph numbers in the transcribed version available on this Web page.

2. The full text of Obama's address is available at the *New York Times* Web site (www.nytimes.com). I cite quotations from the speech by referring the reader to the appropriate paragraph numbers in the transcribed version available on this Web page.

3. For a more complete discussion of religion as a cultural resource see Besecke (1995) and Williams (1995).

4. E. J. Dionne, a Catholic, in a *Washington Post* blog cites a Pew Research Center poll finding that, as of April 2009, Obama's rating among Catholics stood at 65 percent favorable. (See Dionne, 2009.)

REFERENCES

Angus, I. (1992). The politics of common sense: articulation theory and critical com-munication studies. *Communication Yearbook, 15,* 535–570.

Besecke, K. (2005). Seeing invisible religion: Religion as a societal conversation about transcendent meaning. *Sociological Theory, 23,* 179–196.

DeLuca, K. (1999). Articulation theory: A discursive grounding for rhetorical prac-tice. *Philosophy and Rhetoric, 32,* 334–348.

Democrats.org: Renewing America's promise. (2008). Retrieved from http://www .democrats.org/a/party/platform.html

Dionne, E. J. (2008). *Souled out: Reclaiming faith and politics after the religious right.* Princeton: Princeton University Press.

Dionne, E. J. (2009). Obama, Catholics, and Notre Dame. *Washington Post.* Retrieved from http://voices.washingtonpost.com/postpartisan/2009/04/obama -and-notredame-the-other.html

Gehring, J., & Campbell, S. (2009). What makes liberals and conservatives angry? Abortion reduction. Retrieved from http://blog.sojo.net/2009/03/25/what-makes -liberals-and-conservatives-angry-abortion-reduction

Gibbs, N., & Duffy, M. (2007). How the democrats got religion. *Time.* Retrieved from http://www.time.com/time/politics/article/0,8599,1642649,00.html

Greene, R. W. (1998). Another materialist rhetoric. *Critical Studies in Mass Communication, 15,* 21–41.

Grossberg, L. (1992). *We gotta get out of this place: Popular conservatism and post-modern culture.* New York: Routledge.

Guthrie, S. (2005, April). Soul-searching among Democrats. *Christianity Today,* pp. 78–79.

Hall, S. (1986). On postmodernism and articulation. *Journal of Communication Inquiry, 10,* 45–60.

Hanczor, R. S. (1997). Articulation theory and public controversy: Taking sides over *NYPD Blue. Critical Studies in Mass Communication, 14,* 1–30.

Jasinski, J. (2001). *Sourcebook on rhetoric: Key concepts in contemporary rhetorical studies.* Thousand Oaks, CA: Sage.

Kennedy, J. F. (1963). American University commencement address. Retrieved from http://americanrhetoric.com/speeches/jfkamericanuniversityaddress.html

Kimble, J. (2009). John F. Kennedy, the construction of peace, and the pitfalls of androgynous rhetoric. *Communication Quarterly, 57,* 154–170.

Kirkpatrick, D. (2007, October 28). The evangelical crackup. *New York Times.* Retrieved from http://www.nytimes.com/2007/10/28/magazine/28Evangelicals-t .html

Laclau, E. (1977). *Politics and ideology in Marxist theory.* London: New Left Books.

Laclau, E., & Mouffe, C. (2001). *Hegemony and socialist strategy: Towards a radical democratic politics* (2nd ed.). London: Verso.

Morley, J. (2002). Fetal mistake. Retrieved from http://www.slate.com/id/2062056

Mumby, D. (1992). Communication, postmodernism, and the politics of common sense. *Communication Yearbook, 15,* 571–581.

Murphy, J. (2004). The language of liberal consensus: John F. Kennedy, technical reason, and the "new economics" at Yale University. *Quarterly Journal of Speech, 90,* 133–162.

Obama, B. (2009, May 17). Remarks by the President at commencement address at the University of Notre Dame. *New York Times.* Retrieved from http://www .nytimes.com/2009/05/17/us/politics/17text-obama.html

Olsen, T. (2006). Democrats hand weekly radio address to Jim Wallis. Retrieved from http://www.christianitytoday.com/ct/2006/decemberweb-only/149-31.0.html

Polter, J. (2009, June). Bridge over troubled water. *Sojourners,* p. 12.

Rosin, H. (2007, January). Closing the God gap: How a pair of Democratic strategists are helping candidates talk about their faith. *The Atlantic.* Retrieved from http://www.theatlantic.com/doc/prem/200701/god-gap

Stormer, N. (2004). Articulation: A working paper on rhetoric and *taxis. Quarterly Journal of Speech, 90,* 257–284.

Waldman, S. (2008, August 19). The real story of the Democrat's abortion plank. *Wall Street Journal.* Retrieved from http://blogs.wsj.com/capitaljournal/2008/08/19/the-real-story-of-the-democrats-abortion-plank

Wallis, J. (2005). *God's politics: Why the right gets it wrong and the left doesn't get it.* New York: HarperSanFrancisco.

Wallis, J. (2008). *The great awakening: Reviving faith & politics in a post-religious right America.* New York: HarperOne.

Warner, J. (2008, August 14). Walking the abortion plank. *New York Times.* Retrieved from http://warner.blogs.nytimes.com/2008/08/14/walking-the-abortion-plank/?scp=5&sq=democrat%20platform%20change%20on%20abortion%202008&st=cse

Williams, R. H. (1995). Constructing the public good: Social movements and cultural resources. *Social Problems, 42,* 124–144.

Young, I. (2000). *Inclusion and democracy.* New York: Oxford University Press.

Part IV

Religion in Gubernatorial and Congressional Campaigns

Chapter 10

Tim Kaine's Catholic Evangelical Rhetoric

Sara Ann Mehltretter

One year after the Republican Convention seemed to resemble a "praise service," according to religion writer Amy Sullivan (quoted in Wallis, 2005, p. 9), one year after Karl Rove aggressively reached out to conservative religious voters, and one year after Americans at the polls listed religion and moral values as the most important issue in the election, an event that seemed very strange occurred just south of the Mason-Dixon line. Timothy M. Kaine, a Catholic Democrat, won the 2005 Virginia gubernatorial election. Kaine not only defeated his Republican opponent, Jerry Kilgore, but as the *Washington Post* commented, the Democrat was able to win the liberal suburbs of Northern Virginia and Fairfax County as well as the more conservative rural districts. Unlike his Democratic predecessor Governor Mark Warner, Kaine won in Loudoun and Prince William counties—areas that were George W. Bush strongholds by tens of thousands of votes in 2004 (Shear, 2005).

In this chapter, I examine Kaine's campaign discourse and argue that by emphasizing a specific story in his campaign rhetoric, Kaine was able to establish himself as a person of faith and of reputable character. Kaine accomplished this by casting his experience as a volunteer worker in Honduras in an argumentative framework familiar to many Protestant voters: the conversion narrative. Kaine's use of his experience as a missionary in campaign discourse did not necessarily "neutralize" the faith issue—the presumed goal of Democratic candidates according to *Washington Monthly*'s political commentators (Murray, 2005, p. 23). Instead, this narrative provided Kaine a character platform unknown to many other Democratic candidates in recent elections.

Kaine's example challenged two assumptions of political strategy in the first decade of the new millennium. National and state elections suggested

that Democrats were unable to bridge the "God gap": more liberal politicians had difficulty in attracting the votes of religious voters (Sullivan,
2008). Writing in *The Atlantic Monthly,* Ross Douthat called this trend
part of "a large-scale religious realignment in national politics" where the
Republican Party is "increasingly composed of religious traditionalists and
centrists" and the Democratic party is a "coalition of religious liberals,
devout secularists, and the religiously indifferent" (2004, p. 52). According
to a 2004 *Time* article, for example, those Americans who considered
themselves "very religious" supported Republican George W. Bush over
Democrat John Kerry 59 percent to 35 percent. The same article featured
John Green of the University of Akron arguing that "the more often [vot-
ers] pray and attend worship services, the more likely they are to vote for
Bush" (Gibbs, 2004, p. 26). Kaine's victory suggested that Democrats could
overcome this "God gap." Furthermore, because Kaine was a *Catholic*
Democrat, his election also demonstrated how religiosity may be able to
transcend the denominational divide among American Christians. As the
United States continues to grow more "intense" in its religious beliefs,
perhaps celebration of religion is one of the keys to religious success,
regardless of denomination.

Tim Kaine was, to dispel any confusion, running as a Democrat. But his
political platform made classification difficult. Kaine went on record as personally and religiously pro-life, but argued that if elected, he would enforce
the laws on the books as executive of the state—both the one allowing
executions and the one protecting a woman's right to obtain an abortion. He
stated numerous times during the campaign that while he believed Jesus was
the son of God, he would never write a law saying so. He also emphasized
traditionally "liberal" issues as part of his platform: promoting prekindergar-
ten educational programs for Virginia, balancing the budget, and massively
overhauling public transportation. Rather than flee from religion, Kaine
specifically engaged the "moral debate" that seemed to plague Democrats
in the 2004 elections and in the more conservative South. As Kaine said in
a late October 2005 interview, "I'm a person of faith, and here's who I am,
and you're entitled to know who I am because you ought to know about
me, what's important to me . . . That'll give you a yardstick for judging my
actions" (quoted in Murphy, 2005, p. A1).

Religious voters—specifically, Christians—represent a large group of
voters in America. According to a Pew Research Center report on religion
released in 2006, shortly after Kaine's gubernatorial campaign, 85 percent
of American voters identified religion as important to them, and 67 percent
said that the United States is a Christian country (Kohut & Lugo, 2006). This
project, therefore, rests on the assumption that Democrats have the desire to

overcome the stereotype that they are not able to represent the interest of religious, Protestant voters, to "take back the faith," as liberal evangelical leader Jim Wallis (2005) had suggested. This is not to suggest that all Protestants are of a single political mind, or that all people of faith share similar political concerns. Americans are of mixed minds about the role of religion in politics: in 2006, most agreed that the will of citizens should influence laws more than the Bible (63%), but a "significant minority" (32%) primarily composed of evangelical Christians, believed the Bible should be more important (Kohut & Lugo, 2006). Still, Americans generally favor "more, not less, religion in the country" when it comes to guiding personal principles and American life (Kohut & Lugo, 2006, p. 7).[1]

The primary question, therefore, is, how did Tim Kaine, a Democrat and liberal, address the issue of religion in the Virginia election? While religion was certainly not the singular factor in Kaine's success, his example suggests a rhetorical strategy of connecting with religious voters on a character appeal, rather than an issues appeal. Journalists commented that they could not understand why Kaine's expressions of faith during the campaign were seen as authentic when "only 29 percent of voters" found the Democratic Party to be "religion friendly" around the time of Kaine's gubernatorial campaign (Murray, 2005, p. 23). Some chalked it up to "talking about . . . Catholicism early and often" (Murray, 2005, p. 23), but the answer may be more rhetorically complex.

THE TENSION BETWEEN (MOSTLY) ALIKE FAITHS

Protestants and Catholics do not often see eye to eye. Beyond historical conflicts—theological and armed—the American Protestant Church has a long entrenched history of mistrusting Catholics, particularly Catholic politicians. John F. Kennedy's attempt to win over conservative Protestants in Houston is often heralded as "breaking the religious barrier" between Catholics and Protestants (Friedenberg, 2002, p. 65). Kennedy may have convinced some Americans that he would not accept papal guidance in the presidency, but many historians and communication scholars now agree that his Houston speech galvanized Catholic support more than it assuaged Protestants' fears that Kennedy would not accept papal guidance in the presidency (Cohen, 2008; Jamieson, 1996; Sullivan, 2008). Anti-Catholicism existed and continues to exist on both the left and the right (Gushee, 2008; Jenkins, 2003), making Kaine's decision to emphasize his own faith on the campaign trail potentially dangerous. Yet this strategy appealed to the American tradition of evangelicalism and civil religion.

In his book *The New Anti-Catholicism: The Last Acceptable Prejudice,* Philip Jenkins examines what he calls the "ingrained," almost "invisible" attitudes of anti-Catholicism in the Western world, particularly in the United States (2003, p. 2). Jenkins notes that part of the ease of prejudice against Catholics and the Catholic Church may be that, in the United States, there is a strong tradition of attacking institutions without appearing to attack individuals. Therefore, those referring to "the evil Catholic Church [can] defend this view as a comment on the leadership and politics of the institution without necessarily denouncing ordinary Catholic people" (p. 6). Yet Jenkins argues that statements made against the Church are frequently "generalized" to the large body of Catholics in general (pp. 8–9). Historically, evangelicals and Protestants harbored strong anti-Catholic feelings and expressed them vigorously. In the 1990s, for example, some evangelicals agreed that Catholics "should be exempt" from missionary work "devoted to pagans and adherents of other faiths"; this acceptance brought about "widespread anger from Protestant fundamentalists" (p. 25). Beyond the historical Protestant and nativist anti-Catholic prejudices, Jenkins traces the more recent developments in anti-Catholic sentiment on the left. In the last 50 years, Catholics have been subject to verbal attacks by political liberals and secularists who charge that the Church harbors pedophile priests and that its members are antiwomen and antigay. The result is that Catholics are scorned by conservative religious groups and by liberal Democrats.

Evangelicals and Catholics have formed some connections in the recent past. The Christian Coalition, for example, sought out conservative Catholics in the mid-1990s, both as audiences and speakers at their events (Bendyna, Green, Rozell, & Wilcox, 2000). These alliances, however, tended to focus on specific political issues rather than religious pluralism or reconciliation. Catholics are a strong political group on the issue of abortion, for example, and therefore evangelical Protestants and Catholics tend to ally themselves around so-called Right to Life events. Still, as Jelen (1993) commented, even though conservative Protestants may find "much to admire" in Catholic doctrine, that does not mean they identify themselves as, or even as similar to, Roman Catholics in any way. In fact, the nonidentification may trigger sympathy, indifference, ignorance, or even outright hostility towards Catholics (Jelen, 1993, p. 182).

It is important to consider, however, that conservative, Christian religious groups—often dubbed the religious right—are hardly of one united mindset, faith doctrine, or religious practice. In fact, a danger of religious scholarship is to group Protestants or even Protestant conservatives together. Scholars have clarified the differences among different Protestant groups and their varying cultural values and beliefs. Steven Waldman and John C. Green, for example, (2006) challenged the left-right, liberal-conservative, secular-religious divides and instead suggested that Americans belong to one of twelve cultural tribes, tribes that are "coherent blocs" yet have "overlapping interests and values" (p. 136). Of these twelve tribes in the Waldman and Green taxonomy, American Protestants account for six: (1) the conservative religious right composed of "white evangelical Protestants with traditional beliefs and practices"; (2) the white, nonevangelical "heartland cultural warriors" with traditional beliefs and practices; (3) the white, "moderate evangelicals" defined as evangelicals "with moderate beliefs and practices"; (4) "white-bread Protestants" who are mainline Protestants with moderate beliefs and practices; (5) black Protestants; and (6) Latino Christians (p. 138).[2] Waldman and Green argued that the religious right, heartland culture warriors, and moderate evangelicals are the Republican stronghold, having voted more than 60 percent for Bush-Cheney in 2004. Black Protestants usually voted with Democrats because of social issues, despite being "the most culturally conservative" group (p. 138). White-bread Protestants and Latino Christians represented "swing tribes" that might vote for Democrats or Republicans based on the issues of a particular election. The religious right, according to Waldman and Green, is actually composed of the most conservative evangelical Americans—about 12.6 percent of the electorate in 2004 (p. 136). Yet other scholars have emphasized that evangelicalism is tremendously diverse, and therefore difficult to classify (Gushee, 2008; Kyle, 2006; Stromberg, 1993).

Although often confused, it may be useful to define *evangelism* and *evangelicalism* for the purpose of this discussion. Evangelism refers to the generic act of spreading a faith to nonbelievers. The word comes from the Greek word *euangelos,* meaning a messenger bringing good news (Norris, 1999, p. 300). Although there are evangelists in other religions—such as Judaism and Islam—the term *evangelism* tends to refer to the Christian mission to spread the Gospel and convert the masses to Christianity. Theologian Barry Hankins (2008) suggests that in the Christian lexicon, the terms *evangelism* and *evangelical* are related: Christian evangelism is the "spreading of the good news that Christ's death took away the sins of the world so that individuals who accept Christ can experience salvation"; evangelicals believe in evangelism but also in activism and engagement once nonbelievers have been converted (pp. 2–3).

Contemporary evangelicalism is best understood as an organized faith and political movement within the Christian church. It represents a particular strain of conservative, U.S.-based Protestantism. The roots of the contemporary evangelical movement are found in the attempts "by some moderate fundamentalists in the 1940s, 50s, and 60s to break away from the more separatist, defensive, anti-intellectual tendencies of the fundamentalist movement in which they were raised" (Smith, 2000, p. 13). Evangelicals believe in orthodoxy and personal evangelism, but also place a strong emphasis on the exertion of their redemptive influence within culture. Evangelicalism has "adapted itself to the secular world," but still seeks to change the people in that world; evangelicals do not withdraw from society, but rather embrace their fellow humans as potential converts, and culture itself as something to convert and recreate in the image of Christian beliefs and values (Kyle, 2006, pp. 4–5). Randall Balmer (2006) has commented that evangelicalism is mistakenly conflated with televangelists such as Billy Graham and Jerry Falwell. The faith of American evangelicals, as Balmer wrote,

> is shaped by many forces—their own reading of the Scriptures (which in turn is affected by what translation or study Bible they use), their local church and pastor, the kinds of devotional materials they use, and, perhaps least of all, by Jimmy Swaggert or Jim Bakker or Oral Roberts. (2006, p. 9)

The locality and individuality of each church—particularly in nondenominational evangelical circles—shape and mold understandings of how to engage the world.

Yet the majority of evangelicals, past and present, are united under a few common understandings of the Christian faith. American evangelicalism has grown in popularity during several periods of history, all connected by intense cultural change and crisis. The First Great Awakening occurred during the 1730s through the 1760s, as American colonial identity was being formed and the "city on the hill" mentality was being established. Evangelicalism in the colonies encouraged the colonists to be reborn as Americans, free of the Old World and born into the New World of Christ's glory (Hankins, 2008). The Second Great Awakening, from 1800–1830, similarly highlighted being reborn in Christ and also emphasized that every man and woman could choose the higher path—consistent with Jacksonian democracy and populism of the time (Kyle, 2006). The "culture wars" of today began in the early twentieth century, when religious traditionalists challenged the rise of industry and science (Hunter, 1992). Contemporary evangelicalism traces its roots to the rise of American civil religion in the 1950s and challenges to traditional culture in the 1960s and 1970s (Hankins, p. 138). The many strains of evangelicalism have two common threads. First, the evangelical faith rests on the premise that each individual can—and should—be reborn as a Christian, often referred to as "being saved" or "born again" (Graham, 1989). The second common thread in evangelicalism, therefore, is that after being born again, saved individuals should create a better culture—a more Christian culture—on this earth through their actions. Some interpret their actions to be directly infusing biblical principles into law, while others see a more indirect relationship between evangelical values and secular society.

The evangelicals' perspective of engaging the culture around them suggests an ability to transcend difference and connect in the hopes of promoting God's Kingdom on Earth. Smith argues that the evangelical movement
presents the most promise for civility in the conservative church: most evangelicals emphasize "love, respect, mutual dialogue, taking responsibility for
oneself, aversion to force and confrontation, and tolerance for a diversity of
views" (2000, p. 48). Smith argues that unlike the activists or preachers seen
on television, most evangelicals look to be quiet influences in the world rather
than lead the protest parade.

There are, of course, still fundamental and obvious differences between
contemporary evangelicals and Catholics despite gains in understanding and
political alliances between the two groups since the late 1980s and 1990s.
Some evangelicals still see Catholics as lacking the saving moment and
personal relationship with Jesus Christ—in other words, Catholics are not
considered true, born-again Christians. Evangelicals emphasize the personal
faith, whereas Catholics emphasize the corporate faith under the magisterium
of the Church (Robeck, 2000). Ultimately, as Jenkins concludes, "anti-
Catholicism" may survive developments in either liberal theology or reconciliation with evangelicals because "the ideas and the rhetoric are so powerful
that they can flourish even when they are not directed against specific living
targets" (2003, p. 214). The "Church" is always there as a demon figure.

A primary rhetorical task for Tim Kaine in the Virginia gubernatorial election, therefore, was to win over moderate evangelicals who might dislike or
distrust him as an authentic Christian candidate, without alienating members
of his liberal base who might have harbored anti-Catholic, antireligious
sentiment. Repeatedly, he engaged conversations of faith with a focus on
the more secularly acceptable term *values,* emphasizing that his faith was
important because "a hundred per cent of the people are values voters. . . .
And it's never been otherwise" (quoted in Murphy, 2005, p. A1). Kaine's
conversion story appropriated the rhetoric of evangelism, casting his Catholic
faith experiences within an evangelical framework and ingratiating himself to
evangelical Virginians, while still emphasizing a liberal, Democratic political
program of moral reform.

FINDING A CATHOLIC EVANGELICAL MISSION

Throughout the campaign, Kaine's rhetoric demonstrated a model of political—in
this case Catholic—evangelicalism that may be accessible to other Democrats
looking to reach out to Christian voters. Kaine's use of the conversion narrative
was designed to attract religious voters and persuade them that Kaine was a man

of faith. This model of political evangelicalism is available and highly useful for Democrats of faith wishing to establish their *ethos* with religious voters. If identification is the key to persuasion, as Kenneth Burke (1969) advocated, convincing voters of authentic religiosity would be a key rhetorical task for future Democrats.

Before examining Kaine's conversion narrative, it is important to explain the differences between Catholic and Protestant approaches to engaging secular culture. For American Catholics, the emphasis tends to be on service. This is particularly true of the Jesuits, the order of religious priests who educated Kaine in high school and were an integral part of his experience in Honduras. Indeed, one of the Jesuit mottos is *homines pro aliis*, or "men and women for others" (Schroth, 2004). The Catholic approach to engaging culture and spreading the faith is that by serving others, God is glorified. Feeding the hungry, clothing the naked, and aiding the poor are the works of faith essential to demonstrate one's own devotion to God and also show the face of God to others. This is not to say that Protestants do not complete their own works of mercy. The Protestant church is very involved in helping their fellow man. However, the focus of evangelicals in particular is the Great Commission, or the instruction of Jesus to his disciples to spread the Good News of Christ all over the world.

It follows, therefore, that Catholics and Protestants have different rhetorical emphases when discussing serving others. Catholics tend to focus on physical needs. They might provide food and shelter for the poor, for example, believing that individuals can come to know God and His goodness through the actions of the faithful. Catholics serving often quote St. Francis of Assisi's perspective on evangelism—"Preach the gospel. Use words if necessary"—to demonstrate that physical works are the path to leading people to God. Evangelical Protestants, on the other hand, believe that the most important need any individual can have is to be reborn as a Christian. Meeting a person's spiritual needs is, therefore, the most important "service" a Christian can bring to a fellow human. This is not to say that evangelicals do not serve in a physical way. However, the focus for evangelicals is to follow the words of Jesus in the Gospel of Matthew:

> Then Jesus came to them and said, "All authority in heaven and on earth has been given to me. Therefore go and make disciples of all nations, baptizing them in the name of the Father and of the Son and of the Holy Spirit, and teaching them to obey everything I have commanded you. And surely I am with you always, to the very end of the age." (Matthew 28: 18–20, New International Version)

This passage is commonly referred to as the Great Commission, and in the Book of Matthew, the passage serves as both the final utterance of Christ on earth as well as the final words of the Gospel. The "great commission" of Christians has been colloquially shortened in American Protestantism to the "mission" of Christians on this earth. Protestant youth groups, fellowships, and church members go on "mission trips." Churches support "foreign missions" or even missions here in the United States in an attempt to make believers around the world. In contrast, Catholic high schools, parish groups, and university Newman Clubs go on "service trips." College students who commit one year to serving with the Jesuits are called the Jesuit Volunteer Core, not the Jesuit Mission Core.

This phrasing distinction signals a more substantive difference as well. Catholic narratives about service, particularly overseas, tend to focus on the actions of the Christians on the trip—experiences of providing care for others, the "feeding" of the sheep as Jesus suggested to Peter, the first pope of Roman Catholicism (John 21:17, New International Version). Protestant narratives may discuss care for individuals' physical needs, but ultimately, one cannot hear the testimony of a missions trip without hearing how many people attended a worship service or Bible study, and how many converted to Christianity.

Kaine's retelling of his own personal narrative transformed a Catholic service trip into a Protestant missions trip. This narrative is central to Kaine's personal character as portrayed in the 2005 election—indeed, as an article in *The Washington Monthly* mentioned, it was difficult to "find a voter who *doesn't* know" that Kaine spent time working at a Catholic church in Honduras (Murray, 2005, p. 24). Kaine always referred to the trip as a "mission." Along the campaign trail, his speeches talked about "lessons learned while on mission" and isolated the year as a turning point in Kaine's life (Dwyer, 2005, p. A1). Even Kaine's wife dotingly described their meeting in a way that reinforced this narrative. They met immediately after he returned from Honduras, and Anne described Kaine as "cute" and then explained, "He'd been off on a mission year" (Nuckols, 2005, p. A1). By referring to the trip as a mission, Kaine established common ground with many of his Protestant voters, recasting his Catholic experience in terms of a Protestant narrative.

More than just referring to the trip from the Protestant perspective, however, the narrative of the trip functioned as a conversion narrative for the Virginia Democrat. Conversion narratives are a central part of many denominations of religious rhetoric (Peters, 1994), and certainly are a key component of evangelical rhetoric. As Peter Stromberg (1993) noted, the evangelical conversion narrative is "a practice through which believers seek to establish some connection between the language of Evangelical Christianity and their own immediate situations" (p. 11). A conversion narrative will frequently explain why a person struggled in a past life situation, setting up the "rock-bottom" moment when they realized that faith in Jesus Christ was the Truth. The conversion narrative retells how the Christian became a Christian—or, as some evangelicals might say, how they were saved or reborn. The conversion narrative can also be a reinvigoration of faith, connecting the individual's faith journey to the present situation. It is communicated both as an event and a performance, meaning that it is something that *has* happened, but the communication of the experience—or "witnessing" the conversion narrative to others—is itself something that *is* happening (Stromberg, 1993, p. 14).

Kaine's experience in Honduras was both a past event and something that was still, even years later on the campaign trail, a part of his present character and understanding of the world. He described the trip as "the beginning of a journey to find meaning and purpose" (Nuckols, 2005). Kaine's campaign Web site featured an article written by him called "Finding my Mission in Life" (Kaine, 2005).[3] In this narrative—frequently used in stump speeches along the campaign trail—Kaine recast his experience as a Catholic service worker into a personal conversion narrative and missions testimony. In the narrative, Kaine first emphasized his background. He was raised in a religious family, "where life revolved around church, school, friends, sports, and hard work." The first and last components of life particularly convey Kaine's seriousness of purpose. Church was the most important thing in his young life, and he was a dedicated individual who understood the value of hard work.

Yet Kaine faced a sense of purposelessness during his first year of Harvard Law School. His words remind Christians of being lost in the wilderness, a prevalent narrative theme in both the Old and New Testaments. Like the proverbial prodigal son in the Gospel of Luke, Kaine had grown up a practicing and faithful Catholic, yet did not remain faithful. Halfway across the country from his Midwestern childhood home, in a new, bustling, urban environment, Kaine explained that he "questioned his faith" and his place in the world. He was "self-absorbed" and unable to determine what was important. Rather than pursue a job at a "big law firm," Kaine renounced the easy and plentiful life in favor of "a year" to "work with Catholic missionaries in Honduras." His path toward understanding was not easy. All around him, in Boston and in Honduras, he faced the poor and helpless and sought to alleviate their conditions. Kaine's struggle with his beliefs and purpose in life cast his faith as real and strong. This is an important step toward gaining a religious audience because, for devout evangelicals, "a religion that makes no difference in the life of the believer is not really worthy of the name" (Carter, 2000, p. 30). He, like so many sinful Christians, may have fallen into a path of darkness and questioning, but ultimately, he would turn to the Honduras experience to change his life forever. Kaine's faith appeared real and authentic, as it led him to *change* his life and dedicate a year to God's work.

Kaine's narrative emphasizes the Christian principles of humility. His time in Honduras made the young man reflect, "I see how naive I've been many times, placing stock in things that strike me as very unimportant now" (Nuckols, 2005, p. A1). Christian service can be viewed to be more authentic when it is done from a humble heart. Kaine recollects that when he went to Honduras, he only had "four years of high school classes" of Spanish. The language barrier was "tough," but through the patience of those he served, he "soon fell into a good rhythm." Kaine's ability to work with the mission depended not on his skills, but rather on serving and trusting those around him. He also identified a mentor who helped to solidify his faith and teach him the Christian virtue of humility: Jim O'Leary, an "energetic man whose skill with his hands made up for his fractured Spanish," served as Kaine's spiritual mentor in Honduras. O'Leary "selflessly gave to others," and his faith helped steer Kaine in the right direction. "Working with him changed the direction of my life and grounded me in my faith," Kaine declared. Furthermore, Jim O'Leary and those he served taught him about *authentic* faith. He explained, "Jim and my students were living faith in a much different way than I had ever encountered. It wasn't about words or doctrine. It was about action." Kaine here is drawing on the Christian belief that authentic, lived faith would inherently manifest itself in good work (James 2:14–25, New International Version).

Kaine directly related his Honduras experience to the Gospel narratives of Jesus's ministry. His "conversion" was learning that faith is not about "words or doctrine," but instead about following the example of Jesus and doing good things unto others—keeping the "second great commandment" of God, "Love your neighbor as yourself" (Matthew 22:39, New International Version). Kaine explained that a lived faith followed the path and example of "another poor kid, a carpenter, who grew into a wise man with a message of hope for even the most lost or destitute." Kaine's narrative suggested that his experience in Honduras taught him about the need to live an active, ever-present faith in that "poor kid": Jesus the Lord.

While this is not a traditional conversion narrative—at no point did Kaine say, "And then I confessed my faith in Jesus Christ"—Kaine's mission story still functioned within that framework. Kaine closed his account of his time in Honduras by calling the experience "life-changing" and saying that his time there "shaped what [he] wanted to do" with his life. It was during Kaine's time as a Jesuit volunteer worker in Honduras that he began to see things clearly, through a new lens: that of the newly converted Christian who changes his life after coming to know Jesus. His "mission" in life was to help others, and he seemed to be appointed for and approved of by God. As Kaine stated on the campaign trail, the day before the election, "I made a decision when I came back from Honduras . . . that I am not going to focus on making as much money as I can make. I am going to focus on serving people" (quoted in Dwyer, 2005, p. A1). Running for governor, therefore, was part of this larger mission.

Once Kaine established that he had experienced the living power of the Christian faith, his narrative added to his *ethos* as a practicing Christian and a person who not only believed values should be a part of politics, but as one who clearly was living those values. His wife was not just his partner or even soul mate; she was "a person of faith who wanted to use her gifts to help others rather than simply to advance herself." Tim and Anne Kaine were not traditional politicians who worked without ceasing; instead they led "balanced careers of serving" while "raising three kids." Kaine chose to surround himself with people of faith who fought the "battle against selfishness." He lived his life trying to "do good," a task that he felt was "not really complicated." Kaine's narrative established his "mission in life" as caring for others, rather than choosing to sinfully store up for himself "treasures on earth, where moths and rust destroy, and where thieves break and steal" (Matthew 6:19, New International Version). The Honduras experience recast Kaine as friendly to the evangelical way of engaging the world. He communicated that his actions in life were guided by defeating the battle against selfishness and learning to serve others, a battle that was far easier when you had "a role model . . . someone who does it and shows you how to do it, too." While Kaine mentioned his wife Anne and his mentor O'Leary as two people who helped him on earth, his narrative implied that the "poor carpenter," the man familiar to many Protestant evangelical voters as the role model of their lives, was and is similarly guiding Kaine's decisions and actions. His understanding of living faith worked to establish credibility with a broad spectrum of Christian religious voters, transcending political and denominational divides.

DEMOCRATS AND GOD: A PROBLEM OF *ETHOS*

Kaine was not the first liberal to attempt to attract evangelicals, and he will not be the last to attempt to overcome divides among groups of voters in the United States. Yet his success—as judged by his victory in Virginia and his winning of more conservative Protestant counties—is in marked contrast to the attempts of others. Lattin and Underhill (2006) examined the rhetoric of liberal preacher Jim Wallis and his attempt to transcend political divides. They argued that Wallis failed to transcend this divide because he was "hostile towards conservatism" and failed to "address concerns of the religious right" (p. 220). Lattin and Underhill suggested that transcending "both the left and the right" might be a "task too difficult for anyone" (p. 221). Kaine's success in the 2005 gubernatorial election represents a more positive outlook on the status of faith and politics. His personal narrative established his *ethos* as a person of authentic faith, and the style of his narrative directly addressed would-be concerns of the religious right. An ability to connect with religious voters through a personal narrative framed Kaine's liberal initiatives as part of a Christian mission of helping and serving others. He proved, as he said in his election night victory speech, that "faith in God is a value we all can share regardless of party" (Barnes, 2005, p. A1).

As Virginia's governor, Kaine continued to emphasize a rhetoric of faith and service. In a 2006 commencement address at Virginia Tech University, he encouraged students to "serve others" with whatever talents they possessed (Kaine, 2006a). At the University of Virginia, he again recounted his mission narrative, and confessed that deciding to go on a mission trip taught him, "in a way no lecture or lesson could, that true happiness is found in focusing on how to use your gifts to benefit other people" (Kaine, 2006b). At the 2008 Democratic National Convention, Kaine took the stage and reminded his fellow Democrats that in order to accomplish Barack Obama's change, they would need "faith the size of a mustard seed" to "move mountains." This statement was a reference to Jesus' words to his disciples: "Because you have so little faith. I tell you the truth, if you have faith as small as a mustard seed, you can say to this mountain, 'Move from here to there' and it will move. Nothing will be impossible for you" (Matthew 17:20, New International Version; a similar passage is in Luke 17:5–6, New International Version). The biblical theme of accomplishing great deeds in the name of God was explicitly connected to the political programs of the Democratic Party. Kaine's speech repeatedly referenced the "faith" needed, not only to move mountains, but also to elect Barack Obama and his program for change for the better. He finished his speech with a rousing, "Say it with me—move, mountain. Say it with me again—move, mountain. Mountain, get out of our way!" (Kaine, 2008).

For Democrats today, the problem is *not* talking about God. The problem is one of authentically establishing their connection to God. John Kerry went to weekly mass in the 2004 election—we know this because conservative bishops attempted to bar him from receiving communion. Other Democrats routinely use expressions of faith in their rhetoric. Yet these expressions are not enough. To connect with religious voters who view faith as an important voting issue, Democratic candidates must overcome the stigma of being anti-religion. This stigma is fairly recent—as Amy Sullivan noted, in the 1970s, Jimmy Carter had "religious voters locked up" (2007, p. 38). In the 1980s and 1990s, however, the GOP "aggressively courted" religious voters and after Bill Clinton left the presidency, Democrats became alienated from many traditional religious voters (p. 38). In a 2007 *Time* magazine article, Pew Forum on Religion and Public Life senior fellow John C. Green, however, noted that with low approval ratings of the Bush presidency, more moderate evangelicals—around 22 million voters nationally—might be willing to consider Democrats as their new political allies (Gibbs & Duffy, 2007). Sullivan's 2008 book, *The Party Faithful,* concludes with the observation that while the "praying field" is not yet level, Democrats are starting to make progress in connecting with religious voters (p. 220).

This connection also coincides with what David P. Gushee (2008) has called the rise of the "evangelical center," a group of devout religious voters who reject the extreme religious right's "mood of angry nostalgia and aggrieved entitlement about the Christian role in American society," yet also steers clear of the left's alliance with antiglobalization, espousing of pacifism, and promotion of gender equality (pp. 88, 90). Gushee explains that the top political concerns of the evangelical center include involvement in the democratic process, issues of global justice, religious liberty, human rights, and "explicit rooting of all such moral and policy convictions in appeals to biblical teachings and Christian faith" (p. 91). These voters have not aligned with either Republicans or Democrats, and are therefore changing the bipolar understandings of religious right and secular left.

Democrats wishing to appeal to religious voters must continue to redefine themselves as a new type of Democrat. They must concern themselves with values without being overly moralistic, demonstrating that they are guided by principle but still highly connected to civic life. While religion may not always be the most important issue in an election—the 2008 election was relatively quiet about religion—religion has been relatively "inseparable from American politics for as long as America has had politics, and will likely remain inseparable as long as Americans remain religious" (Carter, 2000, p. 11). Kaine was able to speak to values authentically and openly as a Catholic and as a Democrat, advancing his image of a Christian (Catholic) evangelical who was deeply rooted in his faith—and therefore, a trustworthy candidate for moderate evangelical Virginians. For other Democrats to "copy" this model, however, they will need to pay close attention to their audiences' expectations as well as stay true to their own experiences. Kaine found success by placing his own authentic experiences into a more acceptable social framework for the audience of evangelical Virginians.

NOTES

1. A more recent Pew Research Center report summarized that American religious affiliation is "very diverse and extremely fluid," yet almost universally seen as an important part of American life (Lugo & Kohut, 2008, p. 5).

2. The other tribes included "spiritual but not religious voters," "Jews," "Muslims and others" in the Democrat camp, and "Convertible Catholics" in the swing tribes.

3. Unless otherwise noted, all quotations from Kaine's narrative are taken from the Web-reproduced version of the mission narrative.

REFERENCES

Balmer, R. H. (2006). *Mine eyes have seen the glory: A journey into the evangelical subculture in America.* New York: Oxford University Press.

Barnes, R. (2005, November 9). A triumph for Warner, and a guide for his party. *Washington Post,* p. A1.

Bendyna, M., Green, J. C., Rozell, M. J., & Wilcox, C. Catholics and the Christian right: A view from four states. *Journal for the Scientific Study of Religion, 39,* 321–332.

Burke, K. (1969). *A rhetoric of motives.* Berkeley: University of California Press.

Carter, S. L. (2000). *God's name in vain: The wrongs and rights of religion in politics.* New York: Basic Books.

Cohen, M. A. (2008). *Live from the campaign trail.* New York: Walker & Company.

Dwyer, T. (2005, November 3). For Kaine, a faith in service. *Washington Post,* p. A1.

Friedenberg, R. V. (2002). *Notable speeches in contemporary presidential campaigns.* Westport, CT: Praeger.

Gibbs, N. (2004, July 21). The faith factor. *Time,* pp. 26–32.

Gibbs, N., & Duffy, M. (2007, July 23) How the Democrats got religion. *Time.* Retrieved from http://www.time.com/time/politics/article/0,8599,1642649,00.html

Gushee, D. P. (2008). *The future of faith in American politics: The public witness of the evangelical center.* Waco, TX: Baylor University Press.

Hankins, B. (2006). *American evangelicals: A contemporary history of a mainstream religious movement.* Lanham, MD: Rowman & Littlefield.

Hunter, J. D. (1992). *Culture wars: The struggle to define America.* New York: BasicBooks.

Jamieson, K. H. (1996). *Packaging the presidency: A history and criticism of presidential campaign advertising.* New York: Oxford University Press.

Jelen, T. G. (1993). The political consequences of religious group attitudes. *Journal of Politics, 55,* 178–190.

Jenkins, P. (2003). *The new anti-Catholicism: The last acceptable prejudice.* New York: Oxford University Press.

Kaine, T. (2005). Finding my mission in life. Retrieved from www.governor.virginia.gov/AboutTheGovernor/FromtheGovernorsDesk/mission.cfm

Kaine, T. (2006a). That I may serve. Retrieved from http://www.governor.virginia.gov/MediaRelations/Speeches/2006/VTgraduation.cfm

Kaine, T. (2006b). Captains, cast off your lines. Retrieved from http://www.governor.virginia.gov/MediaRelations/Speeches/2006/UVAgraduation.cfm

Kaine, T. (2008). Democratic national convention speech. Retrieved from http://www.huffingtonpost.com/2008/08/28/tim-kaine-dnc-speech_n_122237.html

Kohut, A., & Lugo, L. (2006, August 24). Many Americans uneasy with mix of religion and politics. *Pew Forum on Public and Religious Life.* Retrieved from http://pewforum.org/docs/index.php?DocID=153#2

Kyle, R. G. (2006). *Evangelicalism: An Americanized Christianity.* New Brunswick, NJ: Transaction Publishers.

Lattin, B. D., & Underhill, S. (2006). The soul of politics: Reverend Jim Wallis's attempt to transcend the religious/secular left and the religious right. *Journal of Communication and Religion, 29,* 205–223.

Lugo, L., & Kohut, A. (2008, February). U. S. religious landscape survey. *Pew Forum on Religion and Public Life.* Retrieved from http://religions.pewforum.org/pdf/report-religious-landscape-study-full.pdf

Murphy, C. (2005, October 31). Catholicism, politics a careful mix for Kaine. *Washington Post,* p. A1.

Murray, M. (2005, October/November). Test of faith. *Washington Monthly,* pp. 23–25.

Norris, K. (1999). *Amazing grace: A vocabulary of faith.* New York: Penguin Group.

Nuckols, C. (2005, October 16). Profile: Who is Timothy M. Kaine? *Virginian-Pilot,* p. A1.

Schroth, R. A. (2004). *The American Jesuits: A history.* New York: NYU Press.

Shear, M. D. (2005, November 9). Democrat Kaine wins in Virginia. *The Washington Post,* p. A1.

Smith, C. (2000). *Christian America? What evangelicals really want.* Berkeley: University of California Press.

Stromberg, P. G. (1993). *Language and self-transformation: A study of the Christian conversion narrative.* New York: Cambridge University Press.

Sullivan, A. (2007, July 23). The origins of the God gap. *Time,* p. 38.

Sullivan, A. (2008). *The party faithful: How and why Democrats are closing the God gap.* New York: Scribner.

Waldman, S., & Green, J. C. (2006, January/February). Tribal relations. *Atlantic Monthly,* pp. 136–142.

Wallis, J. (2005). *God's politics: Why the right gets it wrong and the left doesn't get it.* San Francisco: Harper Collins.

Chapter 11

Dwelling amongst the Righteous

Keith Ellison—Demagogue or Demon?

Julie R. Woodbury

On November 7, 2006, a coalition of liberal, antiwar Minnesota voters established precedent when they sent the state's first black and the nation's first Muslim representative to Washington, D.C. Forty-three-year-old criminal defense attorney Keith Ellison was a popular if not uncontroversial candidate for the Fifth Congressional District seat vacated by Democratic-Farmer-Labor Party (DFL) Representative Martin Sabo, who retired after 28 distinguished years in Congress. Including the city of Minneapolis and surrounding suburbs, the Fifth Congressional District is arguably both the most liberal urban area and most ethnically diverse district in Minnesota. After winning the Democratic primary with 41 percent of the vote on September 12, 2006, Ellison went on to win the seat itself with 56 percent of the vote, defeating Republican candidate Alan Fine, the Green Party's Jay Pond, and Independence Party representative Tammy Lee (Kahn, 2006). Robson, a staff writer with local publication *City Pages,* commented on what winning the district might mean to a successful contender, suggesting that "claiming the party's post-Sabo mantle there is the closest thing to a lock on a long career in national politics, and the power and prestige that come with it, that any Minnesota Democrat could hope to find" (2006a, para. 2).

This could have been the tale of just another charismatic and well-spoken maverick Democrat making it big in the northern Midwest, but it is not. The following is not an analysis of Ellison's religious rhetoric—he is careful about what, and when, he shares—but rather, an exploration of his political success and reactions to his very presence in the national political arena.

Ellison was one of eleven DFLers to have set his sights on the soon-to-be-vacated congressional seat, and although he won the day, "polling twice as many delegate votes as anyone else on the first ballot and receiving the endorsement by unanimous acclaim after three ballots" (Robson, 2006a, para. 3), he ended up in the cross-hairs of not only Republicans, but of Democrats as well—some within days of his party's May 6 endorsement. Ellison sought, from the outset, to bring people together. Upon receiving his party's endorsement, he reached out to the Fifth Congressional District community, saying, "We're starting to figure out that it's really got to be about all of us. We have to unify. We have to come together from the suburb and the city. We have to come together straight and gay, black and white, red and yellow. We have to come together" (Scheck, 2006a, para. 4). Even so, from the beginning, the question of whether Ellison should be in federal office has been divisive.

Welcome to *Race and Religion in the USA 101,* circa 2006.

Keith Ellison is black.

Keith Ellison is Muslim.

And, as became clear, Keith Ellison represents an ongoing threat for some people on both sides of the aisle.

BRED FOR A LIFE OF PUBLIC SERVICE

Ellison's biography is not atypical for an individual raised to political activism. Born in Detroit, Michigan, he was brought up a Roman Catholic in a highly educated and socially progressive household. His father was a psychologist, his mother a social worker, and his grandfather a member of the NAACP in Louisiana at a time when being caught working with that organization frequently meant being lynched. Ellison's family background laid the foundation for his own commitment to justice and equal rights.

> As a young man I was outraged and frustrated by the racism and injustice I saw in my community and the world around me. Those experiences propelled me to become a social activist, using my words and actions to draw attention to the very serious problems of inequality, racial injustice and poverty in our society. As I matured, I had to confront my anger and face it down. I eventually realized that it is easy to be a critic pointing out problems and failings, but it is a far more difficult thing to be part of creating the solution. As my father used to say, "Any jackass can kick a barn down; it takes a carpenter to build it back up." Eventually I understood what my father had been telling me, and I committed to being one of the carpenters. I began to help create a world where everybody counts and where there are no throwaway people. (Ellison, 2006, para. 5–9)

In 1983, while an undergraduate at Wayne State University in Detroit, and after having read *The Autobiography of Malcolm X,* Ellison converted to

Sunni Islam. He was 19. A few years later, while attending the University of Minnesota Law School, he wrote several articles supporting Louis Farrakhan and the Nation of Islam. These articles—and an alleged multiple-year affiliation with the group, including intensive efforts in Minnesota recruiting participants for the 1995 Million Man March—came back to bite him as he campaigned for and even after he won the Fifth District Congressional seat (Robson, 2006a).

Ellison presented an easy target for those who chose to aim at him, both personally and politically. He himself commented on what has been called the "chronically sloppy way he has handled his personal and campaign finances" (Robson, 2006a, para. 6) as well as on his various traffic violations and driver's license suspensions (*Politics in Minnesota,* 2006, para. 3). The most insidious attacks on Ellison, however, were not based on his administrative characteristics but rather on his religion and his past and then-present associations, which may have given his detractors the sense that they could have *carte blanche* to denigrate him and question the motives behind his actions.

Within days of winning the Democratic endorsement, rumors began to circulate about Ellison's suitability for national office. An anonymous e-mail sent to local politicos and news organizations after Ellison's DFL endorsement win detailed his past relationship with Farrakhan and the Nation of Islam. It also provided comments allegedly made by Ellison on race in America, as well as the suggestion that Ellison was an anti-Semite. This implication, which arose shortly after the endorsement, has been attributed to a number of factors. From 1989–1990, using the pseudonym Keith E. Hakim, he penned several columns for the *Minnesota Daily* defending Louis Farrakhan against the charges of others that he was anti-Semitic. Nearly a decade later, in 1998, Ellison publicly supported then-executive director of the Minneapolis Initiative Against Racism (MIAR), Jill Jackson, who was alleged to have said, "Jews are among the most racist white people" (Johnson, 2006; Parsons, 1997).

Weeks after his endorsement win, *Politics in Minnesota,* a newsletter that bills itself as "Minnesota's public affairs news service," recognized Ellison as one of the Fifth District candidates with the best shot at winning Representative Sabo's congressional seat. At the same time, the newsletter commented, "Ellison undoubtedly has said things in the past, both as a law student at the University of Minnesota and as a lawyer for the poor, that will come back to haunt him in the campaign" (2006, para. 22). By this point the statement wasn't so much prophetic as a declaration of the obvious.

Over the course of his candidacy, as well as in the years since, Ellison has been the target of allegations about his motives. These claims have been, for the most part, extensions of biases reflecting assumptions about his religion and the people with whom he has associated. Because Ellison did not see himself as a racist, he did not believe he had any obligation to acknowledge the accusations against him or in any other way explain himself (Robson, 2006a). Nevertheless, as he discovered, even ostensibly false charges of racism can derail a candidate's bid for office. Ellison believed that most people would recognize that the attitudes held by Farrakhan and his Nation of Islam were not the same as those held by mainstream Muslims (Robson, 2006a, para. 8).

This attitude seemed to signal a kind of self-serving political myopia, given the position Ellison himself took against former Republican state legislator Rich Stanek in 2004. Stanek was forced to resign his post as public safely commissioner after admitting to having uttered racial slurs in a deposition in the 1990s; Ellison is attributed with having led the push for that resignation. As journalist Tom Scheck of Minnesota Public Radio wrote:

> DFL Rep. Keith Ellison of Minneapolis questions the timing of the apology. Ellison called a news conference on Friday morning to call for Stanek's resignation. He suggests Stanek was apologizing to save his job. He says Stanek has continued to promote controversial legislation that harms the community. Ellison noted as a legislator Stanek objected to the collection of data on racial profiling by police. "I do believe in racial reconciliation, but you know what? When somebody makes an apology on the eve of them being confirmed for a job that they want, I sort of doubt the sincerity of that apology," he said. (2006b, para. 7–8)

According to an interview conducted by Minneapolis *Star Tribune* reporter Rochelle Olson (2006), until his Jewish friends pointed out to Ellison that he had to respond to his detractors—and suggested that he begin by clarifying his statements and position with the Jewish community—Ellison didn't realize the potential scope of the problem. In a letter to the Jewish Community Relations Council (JCRC), Ellison wrote that during the 18 months in the mid-1990s when he had had ties to the Nation of Islam, he had failed to "scrutinize the positions of the group and its leader, Louis Farrakhan, and 'wrongly dismissed concerns that they were anti-Semitic. I should have come to that conclusion earlier than I did. I regret that I didn't'" (quoted in Olson, 2006, p. B1). Ellison continued, noting that he'd seen "in the Nation of Islam, and specifically the Million Man March [in 1995], an effort to promote African-American self-sufficiency, personal responsibility, and community economic development." Of his 1998 defense of MIAR's Jill Jackson, Ellison wrote, "I believe that Ms. Jackson's alleged remark was clearly bigoted, discriminatory, inappropriate, and even ridiculous," adding that "while some leaders defended her comments, he 'spoke out in favor of increased dialogue between the Jewish and African-American communities'" (quoted in Olson, 2006, p. B1). Ellison further asserted during that same interview that he'd written the May 28 JCRC letter to "reassure allies and friends of my long-term support for civil and human rights" (p. B1). That this was not universally understood to be his position became clear when members of the public as well as other candidates began to take potshots at him on the basis of his religious affiliation.

Attorney Dan Rosen, a member of the Jewish Community Relations Council who had seen the letter prior to the publication of Olson's interview, said, "Given Ellison's public multiyear association with a vicious anti-Semitic organization, and given his past writing, I have to be skeptical of statements he makes in the context of an election campaign'" (quoted in Olson, 2006, p. B1). Taking the position that Ellison's past affiliation with the Nation of Islam should disqualify his candidacy, Rosen posited one circumstance under which he believed the man might be justified in running for office. "If Keith Ellison establishes a record of advocating for Jews and the Jewish Community that is as lengthy and enthusiastic as his record of advocacy for anti-Semites and anti-Semitic organizations, then at that time we can weigh his two records and decide who the real Keith Ellison is. We haven't reached that time" (quoted in Scheck, 2006b, para. 20).

Mark Rotenberg, head of Minnesotans Against Terrorism, general counsel of the University of Minnesota, and a Jewish Minneapolis resident who supported Ellison's opponent Ember Reichgott Junge, said, "folks are extra-concerned about his past association with known anti-Semites, antiwhites and anti-Catholic spokesmen. There are other strong, experienced, progressive Democrats in this race who don't have that kind of heavy baggage" (quoted in Olson, 2006, p. B1). Reichgott Junge refrained from publicly questioning Ellison on the issue of anti-Semitism, preferring to concentrate on her own campaign. She did comment, however, that questions had arisen concerning Ellison's suitability for federal office. Minneapolis City Council member Paul Ostrow was less reticent, stating, "It is disappointing that it took until now for Representative Ellison to acknowledge and disown the anti-Semitism of the Nation of Islam and Louis Farrakhan. When you run for federal office, you run on your record and your past" (quoted in Olson, 2006, p. B1).

While the majority of the community seemed willing to give Ellison the benefit of the doubt based on his Minnesota legislative record, an appreciable number of people remained concerned. Ellison supporters were temperate in their acceptance of the candidate. Former University of Minnesota law school classmate Dan Weiss, a member of the Law School's Jewish Caucus, said that although he was aware of Ellison's support for the Nation of Islam, he and another Jewish law classmate had never gotten the impression that Ellison himself was anti-Semitic, despite the fact that he "would downplay or ignore some of the hateful messages portrayed by [the group]" (quoted in Scheck, 2006b, para. 11). Even so, Weiss believed that Ellison needed to clear the air about his involvement, stating, "If you're going to latch onto a very strong, but racist, movement, you have to be sure to explain why that happened so people in the community . . . know that you really have changed" (quoted in Scheck, 2006b, para. 13).

Several members of the JCRC board supported the candidate without reservations. DFL elections lawyer Alan Weinblatt commented that after having listened to Ellison's public speeches and then having met with him, he was comfortable with the candidacy. "I view this as an awesome opportunity for the citizens of Minneapolis . . . to send somebody to Congress who has a unique background" (quoted in Olson, 2006, p. B1). St. Paul City Council member Jay Benanav, a Jewish Holocaust survivor, said that he'd worked with Ellison and that the concerns being voiced were "not well founded with regards to anti-Semitism, anti-Israel" (quoted in Olson, 2006, p. B1).

Representative Frank Hornstein (DFL-Minneapolis), with whom Ellison worked in the state legislature, called Ellison "a friend of the Jewish community," pointing to Ellison's effort to censure another state representative who made questionable comments about the Holocaust. He believed that electing Ellison would make a strong statement:

> To have a potentially historic election, the first Muslim ever elected to Congress and to have the first Muslim ever elected to Congress be a strong friend of the Jewish community and someone who is very sensitive to our concerns both domestically and internationally, is a real plus. (quoted in Scheck, 2006b, para. 14–15)

As the Minneapolis Jewish community squared off on the issue of whether or not the candidate was, indeed, racist, Ellison persevered in his attempts to distance himself from the politics of Farrakhan and The Nation of Islam. In a June interview with Tom Scheck (2006b) of Minnesota Public Radio, Ellison said "My ideas about Minister Farrakhan have changed in a number of important ways." Scheck interpreted the substantive parts of this interview, writing that Ellison

> favored Louis Farrakhan's teachings on certain subjects, like black self sufficiency and personal responsibility . . . his law-school writings and other activities were independent of any outside groups . . . [and he states that he hadn't] had any involvement with the group since that time and has never been a member of the organization. (2006b, para. 16)

Ellison admitted that he had been "wrong to dismiss concerns about the group's anti-Semitic views and has learned to scrutinize the groups with which he works" (quoted in Scheck, 2006b, para. 17). "Human beings are complex, we evolve," he said. "We ought to let each other evolve. We ought to let each other be better than they were today. If someone is the same as they were 16 years ago, that would be the very definition of stuck in a rut, wouldn't it?" (quoted in Scheck, 2006b, para. 18).

It did not take long, however, for an already divided political field to become ugly. Ten days after Ellison's letter was submitted to the Jewish Community Relations Council, al-Qaeda second-in-command Abu Musab Al-Zarqawi was killed. A weblog created to promote the campaign of Republican U.S. Senate hopeful Mark Kennedy showcased a photograph of Zarqawi accompanied by the caption "Condolences can be sent to Ellison HQ." Almost simultaneously, the claims that Ellison was anti-Semitic surfaced in the mainstream media. *Star Tribune* columnist Katherine Kersten expressed surprise at Ellison's ongoing campaign for federal office, offering a hypothetical situation: "Imagine that a Republican seeks his party's endorsement for the U.S. House of Representatives, despite having been allied with a white supremacist organization just a decade earlier . . . That man wouldn't get his party's endorsement" (2006, para. 1).

Arguably the greatest amount of trouble for Ellison stemmed from postings on *MinnesotaDemocratsExposed,* a conservative blog run by local Republican Michael Brodkorp, and *PowerLine,* the national conservative blog known for having helped to bring down CBS News anchor Dan Rather. Shortly after Ellison's endorsement victory, Brodkorp posted the articles Ellison had written in 1988 and 1989 for the University of Minnesota student newspaper under the pen name of Keith Hakim—articles that supported Farrakhan, requested reparations for African Americans, and called for the establishment of a black nation within the borders of the United States. Subsequent blog posts itemized Ellison's apparent disinclination to pay traffic tickets (he was reported to have had at least 55 parking or traffic tickets, including 17 moving violations), the fact that his driver's license had been revoked, his alleged failure to file taxes, and his incomplete campaign finance reports. Between May and early September, one of the founders of *PowerLine,* Minneapolis resident Scott Johnson, wrote 20 blog entries about Ellison, focusing on "Mr. Ellison's presence and statements at rallies defending gang members accused of violence against police" (Gerstein, 2006, para. 20). By July, pundits at *Politics in Minnesota* had decided that the race was over for Ellison. Under the caption "Dead Man Walking," the newsletter suggested that the only person who didn't recognize that his bid for Congress was over was Keith Ellison himself (2006, para. 1).

AFFILIATION ≠ ATTRIBUTION

Summer 2006 was a difficult time for Ellison, as he was forced to deal with what *Minnesota Politics* columnist Britt Robson described as the "relentless criticism of his campaign in the media and blogosphere" (2006a, para. 3). In late June, *Politics in Minnesota*'s Republican editor, Sarah Janecek, told *Roll Call* that the fact the Democrats endorsed Ellison in spite of his ties to the Nation of Islam and his failure to pay parking tickets was a "classic example of liberal moral relativism . . . A lot of people are willing to gloss over his past because he's black" (quoted in Robson, 2006b, para. 1). In mid-August, Robson called Janecek on what appeared to be a fine bit of hypocrisy, writing:

> Since *PowerLine* has been lauding Conn. Sen. Joe Lieberman ever since Lieberman was defeated in the recent Democratic primary, and since Ellison's most formidable opponent, Ember Reichgott Junge, told *City Pages* earlier this month that she co-chaired Lieberman's 2004 presidential bid in Minnesota because he is "a man of integrity," an article in today's edition of the online magazine *Salon* might be instructive. It quotes Lieberman as saying of Louis Farrakhan, "I have respect for him . . . I admire what Minister Farrakhan is doing." Let's see if there is as much of a media shit-storm directed at Junge as there was against Ellison for supporting the Million Man March (which occurred five years before Lieberman's kind words for the Minister). And let's see if *PowerLine* and MDE [the Minnesota Democrats Exposed blog], and yes, Janecek, condemn Lieberman for his remarks. Let's see if they impugn Junge's staunch support for an open admirer of Farrakhan and demand clarification on her position vis-a-vis Lieberman and Farrakhan. Let's see, in other words, whether there is conservative moral relativism and a glossing over of Lieberman's and Junge's past because they happen to be white. (2006a, para. 2–3)

Ellison himself refrained from engaging in such negative politicking, preferring to spend his energy on a grassroots, door-to-door campaign in which he reached out to nontraditional voters. In spite of the ongoing agitation in the press and the blogosphere, by the latter part of August 2006 it was becoming evident that the tide of public opinion, at least in Minnesota's Fifth Congressional District, was skewing in favor of Ellison over the other Democratic contenders. A tally taken the evening of August 22 at Take Action Minnesota, a nonprofit formed by the merger of Progressive Minnesota and the Minnesota Alliance for Progressive Action, showed that an "overwhelming" 80 percent of the membership supported the candidate (Robson, 2006c, para. 1). On September 7, Ellison's campaign received what was considered by many in the blogosphere to be a pivotal boost: Mordecai Spektor, publisher of the *American Jewish World,* a weekly serving Minnesota's Jewish community, endorsed the candidate. The endorsement, published as an editorial on *Tzvee's Talmudic Blog,* included the following comments:

> There are three fairly conventional candidates who would bring particular strengths to service in the U.S. House and would likely provide competent representation for their constituents. However, voters could make an emphatic statement—one that would gain national and international attention—by casting their ballots for Keith Ellison. The 43-year-old state representative would bring a singular passion and intelligence to the job . . . In many ways, Ellison represents the progressive populist vision that Minnesota lost with the untimely passing of Paul Wellstone in 2002. Ellison acted as the lawyer for the House DFL caucus in an ethics proceeding against former representative Arlon Lindner, who contended that gays were not victims of Nazi oppression in the Holocaust. Ellison understands the importance of guarding against Holocaust denial and revisionism, and links the lessons of the Shoah to more recent cases of genocide in Rwanda and Darfur. Further, he supports the State of Israel and the continuation of U.S. aid to Israel. He holds to the mainstream position of a negotiated two-state solution regarding the long-standing Israeli-Palestinian conflict . . . We think that Keith Ellison has the attributes to be a dynamic and effective representative in Congress. In Ellison, we have a moderate Muslim who extends his hand in friendship to the Jewish community and supports the security of the State of Israel. He is a person with a vision of a more humane and equitable society and he is the candidate we favor in the Fifth District DFL election.

The Minneapolis Jewish community split over Spektor's endorsement. As Tzvee so succinctly put it, "Jews back a Muslim for Congress. Any way you slice and dice it that is classic news" (2006, para. 7).

In this case, it was as much news to the Fifth Congressional District's Jewish population as it was to everybody else. The ink had barely dried on Ellison's primary win before his GOP opponent, Alan Fine, administered a "blistering criticism" and condemned him as "unfit to represent voters in the fifth district" (Scheck, 2006c, para. 1). Ellison immediately issued a response, deploring the tactics that were being used against him and reaching out to the disenfranchised populations most likely to respond to his message of hope.

> The remarks about which I've been asked to respond to are diametrically opposed to what our campaign has been about, what my career as a public servant and a grassroots organizer has been about. To engage them is to be sullied by them.
>   This campaign is about inclusion, not alienation. This campaign is about reaching across the needless barriers that divide us, not erecting them. Last night's primary election's record turnout is all the evidence I need to know that our message of enfranchisement, of peace and a society where there are no

throwaway people, resonated with voters. In fact, it brought more people into the democratic process. The remarks made this afternoon by my Republican opponent are calculated to do just the opposite.

I intend to continue reaching out to the marginalized, to the disenfranchised, the dispossessed and inviting them in, to join us as we take our country back from those who would pander to our worst fears. This campaign will continue to speak to our highest hopes. And together, I am confident those hopes can be realized. (quoted in Scheck, 2006c, para. 2–4)

It came as a surprise, even in a campaign characterized by surprises, when Ira Forman, Executive Director of the Washington, D.C.-based National Jewish Democratic Council, issued a statement asking Minnesota GOP candidate Alan Fine, the Minnesota Republicans, and other Republican organizations to end their "unbalanced and irrational attacks" on Ellison. Among the highlights of Forman's statement, which chided Ellison's opponents, were the following:

Republicans can't beat Keith Ellison on the merits of their policy positions. So instead, they appear to be using his religion as a weapon to question his patriotism. These kinds of scare tactics are disgraceful and have no place in mainstream politics . . . Republicans are taking intolerance and hypocrisy to a whole new level, even for them . . .

Keith has recognized his past mistakes and renounced his brief association with the Nation of Islam and has condemned the anti-Semitic statements and beliefs of Louis Farrakhan and Khalid Muhammed. Keith has demonstrated his support for Israel and issues of importance to the Jewish community. His explanation of his past has been accepted by Minnesota's organized Jewish community, and it is only the GOP attack machine who seems intent on not moving on. Republican Jews who attack Keith Ellison do not represent the mainstream of the American Jewish community, and they owe all of us an apology for invoking their Judaism in this shameful partisan hack job (Forman, 2006, para. 3–7)

Speaking after his successful primary bid, Ellison stated, "We came together, all colors, all faiths, all of us . . . we said from the very beginning this campaign is about everybody counts" (quoted in Lohn, 2006, *para. 4*). Ellison's statement reflected what many Americans believe are the highest standards of a democratic nation, suggesting that the political process represents a level playing field. Unfortunately, this was not necessarily the case, because although Ellison has always maintained that he "lives his life 'in a way not to make religion a big deal,'" from the moment he decided to run, his religion became just that—a big deal (Amanullah, 2006, para. 2).

Ellison was aware that his religion was a topic of both speculation and concern before, during, and since his successful 2006 campaign. Although usually silent about matters relating to faith, Ellison has willingly admitted that the Qur'an provides a foundation for his core ideas on social justice and reform. While speaking to a group of metropolitan Detroiters in late December 2006, after having won Minnesota's Fifth Congressional District seat, Ellison remarked upon the relationship between his religion and his political convictions, saying, "I'm not a religious leader, I've never led religious services of any kind . . . I'm not here to be a preacher, but in terms of political agenda items, my faith informs these things" (quoted in Warikoo, 2006a, para. 2).

Ellison's faith also informed his desire to hold a Qur'an during a pictorial reenactment of his swearing-in ceremony. The furor that arose over his stated intention to do so underscored the public's lack of understanding about how the formalities are actually executed. In fact, the official ceremony in which new representatives are sworn in to the U.S. House of Representatives is done *en masse* and without any books. During the swearing-in for the 110th Congress, not only Christian members (predominantly Roman Catholic, Baptist, and Methodist), but also Jewish members (who for the first time outnumbered the Episcopalians), two new Buddhist members, agnostic members, a Quaker member, and Ellison (the Muslim member) all pledged "true faith" and allegiance to uphold the Constitution (Evans, 2007). The official ceremony was not expected to create an issue.

Ellison recognized that his desire to put his hand on the Qur'an during the reenactment of the swearing-in ceremony resonated with some people and threatened others. He articulated the potential discomfort, saying,

> Many people see their religion as an identity thing, much in the same way Crips or Bloods [street gangs] might say, "I'm this, this is the set I'm rolling with'" . . . They've never actually tried to explore how religion should connect us, they're into how religion divides us . . . They haven't really explored . . . how my faith connects me to you (quoted in Warikoo, 2006a, para. 12).

Ellison also recognized that the Qur'an controversy—or, rather, the fact that there was one—begged a question. When electing an individual to office, is it his or her attributes or affiliations that matter more? "I'm a little incredulous about why anyone would care about what I'm going to swear on," he said. "In fact, if I swore on a book that wasn't of my tradition . . . would you trust me?" (quoted in Warikoo, 2006a, para. 8). Pragmatically, Ellison observed that to the extent that the issue "made people dust off their Constitution and actually read it," it was not a bad thing (quoted in Warikoo, 2006b, para. 12).

Aware that his decision would resonate widely, and perhaps hoping to defuse some of the anticipated opposition, Ellison invited opportunities to air the issue with the media. During a December 26, 2006, interview with CNN's Wolf Blitzer, Ellison talked candidly about what was already becoming known as the swearing-in controversy.

> When I'm officially sworn in, I will do it the same, exact way as every Congressperson-elect who is sworn in. We will all stand up and, in unison, lift our hand and swear to uphold that Constitution. And then later, in a private ceremony, of course, I'll put my hand on a book that is the basis of my faith, which is Islam. And I think that this is a beauty. This is a wonderful thing for our country, because Jewish members will put their hands on the Torah, Mormon members will put their hand on the Book of Mormon, Catholic members will put their hand on the book of their choice. And members who don't want to put their hand on any book are also fully free to do that. That's the American way. But I think that we need to not focus on what religious text any Congress member might want to use. Let's focus on the text that binds us together. That's the Constitution. That's a great document, and I'm looking forward very much to raising my hand and swear to uphold that Constitution. (quoted in Phillips, 2006, para. 8–10)

In the face of the negative discourse generated over the issue, journalists weighed in. *Washington Informer* columnist Askia Muhammed reminded his readers about the constitutional provision relevant to the swearing-in:

> Article VI of the U.S. Constitution is clear and unequivocal concerning Ellison. "The Senators or Representatives . . . shall be bound by an oath or affirmation, to support this Constitution; but no religious test shall ever be required as a qualification to any office of public trust under the United States," it says. (Muhammed, 2007, para. 18)

Constitutional precedent notwithstanding, conservatives, particularly some of the more outspoken members of the religious right, took the opportunity to express consternation. Although Jewish himself, *TownHall.com* columnist Dennis Prager wrote that permitting members of Congress to swear in using whatever book they choose "undermines American civilization." He chastised Ellison, writing:

> When all elected officials take their oaths of office with their hands on the very same book, they all affirm that some unifying value system underlies American civilization. If Keith Ellison is allowed to change that, he will be doing more damage to the unity of America and to the value system that has formed this country than the terrorists of 9-11. It is hard to believe that this is the legacy most Muslim Americans want to bequeath to America. But if it is, it is not only Europe that is in trouble. (2006, para. 11)

Joe Kaufman, chair of the self-proclaimed terrorism watchdog group *Americans Against Hate* and the founder of *CAIR Watch,* which keeps an eye on the Council of American-Islamic Relations (a civil rights group), wrote, plaintively, on January 4, 2007: "When Congressman Ellison places his hand today on the Qur'an, to which people is he swearing an oath to protect? Is it the American public—many of which went blindly into the voting booths to choose him—or is it his friends, our enemies?" (2007, para. 13).

Ellison did the reenactment with his hand on the Qur'an—but not just *any* Qur'an. He used a two-volume 1764 edition that was published in London, had been previously owned by Thomas Jefferson, and had been loaned to Ellison for the occasion by the rare books and special collections division of the Library of Congress. In a telephone interview with an ABC correspondent in early January 2007, Ellison said,

> It demonstrates that from the very beginning of our country, we had people who were visionary, who were religiously tolerant, who believed that knowledge and wisdom could be gleaned from any number of sources, including the Qur'an. A visionary like Thomas Jefferson was not afraid of a different belief system. This just shows that religious tolerance is the bedrock of our country, and religious differences are nothing to be afraid of. (quoted in Frommer, 2007, para. 3–4)

Ellison's campaign and subsequent election win drew comments from around the globe, including the Arab world. In November 2006, *Al-Jazeera USA* guest columnist Abdus Sattar Ghazali, the executive editor of the online magazine *American Muslim Perspective,* lauded Ellison's congressional win and quoted the executive director of the Muslim Public Affairs Council, Salam Al-Marayati: "The only way towards success in American society is by civic engagement and political participation" (quoted in Ghazali, 2006, para. 4). The observation reflected comments made in Ellison's victory speech: "We showed that we are stronger when we build bridges between communities rather than trying to divide and conquer . . . I am working for an America where everybody counts, where everybody matters and where peace is our guiding principle" (quoted in Ghazali, 2006, para. 3).

As part of a frequently apathetic electorate, we might be forgiven for asking "What's the big deal here? Why *should* we care about this race—about this politician?" Staff reporter Josh Gerstein, writing for the *New York Sun,* articulated the answer one week before the September primary when he pointed out that although it seemed possible that Ellison would become not only the first African American to serve Minnesota but the first Muslim American ever to serve in Congress, it was equally possible that he would be defeated because of "hard-hitting posts by conservative bloggers" (2006, para. 1). The dynamic established between conservative bloggers, the media, and the candidate had, by this time, become a matter of interest to political scientists across the nation. As Lawrence Jacobs of the University of Minnesota wrote,

"The bloggers, they brought out the blowtorches and said, 'You're not really asking the tough questions here'" (quoted in Gerstein, 2006, para. 4).

City Pages columnist Britt Robson, writing the day after the primary, suggested that "no Minnesota candidate has ever encountered the vigor and concentration of negative fervor from the blogs that was borne by the Ellison campaign" (2006d, para. 4). She predicted that the months between September and November would continue to be difficult ones for Ellison. Indeed, minutes after the polls closed on the September 12 primary, blogger Brodkorp of *MinnesotaDemocratsExposed.com* posted "Trust me—there is more exposing of Ellison to be done and I'm just the blogger to do it" (quoted in Robson, 2006d, para. 5).

CONCLUSION

The current volume explores Democrats and how they deal with issues relating to religion. Why, then, offer a chapter focusing on Ellison, a Muslim who makes a concerted effort to refrain from public comment about religion? Joseph M. Knippenberg, Professor of Politics and Associate Provost for Student Achievement at Oglethorpe University, writes:

> It is almost a commonplace of political punditry to note the "religion gap" between the Republicans and Democrats. Those who attend church frequently tend to vote Republican, while those who seldom or never darken the door of a sanctuary tend to vote Democratic. This difference is but one aspect of the "culture war" diagnosed by University of Virginia sociologist James Davison Hunter more than a decade ago: religious traditionalists seem to be on one side and secular progressives on the other. One side talks of God, prayer, providence, and moral duty, the other of science, reason, progress, and choice. To put it another way, Republicans seem to be willing to accommodate religion in the public square, while Democrats seem almost reflexively to insist upon separation of church and state. (2004, para. 1)

With the nomination of Ellison, what we on the sidelines were able to see is that even under circumstances where religion should not be the subject, the potentially controversial religious views of a candidate can become the object. Ellison's campaign showed that as powerful as political pundits, the blogosphere, and negative politicking can be, transparency, contrition, grassroots advocacy, and a positive, honorable campaign can still hold sway on the political front. Ellison, the man, draws his inspiration from the Qur'an, but the values he espouses are consistent with those of the founders of our nation:

I believe in a value system that invests in people and asks citizens to work for the common good. I decided to run for office because I believe our government has a positive role to play in creating a better future for all people. We need leaders who are committed to peace, a clean and sustainable environment, strong public schools and a health care system that works for all people. I am that leader and will continue to be that leader as a congressman from Minnesota. (Ellison, 2006, para. 13–14)

REFERENCES

Amanullah, S. (2006, September 14). U.S. elections: the lessons of Keith Ellison. *Altmuslim.com.* Retrieved from http://www.altmuslim.com/a/a/2385

Ellison, K. (2006, July 19). The value system that's behind my candidacy: It's about family, faith, and a need to work for social justice and the common good. *Minneapolis Star Tribune.* Retrieved from http://www.keithellison.org/StribOpEd.htm

Evans, J. L. (2007, January 4). The spirituality of the U. S. Congress. *Sightings.* Martin Marty Center at the University of Chicago Divinity School. Retrieved from http://jmm.aaa.net.au/articles/19007.htm

Forman, I. (2006, September 21). NJDC calls on Alan Fine and Republicans to apologize for hate-filled attacks on Keith Ellison. *NJDCBlog: The Online Voice for Jewish Democrats.* Retrieved from http://njdc.typepad.com/njdcs_blog/2006/09/njdc_calls_on_a.html

Frommer, F. J. (2007, January 4). Congressman uses Thomas Jefferson's Qur'an at swearing in. *The Seattle Times.* Retrieved from http://seattletimes.nwsource.com/html/politics/2003509142_webellison04.html

Gerstein, J. (2006, September 5). Historic primary takes shape in Minnesota. *New York Sun.* Retrieved from http://www.nysun.com/national/historic-primary-takes-shape-in-minnesota/39030

Ghazali, A. S. (2006, November 10). Keith Ellison: First Muslim elected to US Congress. *Al-Jazeera USA.* Retrieved from http://www.aljazeerah.info/Opinion%20editorials/2006%20Opinion%20Editorials/November/10%20o/Keith%20Ellison%20First%20Muslim%20Elected%20to%20US%20Congress%20By%20Abdus%20Sattar%20Ghazali.htm

Johnson, S. W. (2006, October 9), Louis Farrakhan's first congressman. *The Weekly Standard.* Retrieved from http://www.weeklystandard.com/Content/Public/Articles/000/000/012/764obcsx.asp

Kahn, A. (2006, November 8). Ellison breaks ground as Muslim, black. *St. Paul Pioneer Press.* Retrieved from http://www.pluralism.org/news/article.php?id=14067

Kaufman, J. (2007, January 4). Keith Ellison's friends, our enemies. *Frontpagemag.com.* Retrieved from http://www.frontpagemag.com/readArticle.aspx?ARTID=768

Kersten, K. (2006, June 8). Let's not forget Ellison's support of Nation of Islam. *Minneapolis Star Tribune.* Retrieved from http://nl.newsbank.com

Knippenberg, J. M. (2004, August). Have the Democrats gotten religion? *Ashbrook Center for Public Affairs.* Retrieved from http://www.ashbrook.org/publicat/guest/04/knippenberg/religion.html

Lohn, M. (2006, September 13). Democrat could be 1st Muslim in Congress. *Muslim American Society.* Retrieved from http://www.masnet.org/news.asp?id=3744

Muhammed, A. (2007, January 18). It's time to stop 'hatin' on Muslims in Washington. *Washington Informer.* Retrieved from http://news.newamericamedia.org/news/view_article.html?article_id=b15af77e979558c02bf66b39421abc68

Olson, R. (2006, June 3). Ellison letter addresses his past ties: The DFL-endorsed congressional candidate said he failed to study Louis Farrakhan's positions when he was involved with the Nation of Islam. *Minneapolis Star Tribune,* p. B1.

Parsons, J. (1997, February 3). Defections threaten anti-racism panel. *Minneapolis Star Tribune,* p. B1.

Phillips, K. (2006, December 26). Lone Muslim Congressman speaks out. *New York Times Caucus.* Retrieved from http://thecaucus.blogs.nytimes.com/2006/12/21/the-lone-muslim-congressman-speaks-out

Politics in Minnesota. (2006, July 12). Weekly report. Retrieved from http://www.politicsinminnesota.com/politics-minnesota-weekly-report-vol-2-issue-6-7-12-2006

Prager, D. (2006, November 28). America, not Keith Ellison, decides what book a congressman takes his oath on. *Townhall.com.* Retrieved from http://www.townhall.com/columnists/DennisPrager/2006/11/28/america,_not_keith_ellison,_decides_what_book_a_congressman_takes_his_oath_on

Robson, B. (2006a, August 30). Running man. *City Pages.* Retrieved from http://www.citypages.com/databank/27/1343/article14661.asp

Robson, B. (2006b, August 18). Junge, Lieberman, Farrakhan and "moral relativism." *City Pages.* Retrieved from http://blogs.citypages.com/blotter/2006/08/junge_lieberman_farrakhan_and.php

Robson, B. (2006c, August 22). Ellison wins overwhelming endorsement from Take Action Minnesota. *City Pages.* Retrieved from http://blogs.citypages.com/blotter/2006/08/ellison_wins_overwhelming_endo.php

Robson, B. (2006d, September 13). Soul food: Ellison answers critics, replenishes DFL. *City Pages.* Retrieved from http://blogs.citypages.com/blotter/2006/09/soul_food_ellison_answers_crit.php

Scheck, T. (2004, April 16). Stanek resigns as public safety commissioner over racial slur controversy. *MPR News Q: Minnesota's Online News Source.* Retrieved from http://news.minnesota.publicradio.org/features/2004/04/16_scheckt_stanek

Scheck, T. (2006a, May 6). Keith Ellison wins endorsement in 5th District. *MPR News Q: Minnesota's Online News Source.* Retrieved from http://minnesota.publicradio.org/display/web/2006/05/06/5dist

Scheck, T. (2006b, June 30). Keith Ellison dogged by his past. *MPR News Q: Minnesota's Online News Source.* Retrieved from http://minnesota.publicradio.org/display/web/2006/06/22/ellisonprofile

Scheck, T. (2006c, September 13). Alan Fine fires away at Keith Ellison. *MPR News Q: Minnesota's Online News Source.* Retrieved from http://minnesota.publicradio. org/collections/special/columns/polinaut/archive/2006/09/alan_fine_fires.shtml

Tzvee. (2006, September 7). Minnesota's Jewish newspaper endorses Muslim candidate for congress. *Tzvee's Talmudic Blog.* Retrieved from http://tzvee.blogspot .com/2006_09_01_archive.html

Warikoo, N. (2006a, December 28). Ellison says faith won't be exploited. *Detroit Free Press,* p. A3.

Warikoo, N. (2006b, December 26). 1st Muslim congressman thrills crowd in Dearborn. *Detroit Free Press.* Retrieved from http://www.discoverthenetworks .org/Articles/1st%20Muslim%20Congressman%20Thrills.htm

Index

Sojourners magazine, 130, 133. *See also*
religious left; Wallis, Jim
Southern Baptists. *See* Baptists
Spanish Inquisition, 138, 143, 145, 146
Sullivan, Amy, 65, 98, 106, 177,
189–90
Supreme Court, 12, 19–21, 101, 125,
129
Swaggert, Jimmy, 182

testimony, 6–7, 81, 131, 134, 136–37,
148–49nn6–7, 185–86
theology, 2, 28, 43, 76–77, 80, 94–96,
98–99, 130–31, 146, 162, 179, 181,
183. *See also* doctrine
Torah, 142, 204. *See also* Bible; Old
Testament

Unitarians, 13, 16, 125
United States Constitution. *See*
Constitution
United States Supreme Court. *See*
Supreme Court
Urban VIII (pope), 146

values, 2–3, 5, 18, 26, 28–29, 32–36,
44–45, 50, 53, 56–57, 63–65, 67,
71–72, 75, 78, 82, 85–87, 89, 98,

101, 105, 107, 129, 134–35, 137,
139–41, 155, 157, 160, 162, 165,
167–68, 177, 180–83, 188, 190, 207.
See also morals and morality
Vatican, 46–47. *See also* Catholicism
and Catholics; popes; *specific popes*

Wallis, Jim, 6, 64, 98, 130, 135, 140,
148n3, 148n5, 157–58, 161–65,
168–69, 171, 177, 179, 188. *See
also* conservative radicalism; *God's
Politics* (Wallis); religious left;
Sojourners (group); *Sojourners*
magazine
wall of separation between church and
state. *See* church-state separation;
Constitution; Jefferson, Thomas;
secularism and secularity
Warren, Rick, 84
Washington, George, 13
West, Cornel, 6, 117–26
White House Office of Faith-Based
and Neighborhood Partnerships. *See*
faith-based organizations
White House Office of Faith-Based
Initiatives. *See* faith-based
organizations
Wright, Jeremiah, 34

About the Contributors

Allison J. Ainsworth is an assistant professor of communication at Gainesville State College and a member of the teaching faculty of the Institute for Environmental and Spatial Analysis. She is the author of *The Essential Guide to Presentation Software.* Her areas of specialty are environmental studies and geospatial data analysis, business and professional communication, interpersonal communication in intercultural contexts, and education. She is currently serving as chair of the Community College Section and as member of the Legislative Assembly of the National Communication Association.

Samuel Boerboom is a visiting assistant professor in the Department of Communication Studies at Gustavus Adolphus College where he teaches courses in public discourse, argumentation, and political rhetoric. His research interests include rhetoric and religion, rhetorical theory, communication ethics, and sexuality discourse. His work has appeared in the *Journal of Mass Media Ethics.*

Daniel D. Gross is a professor of communication at Montana State University, Billings. He teaches courses in communication and rhetorical theory. He has published several articles in state and regional communication journals. His primary research interest is narrative theory.

Paul Haridakis is an associate professor of communication studies at Kent State University. He conducts research in media use and effects, law, public policy, sports communication, and political communication. His recent research has focused on First Amendment issues and political social media use.

Christina M. Knopf is an assistant professor in the Department of English & Communication at the State University of New York, Potsdam. She earned her PhD at the University at Albany, SUNY, specializing in cultural sociology and political communication. In addition to public expressions of faith and religion, Dr. Knopf's research interests include "civil-military dialectics." She regularly presents her work at the annual meetings of the National and Eastern Communication Associations and the Rhetoric Society of America.

Lenore Langsdorf is professor emerita at Southern Illinois University, Carbondale. Her research interests in the philosophy of communication center on the usefulness of process pragmatism and hermeneutic phenomenology for understanding and strengthening communicative interaction.

Sara Ann Mehltretter is a doctoral candidate in the Department of Communication Arts and Sciences at Pennsylvania State University. Her research interests include political rhetoric, social movements, deliberative democracy, and the rhetoric of religion. Her publications have appeared in *Journal of Communication & Religion* and *Voices of Democracy*.

Jeffrey L. Morrow is an assistant professor in theology at the Immaculate Conception Seminary School of Theology at Seton Hall University. His research focuses on the history of biblical interpretation. His work has appeared in numerous journals, including *Global Media Journal, Renascence, New Blackfriars, Fides Quaerens Intellectum,* and *Christianity & Literature*.

James T. Petre is a doctoral candidate at Southern Illinois University, Carbondale specializing in rhetoric and philosophy of communication. His research explores intersections of politics, economics, and history through a rhetorical lens. He served as editor of *Kaleidoscope: A Graduate Journal of Qualitative Communication Research* for the 2009–2010 academic year.

Penni M. Pier is an associate professor of communication arts at Wartburg College where she directs the basic public speaking course, teaches courses in rhetoric and persuasion, and is the director of the Women's Studies Program. Her research interests include political communication, gender, and rhetoric. She is the coauthor of three books that analyze political campaigns and the rhetorical strategies used by political figures.

C. Thomas Preston, Jr., is professor of communication at Gainesville State College. He holds degrees from the University of North Carolina, Chapel Hill and the University of Nebraska, Lincoln. As a communication generalist, his main research interests include intercultural communication (particularly Sino-U.S. communication), sports communication, public address, and argumentation. Having published over 40 articles and presented over 50 convention papers, he is a recipient of the L. E. Norton Award and E. R. Nichols Award with Pi Kappa Delta and two American Forensic Association research awards.

Paul R. Raptis is an assistant professor of communication at Gainesville State College where he teaches courses in public speaking and interpersonal communication. He also has taught a course in media, culture, and society at Zhengzhou University in China as part of a study-abroad program. His research interests include argumentativeness and verbal aggressiveness, teacher immediacy, and training and adult education. His work has appeared in *Communication Research Reports.*

Brent S. Roberts is director of library services at Montana State University, Billings. He received his MLIS from the University of Washington and his MS in public relations from MSU, Billings. He teaches courses in business communication, information literacy, intercultural communication, interpersonal communication, and Japanese.

Biff Rocha is an assistant professor of theology at Benedictine College in Atchison, Kansas. He holds an MA in speech communication and rhetoric from Miami University in Oxford, Ohio, and is currently completing his doctorate in theology at the University of Dayton. His areas of interest are religious rhetoric and American Catholicism.

David Weiss is an assistant professor of media studies at Montana State University, Billings. His research interests include media ecology, popular culture, and political communication. His work has appeared in *The Howard Journal of Communications, Popular Communication, Theory in Action,* Sage's *Encyclopedia of Communication Theory,* and numerous scholarly anthologies. He is currently coediting a collection of essays on the rhetoric of American exceptionalism.

Julie R. Woodbury is a visiting assistant professor at Hamline University. She received her PhD at the University of Minnesota. Her research interests include First Amendment law, political rhetoric, persuasion, ethics, and social interaction. She has published work in the areas of curricular support and new media.

Breinigsville, PA USA
01 October 2010
246513BV00002B/1/P